SEVEN SEAS ENTERTAINMENT PRESENTS

BUY THE LAND and CULTIVATE IT
IN A DIFFERENT WORLD
VOLUME 4

story by **ROKUJUUYON OKAZAWA**   art by **JUN SASAMEYUKI**   character designs by **YUICHI MURAKAMI**

TRANSLATION
Jess Leif

ADAPTATION
Amanda Lafrenais

LETTERING
Isabell Struble

LOGO DESIGN
George Panella

COVER DESIGN
Nicky Lim

PROOFREADER
Leighanna DeRouen

COPY EDITOR
B. Lillian Martin

EDITOR
Abby Lehrke
K. McDonald

PRODUCTION DESIGNER
Eve Grandt

PRODUCTION MANAGER
Lissa Pattillo

PREPRESS TECHNICIAN
Melanie Ujimori
Jules Valera

EDITOR-IN-CHIEF
Julie Davis

ASSOCIATE PUBLISHER
Adam Arnold

PUBLISHER
Jason DeAngelis

Isekai de Tochi wo katte Noujou wo tsukurou volume 4
© OKAZAWA ROKUJUUYON, SASAMEYUKI JUN/OVERLAP,
GENTOSHA COMICS 2021
Originally published in Japan in 2021 by GENTOSHA COMICS INC., Tokyo.
English translation rights arranged with GENTOSHA COMICS INC., Tokyo.
through TOHAN CORPORATION, Tokyo.

Seven Seas press and purchase enquiries can be sent to Marketing Manager Lianne
Sentar at press@gomanga.com. Information regarding the distribution and purchase of
digital editions is available from Digital Manager CK Russell at digital@gomanga.com.

Seven Seas and the Seven Seas logo are trademarks of
Seven Seas Entertainment. All rights reserved.

ISBN: 978-1-68579-604-4
Printed in Canada
First Printing: July 2023
10 9 8 7 6 5 4 3 2 1

READING DIRECTIONS

This book reads from *right to left*,
Japanese style. If this is your first time
reading manga, you start reading from
the top right panel on each page and
take it from there. If you get lost, just
follow the numbered diagram here.
It may seem backwards at first,
but you'll get the hang of it! Have fun!!

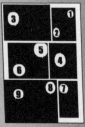

Follow us online: www.SevenSeasEntertainment.com

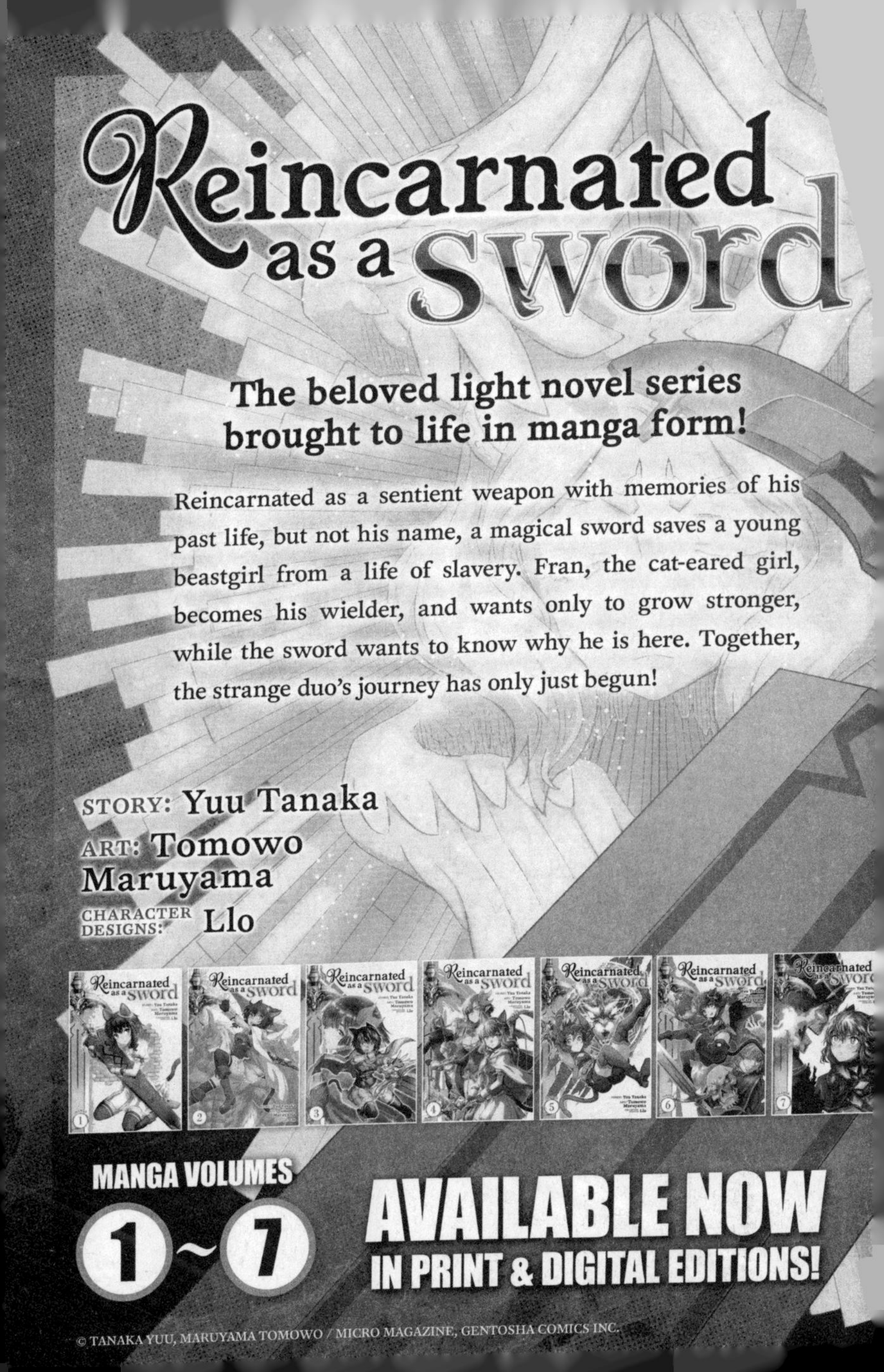
Reincarnated as a Sword
The beloved light novel series brought to life in manga form!
Reincarnated as a sentient weapon with memories of his past life, but not his name, a magical sword saves a young beastgirl from a life of slavery. Fran, the cat-eared girl, becomes his wielder, and wants only to grow stronger, while the sword wants to know why he is here. Together, the strange duo's journey has only just begun!
STORY: Yuu Tanaka
ART: Tomowo Maruyama
CHARACTER DESIGNS: Llo
MANGA VOLUMES 1~7
AVAILABLE NOW IN PRINT & DIGITAL EDITIONS!
© TANAKA YUU, MARUYAMA TOMOWO / MICRO MAGAZINE, GENTOSHA COMICS INC.

SHOOO
THE
ROYAL
MY HON
AT RIS
I DO
RISE TO
CHALLEN

Arowana

The Crown Prince of the Merpeople Kingdom. He originally intervened to take his sister home, but came to recognize Kidan as the Chosen One, and entrusted his sister with him.

Veel

The Grinzell Dragon. Though she's supposed to be training as heir to the Geyser Dragon, she's always just loafing around the farm.

Sensei

The Lord of the Undead, the Unliving King. The master of a nearby dungeon and Kidan's neighbor.

LORD ZEDAN ...

Zedan

The Demon Lord. He arrived at Kidan's farm in pursuit of Astareth, and ended up forming a friendship with Kidan and the others. Together with Astareth, he returned to the Land of the Demons.

Belena and Bati

Aides to Astareth. They are her loyal followers and left the Land of Demons with her. Belena is from a noble Demon Tribe family.

Astareth

One of the Four Heavenly Kings of the Demon Lord: Astareth of Chaos. Though chased out of the Demon Tribes, after marrying Zedan she was able to return to her homeland.

Story

Though he was among a group of humans summoned to another world, Kidan was swiftly tossed aside for not possessing a skill like the others. Unfazed, he decides to dedicate himself to a second chance at life by buying and cultivating a plot of land in the wild frontier. Along the way he ends up with a wife, Plattie, and together they befriend the Undead King, a dragon, and the prince of the Merpeople. Astareth, chased away from the Land of Demons after an ambush, would find refuge with them, soon joined by Demon Lord Zedan. The two would wed before returning to the Land of Demons together.

Contents

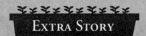

EXTRA STORY

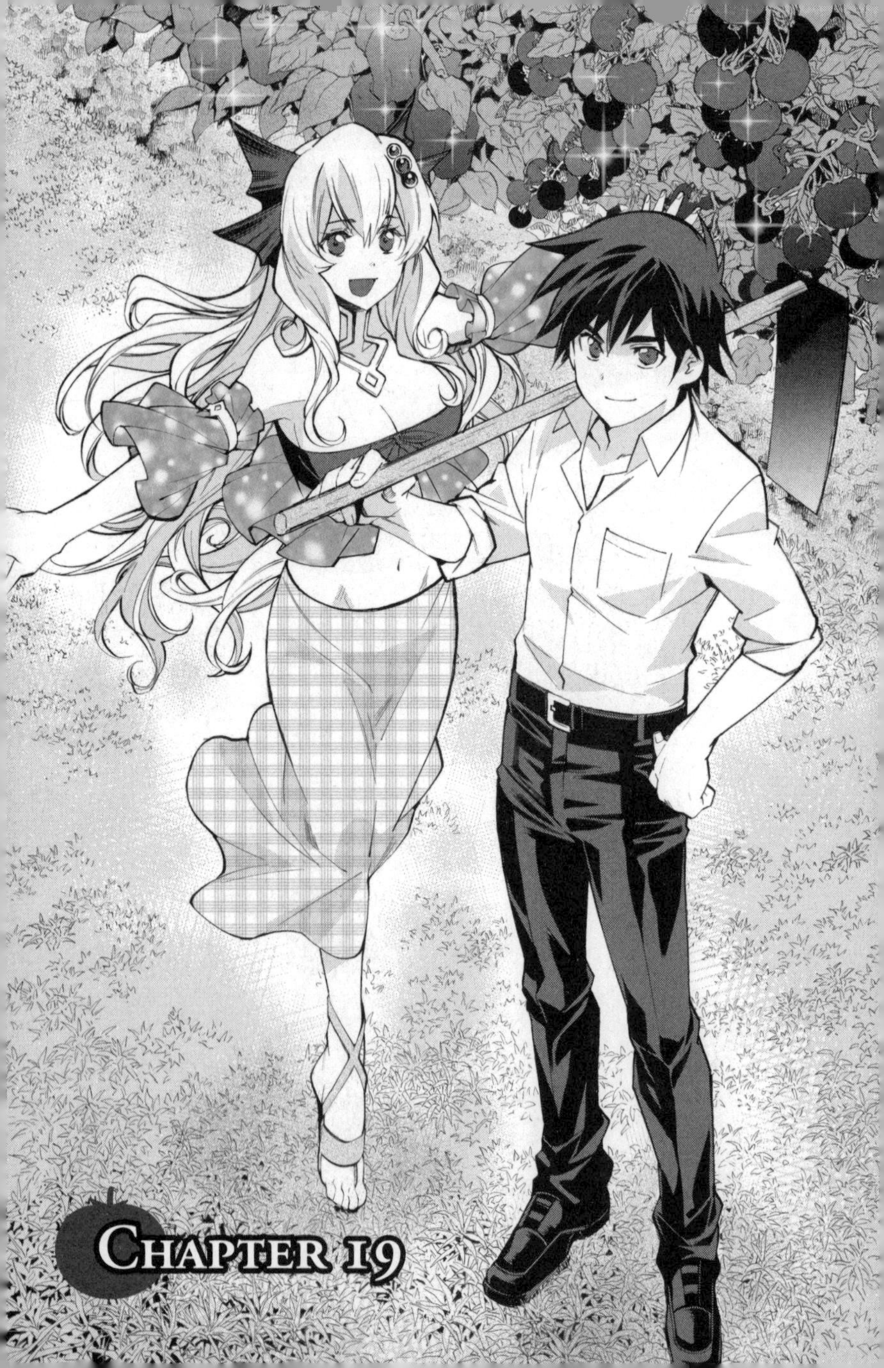
CHAPTER 19

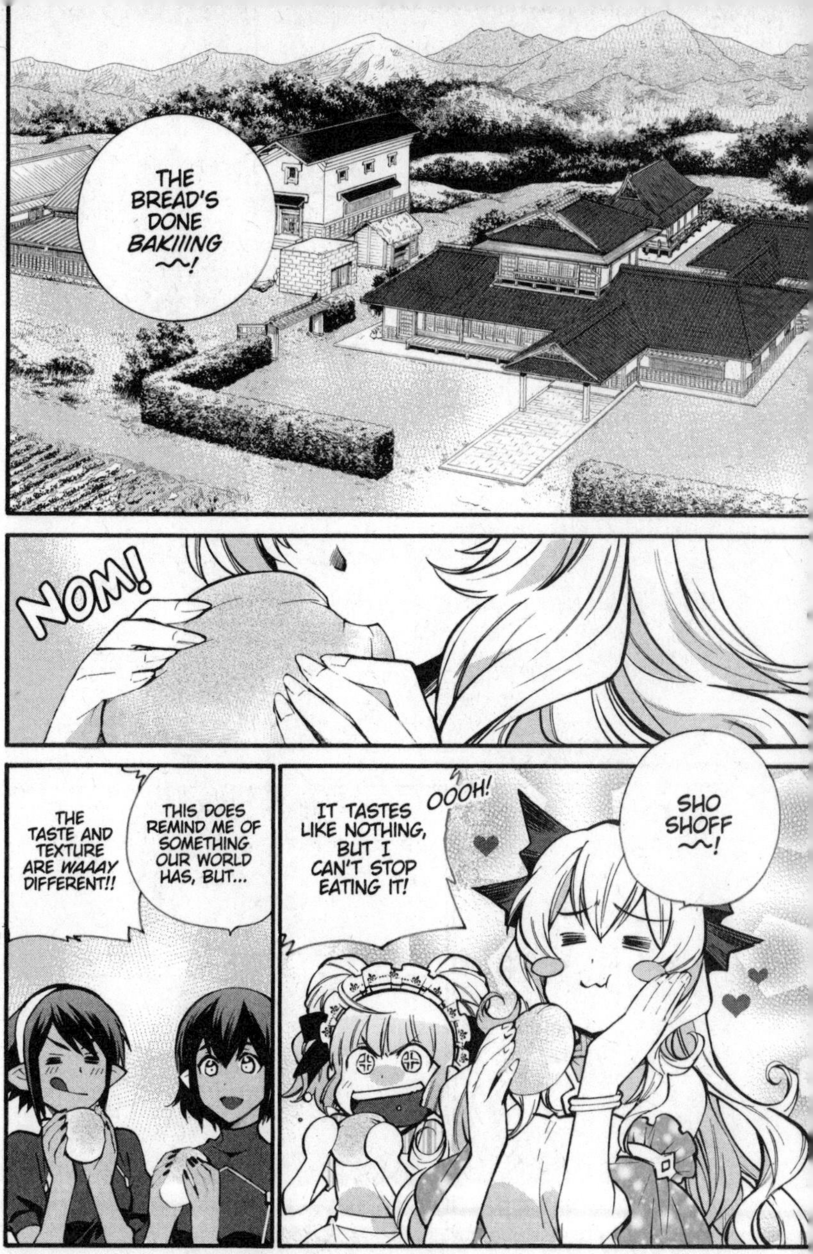
THE BREAD'S DONE BAKIIING ~~!
NOM!
SHO SHOFF ~~!
OOOH!
IT TASTES LIKE NOTHING, BUT I CAN'T STOP EATING IT!
THIS DOES REMIND ME OF SOMETHING OUR WORLD HAS, BUT...
THE TASTE AND TEXTURE ARE WAAAY DIFFERENT!!

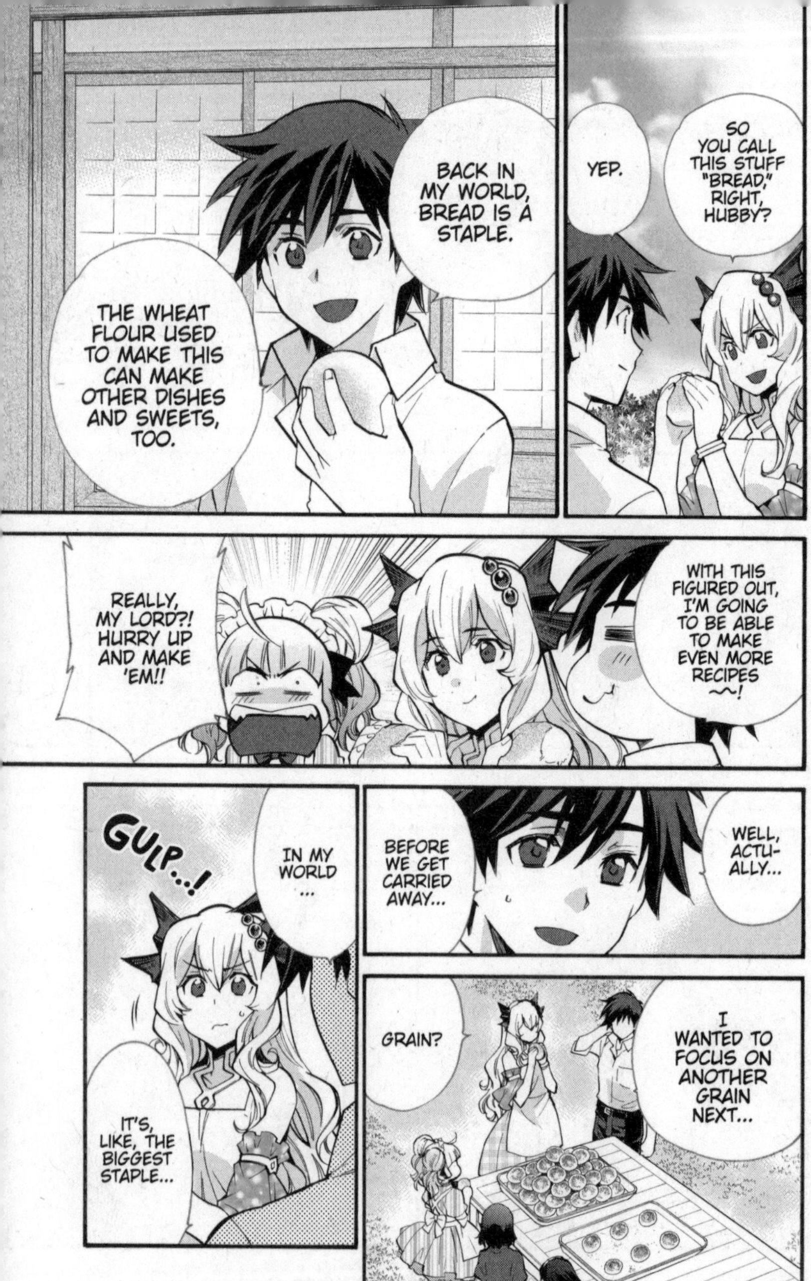
SO YOU CALL THIS STUFF "BREAD," RIGHT, HUBBY?
YEP.
BACK IN MY WORLD, BREAD IS A STAPLE.
THE WHEAT FLOUR USED TO MAKE THIS CAN MAKE OTHER DISHES AND SWEETS, TOO.
WITH THIS FIGURED OUT, I'M GOING TO BE ABLE TO MAKE EVEN MORE RECIPES ~!
REALLY, MY LORD?! HURRY UP AND MAKE 'EM!!
WELL, ACTU-ALLY...
BEFORE WE GET CARRIED AWAY...
I WANTED TO FOCUS ON ANOTHER GRAIN NEXT...
GRAIN?
IN MY WORLD ...
GULP...!
IT'S, LIKE, THE BIGGEST STAPLE...

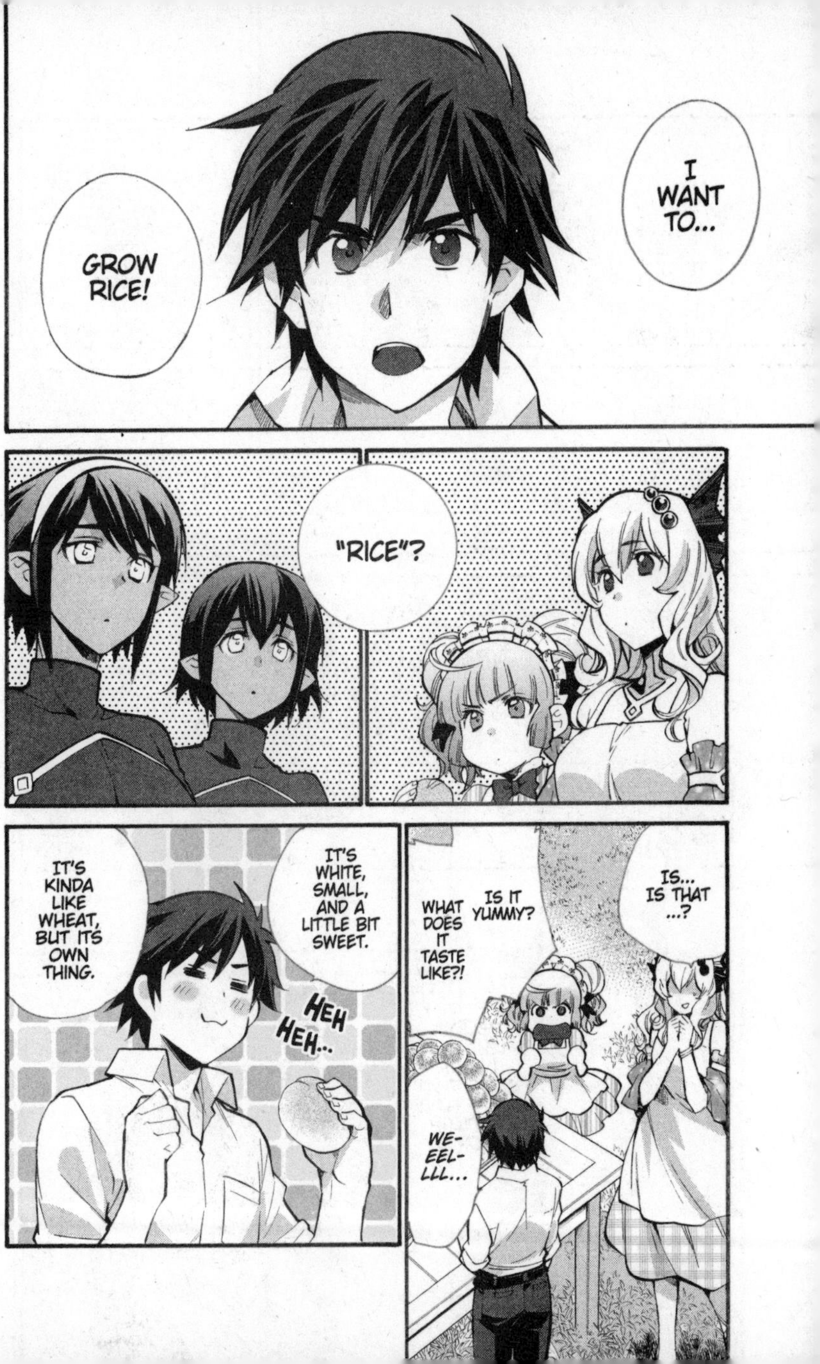
I WANT TO...
GROW RICE!
"RICE"?
IS... IS THAT ...?
IS IT YUMMY?
WHAT DOES IT TASTE LIKE?!
WE-EEL-LLL...
IT'S WHITE, SMALL, AND A LITTLE BIT SWEET.
IT'S KINDA LIKE WHEAT, BUT ITS OWN THING.
HEH HEH...

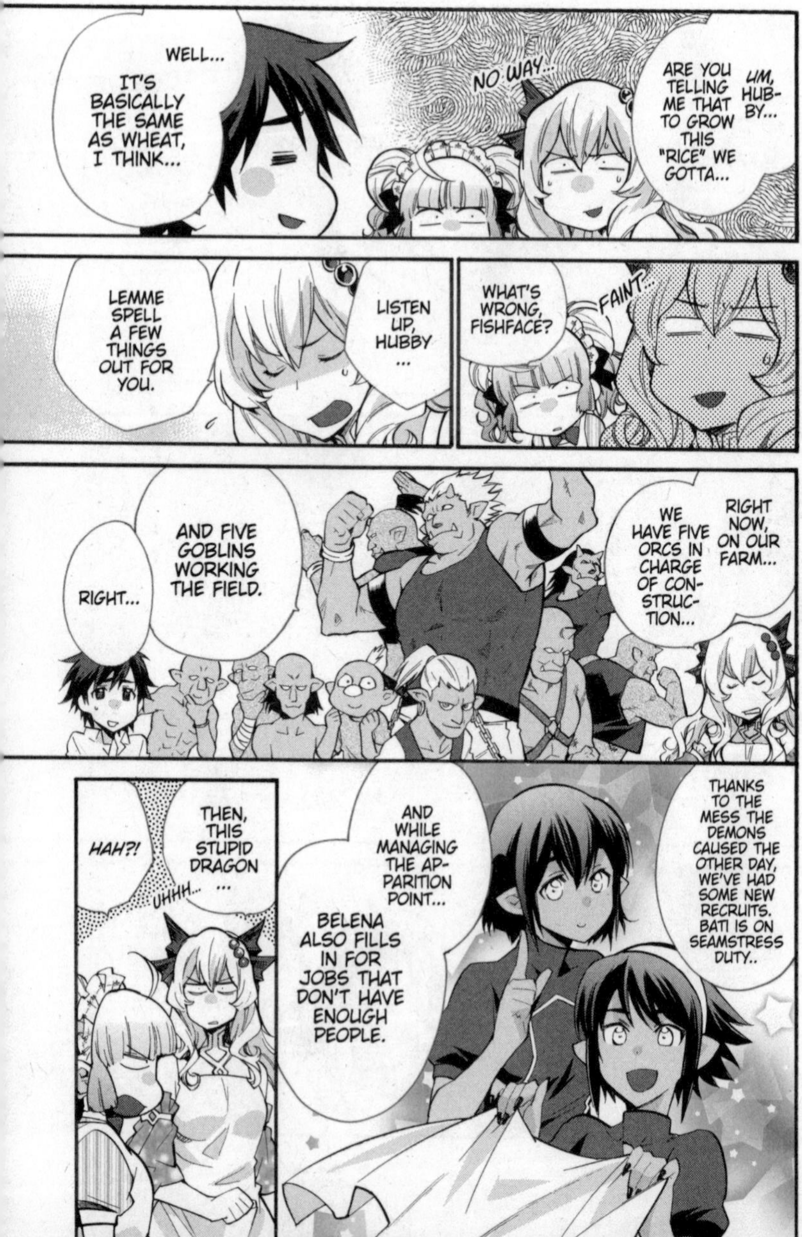
UM, HUBBY...
ARE YOU TELLING ME THAT TO GROW THIS "RICE" WE GOTTA...
NO WAY...
WELL...
IT'S BASICALLY THE SAME AS WHEAT, I THINK...
FAINT...
WHAT'S WRONG, FISHFACE?
LISTEN UP, HUBBY ...
LEMME SPELL A FEW THINGS OUT FOR YOU.
RIGHT NOW, ON OUR FARM...
WE HAVE FIVE ORCS IN CHARGE OF CONSTRUCTION...
AND FIVE GOBLINS WORKING THE FIELD.
RIGHT...
THANKS TO THE MESS THE DEMONS CAUSED THE OTHER DAY, WE'VE HAD SOME NEW RECRUITS. BATI IS ON SEAMSTRESS DUTY..
AND WHILE MANAGING THE APPARITION POINT...
BELENA ALSO FILLS IN FOR JOBS THAT DON'T HAVE ENOUGH PEOPLE.
THEN, THIS STUPID DRAGON ...
UHHH...
HAH?!

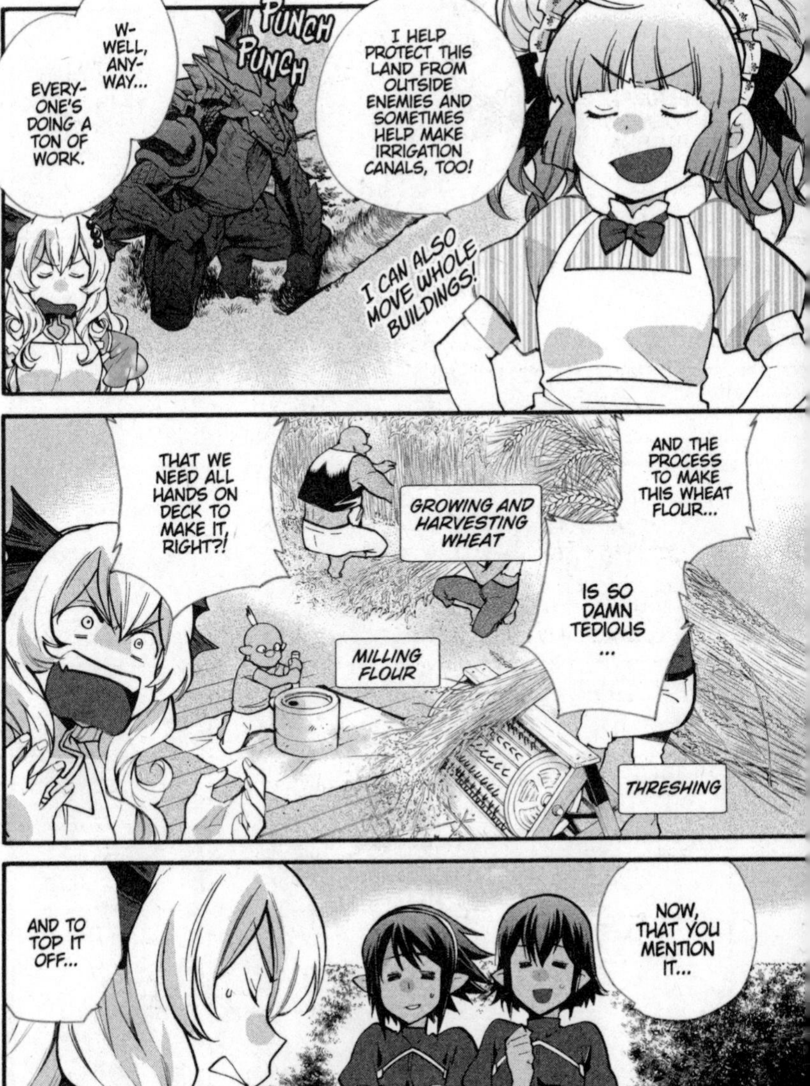
I HELP PROTECT THIS LAND FROM OUTSIDE ENEMIES AND SOMETIMES HELP MAKE IRRIGATION CANALS, TOO!
I CAN ALSO MOVE WHOLE BUILDINGS!
PUNCH
PUNCH
W-WELL, ANYWAY... EVERYONE'S DOING A TON OF WORK.
AND THE PROCESS TO MAKE THIS WHEAT FLOUR...
IS SO DAMN TEDIOUS...
GROWING AND HARVESTING WHEAT
THRESHING
MILLING FLOUR
THAT WE NEED ALL HANDS ON DECK TO MAKE IT, RIGHT?!
NOW, THAT YOU MENTION IT...
AND TO TOP IT OFF...

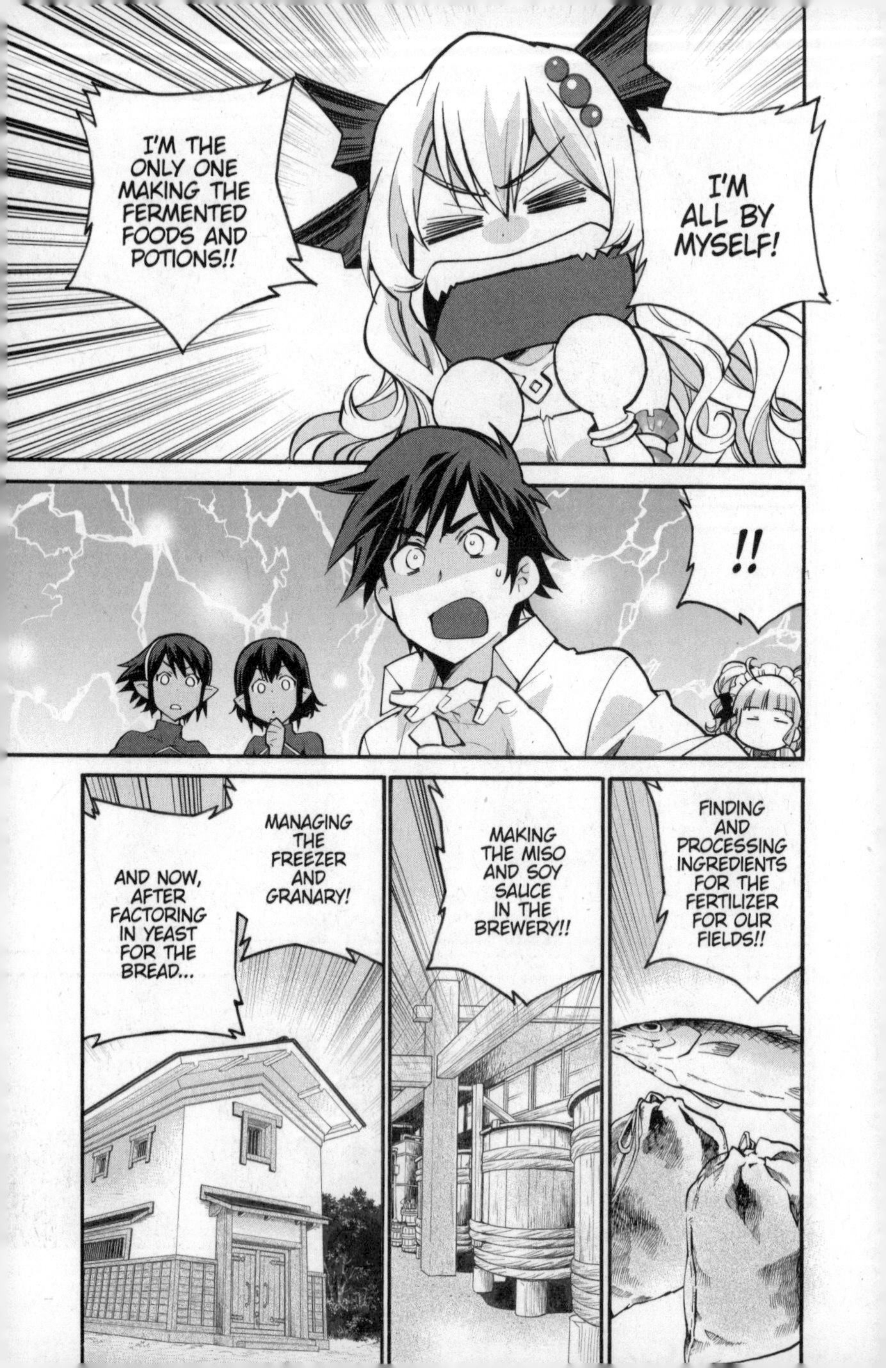
I'M ALL BY MYSELF!
I'M THE ONLY ONE MAKING THE FERMENTED FOODS AND POTIONS!!
!!
FINDING AND PROCESSING INGREDIENTS FOR THE FERTILIZER FOR OUR FIELDS!!
MAKING THE MISO AND SOY SAUCE IN THE BREWERY!!
MANAGING THE FREEZER AND GRANARY!
AND NOW, AFTER FACTORING IN YEAST FOR THE BREAD...

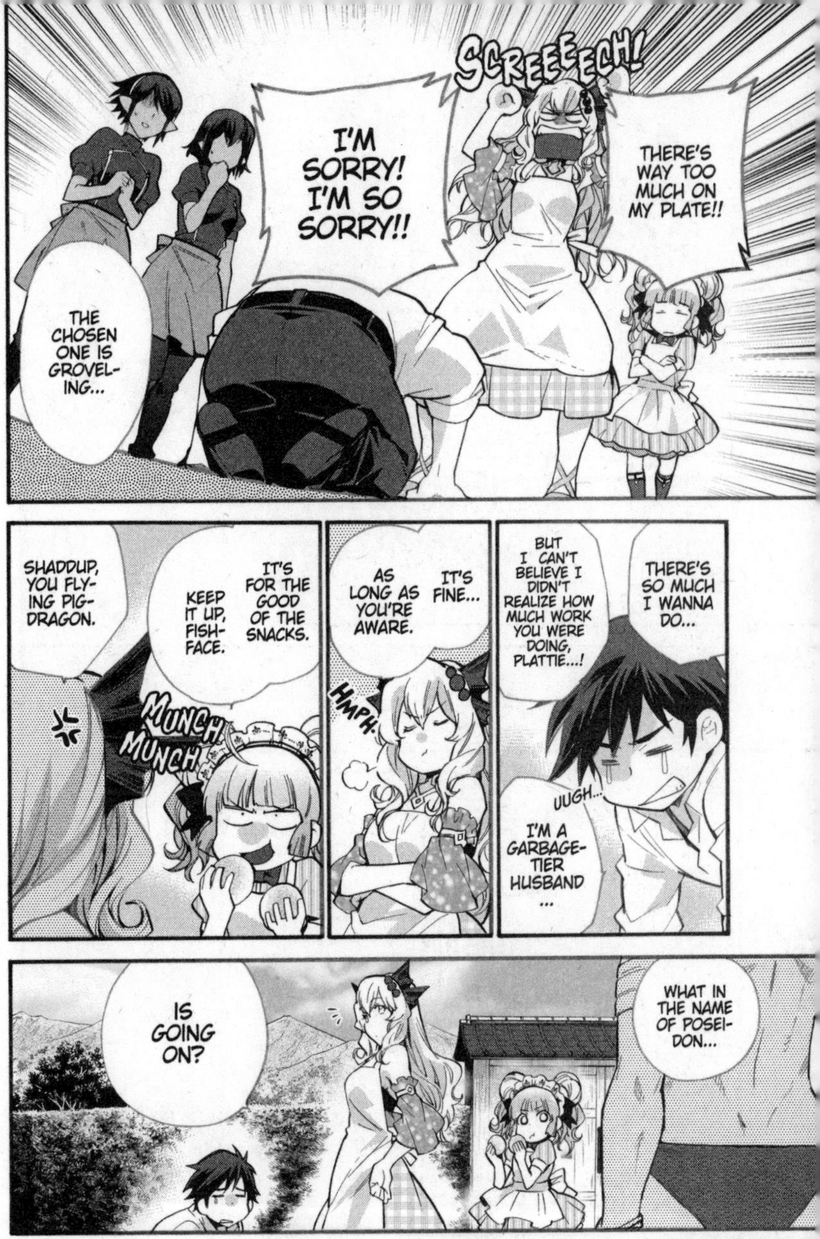
SCREEEECH!
THERE'S WAY TOO MUCH ON MY PLATE!!
I'M SORRY! I'M SO SORRY!!
THE CHOSEN ONE IS GROVELING...
THERE'S SO MUCH I WANNA DO...
BUT I CAN'T BELIEVE I DIDN'T REALIZE HOW MUCH WORK YOU WERE DOING, PLATTIE...!
UUGH...
I'M A GARBAGE-TIER HUSBAND ...
IT'S FINE...
AS LONG AS YOU'RE AWARE.
HMPH.
IT'S FOR THE GOOD OF THE SNACKS.
KEEP IT UP, FISH-FACE.
MUNCH MUNCH
SHADDUP, YOU FLYING PIG-DRAGON.
WHAT IN THE NAME OF POSEIDON...
IS GOING ON?

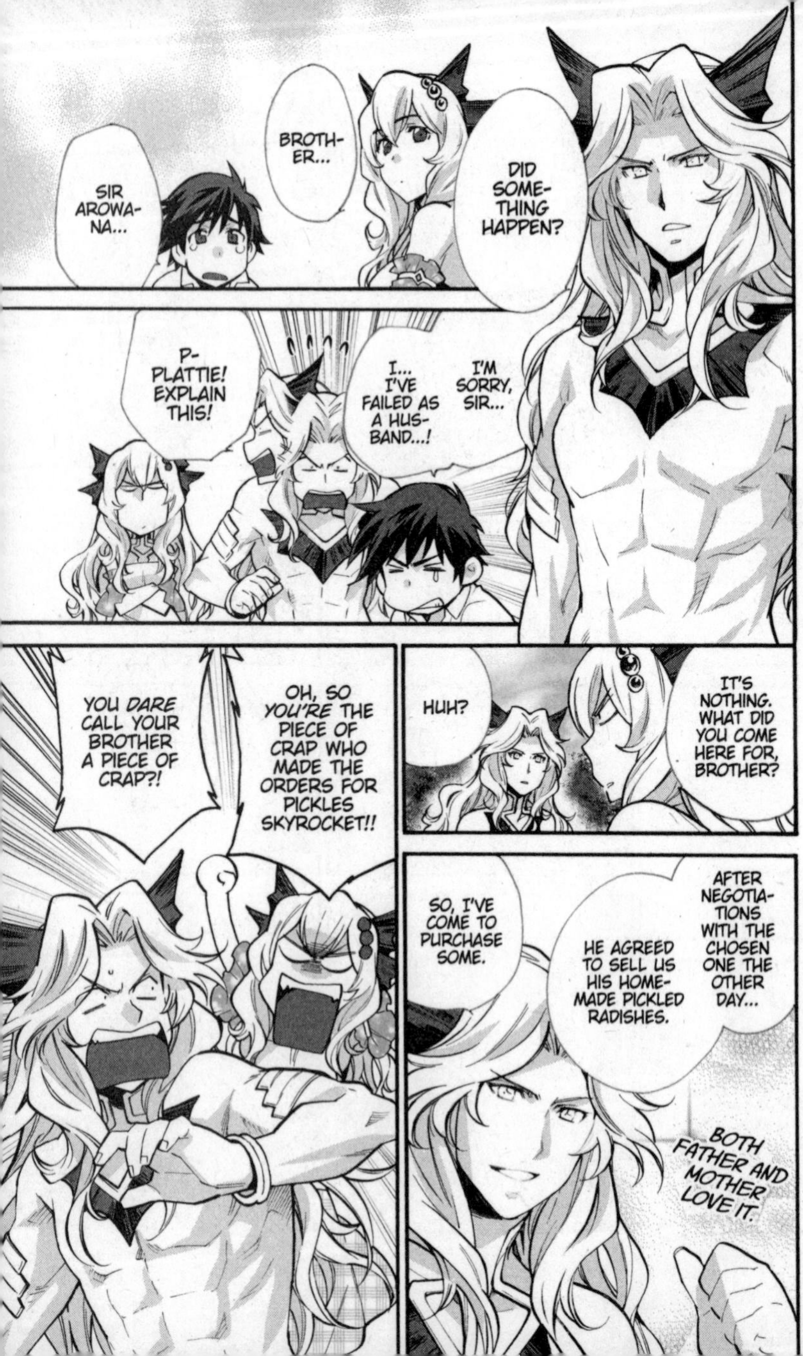
DID SOMETHING HAPPEN?
BROTHER...
SIR AROWANA...
I'M SORRY, SIR...
I... I'VE FAILED AS A HUSBAND...!
P-PLATTIE! EXPLAIN THIS!
IT'S NOTHING. WHAT DID YOU COME HERE FOR, BROTHER?
HUH?
AFTER NEGOTIATIONS WITH THE CHOSEN ONE THE OTHER DAY...
HE AGREED TO SELL US HIS HOMEMADE PICKLED RADISHES.
SO, I'VE COME TO PURCHASE SOME.
BOTH FATHER AND MOTHER LOVE IT.
OH, SO *YOU'RE* THE PIECE OF CRAP WHO MADE THE ORDERS FOR PICKLES SKYROCKET!!
YOU *DARE* CALL YOUR BROTHER A PIECE OF CRAP?!

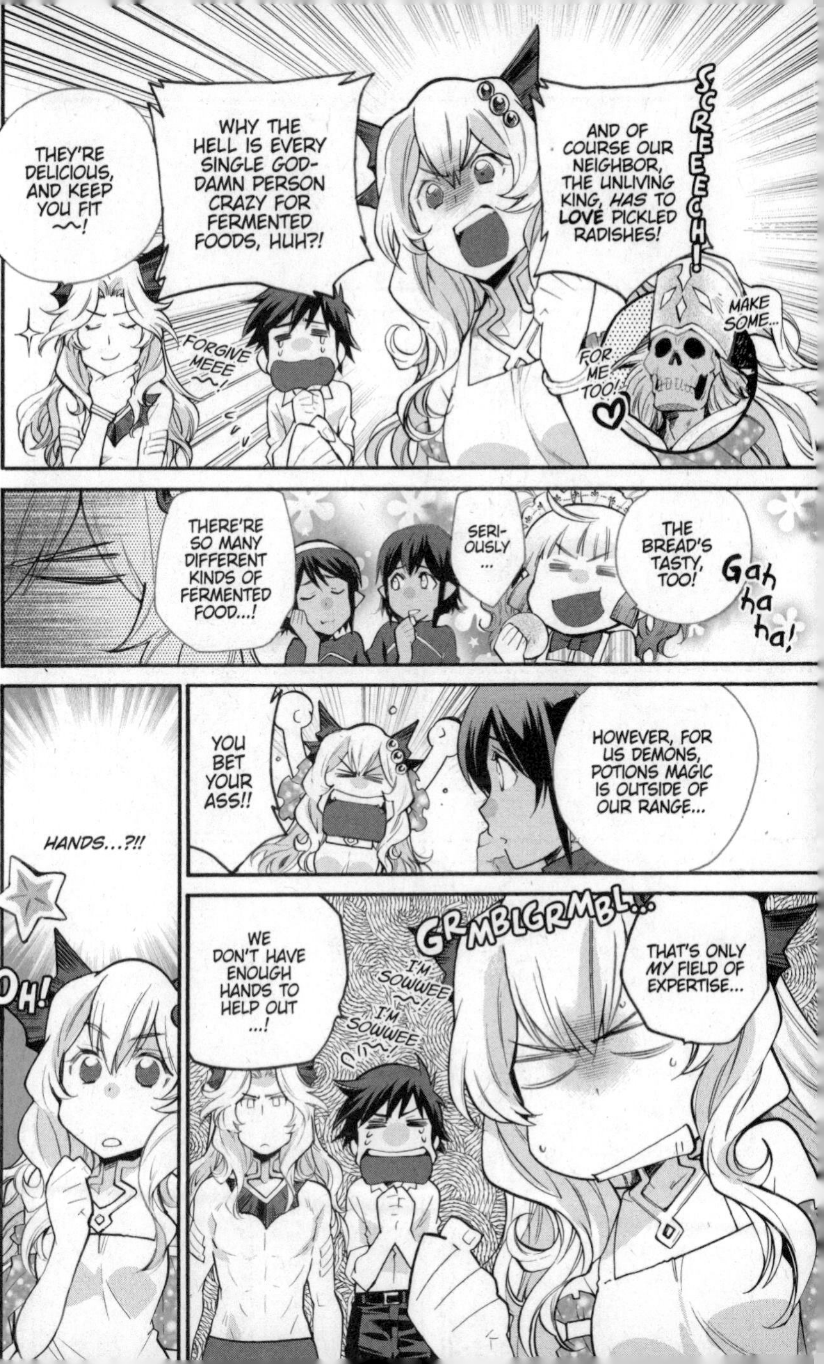
SCREEECH!
AND OF COURSE OUR NEIGHBOR, THE UNLIVING KING, HAS TO LOVE PICKLED RADISHES!
MAKE SOME...
FOR ME TOO!
WHY THE HELL IS EVERY SINGLE GOD-DAMN PERSON CRAZY FOR FERMENTED FOODS, HUH?!
FORGIVE MEEE ~!
THEY'RE DELICIOUS, AND KEEP YOU FIT ~!
Gah ha ha!
THE BREAD'S TASTY, TOO!
SERIOUSLY ...
THERE'RE SO MANY DIFFERENT KINDS OF FERMENTED FOOD...!
HOWEVER, FOR US DEMONS, POTIONS MAGIC IS OUTSIDE OF OUR RANGE...
YOU BET YOUR ASS!!
THAT'S ONLY MY FIELD OF EXPERTISE...
GRMBLGRMBL...
I'M SOWWEE ~!
I'M SOWWEE ~!
WE DON'T HAVE ENOUGH HANDS TO HELP OUT ...!
HANDS...?!!
OH!

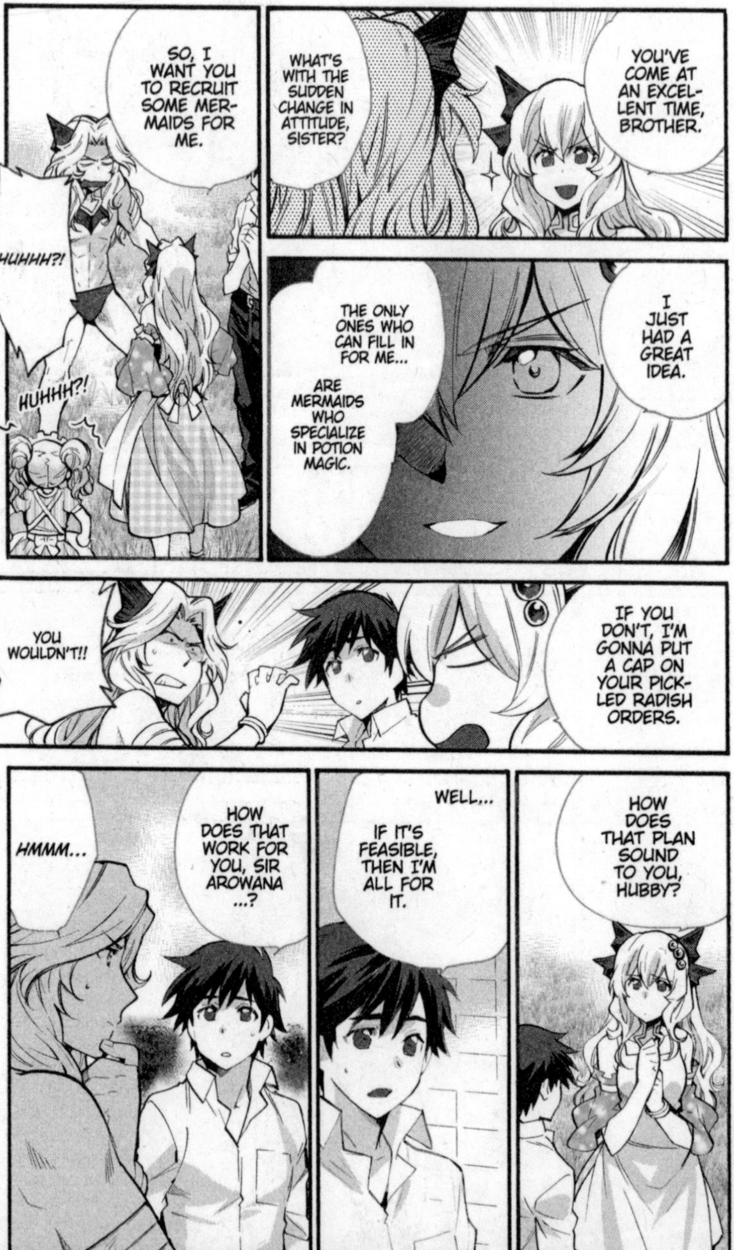
YOU'VE COME AT AN EXCEL-LENT TIME, BROTHER.
WHAT'S WITH THE SUDDEN CHANGE IN ATTITUDE, SISTER?
I JUST HAD A GREAT IDEA.
THE ONLY ONES WHO CAN FILL IN FOR ME...
ARE MERMAIDS WHO SPECIALIZE IN POTION MAGIC.
SO, I WANT YOU TO RECRUIT SOME MER-MAIDS FOR ME.
HUHHH?!
HUHHH?!
IF YOU DON'T, I'M GONNA PUT A CAP ON YOUR PICK-LED RADISH ORDERS.
YOU WOULDN'T!!
HOW DOES THAT PLAN SOUND TO YOU, HUBBY?
WELL...
IF IT'S FEASIBLE, THEN I'M ALL FOR IT.
HOW DOES THAT WORK FOR YOU, SIR AROWANA ...?
HMMM...

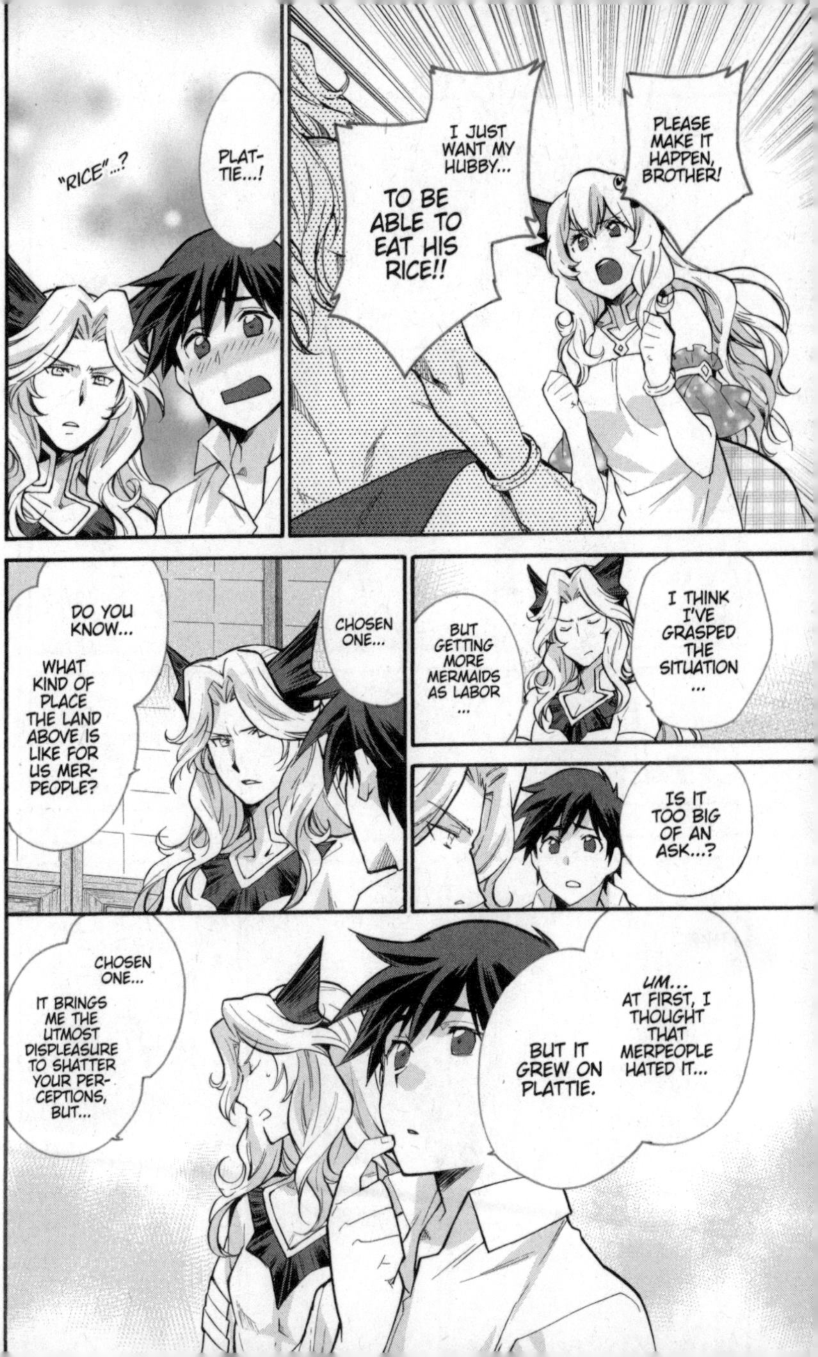
PLEASE MAKE IT HAPPEN, BROTHER!
I JUST WANT MY HUBBY...
TO BE ABLE TO EAT HIS RICE!!
PLAT-TIE...!
"RICE"...?
I THINK I'VE GRASPED THE SITUATION...
BUT GETTING MORE MERMAIDS AS LABOR...
IS IT TOO BIG OF AN ASK...?
CHOSEN ONE...
DO YOU KNOW...
WHAT KIND OF PLACE THE LAND ABOVE IS LIKE FOR US MER-PEOPLE?
UM... AT FIRST, I THOUGHT THAT MERPEOPLE HATED IT...
BUT IT GREW ON PLATTIE.
CHOSEN ONE...
IT BRINGS ME THE UTMOST DISPLEASURE TO SHATTER YOUR PER-CEPTIONS, BUT...

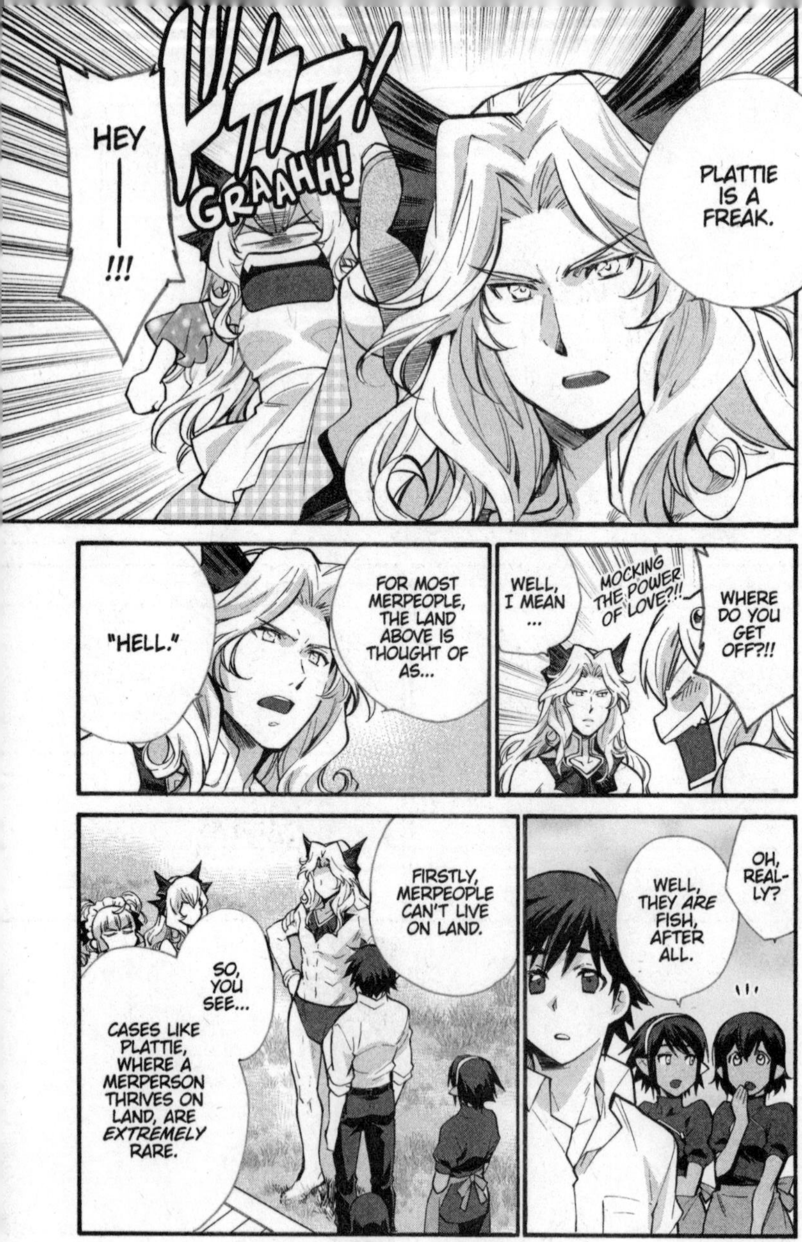
PLATTIE IS A FREAK.
GRAAHH!
HEY——!!!
WHERE DO YOU GET OFF?!!
MOCKING THE POWER OF LOVE?!!
WELL, I MEAN ...
FOR MOST MERPEOPLE, THE LAND ABOVE IS THOUGHT OF AS...
"HELL."
OH, REAL-LY?
WELL, THEY *ARE* FISH, AFTER ALL.
FIRSTLY, MERPEOPLE CAN'T LIVE ON LAND.
SO, YOU SEE...
CASES LIKE PLATTIE, WHERE A MERPERSON THRIVES ON LAND, ARE *EXTREMELY* RARE.

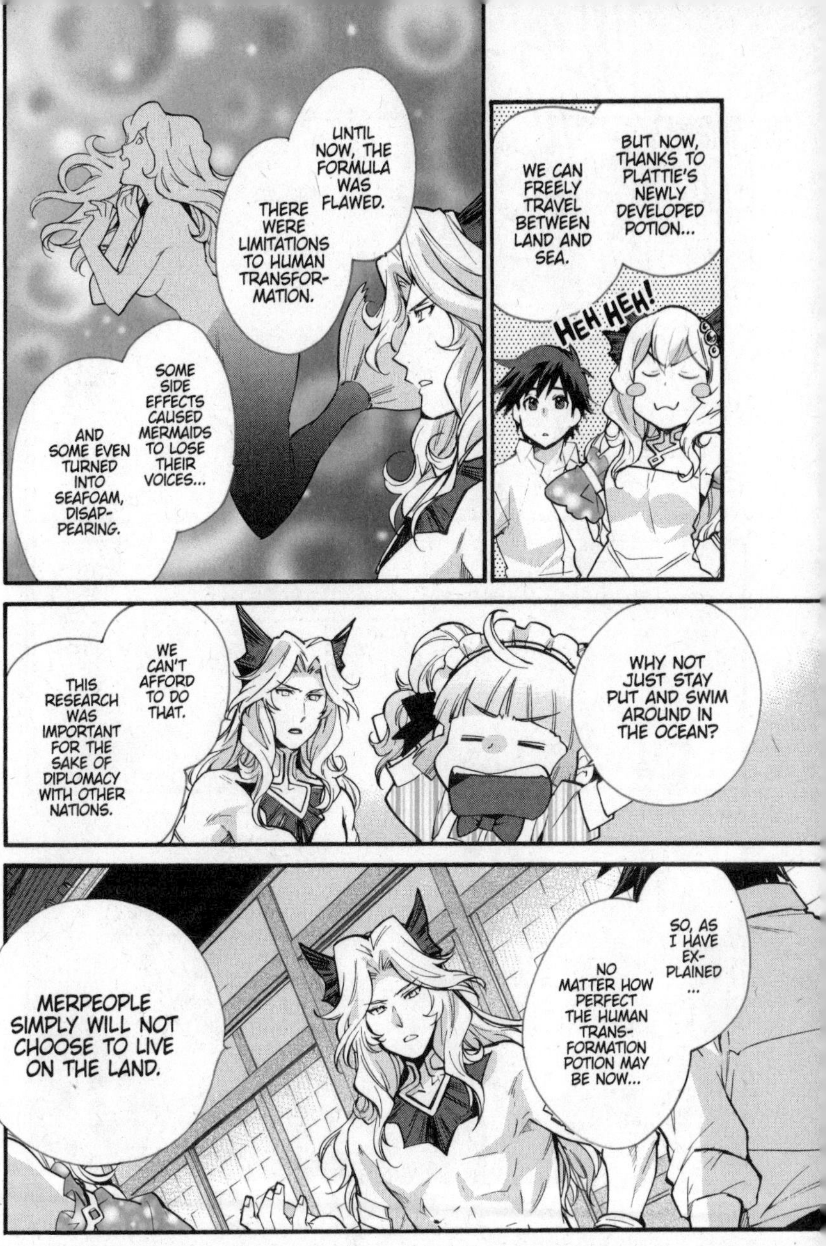
BUT NOW, THANKS TO PLATTIE'S NEWLY DEVELOPED POTION...
WE CAN FREELY TRAVEL BETWEEN LAND AND SEA.
HEH HEH!
UNTIL NOW, THE FORMULA WAS FLAWED.
THERE WERE LIMITATIONS TO HUMAN TRANSFORMATION.
SOME SIDE EFFECTS CAUSED MERMAIDS TO LOSE THEIR VOICES...
AND SOME EVEN TURNED INTO SEAFOAM, DISAPPEARING.
WHY NOT JUST STAY PUT AND SWIM AROUND IN THE OCEAN?
WE CAN'T AFFORD TO DO THAT.
THIS RESEARCH WAS IMPORTANT FOR THE SAKE OF DIPLOMACY WITH OTHER NATIONS.
SO, AS I HAVE EXPLAINED...
NO MATTER HOW PERFECT THE HUMAN TRANSFORMATION POTION MAY BE NOW...
MERPEOPLE SIMPLY WILL NOT CHOOSE TO LIVE ON THE LAND.

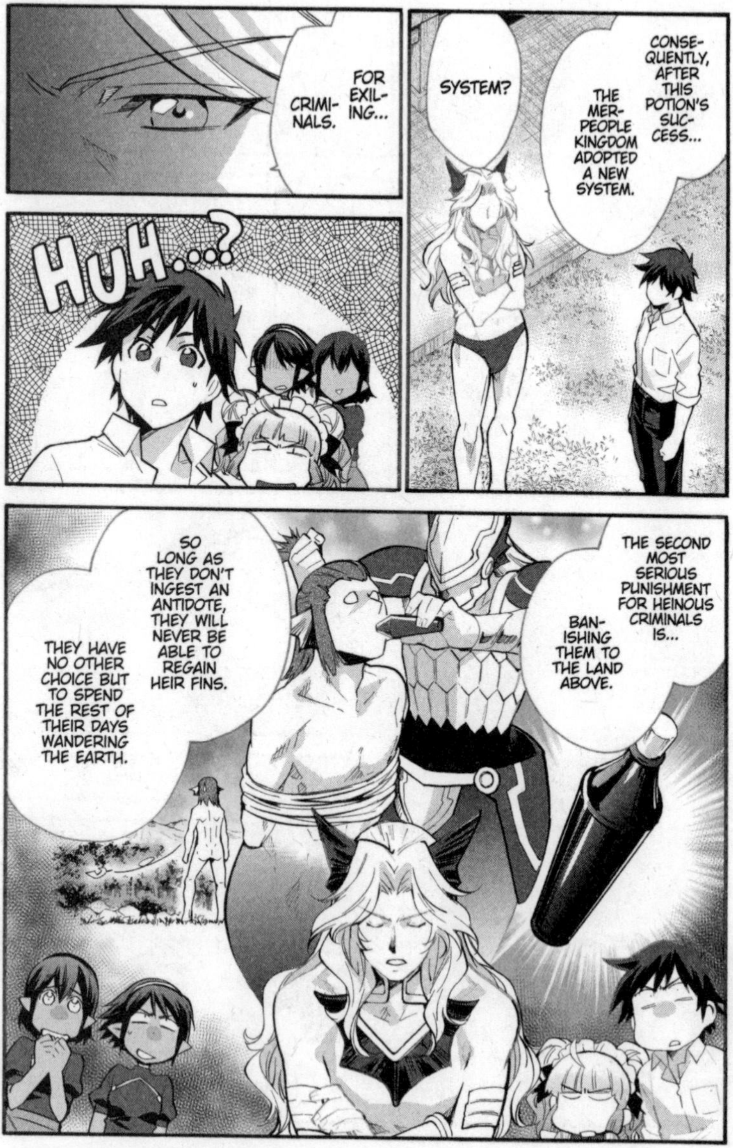
CONSEQUENTLY, AFTER THIS POTION'S SUCCESS...
THE MERPEOPLE KINGDOM ADOPTED A NEW SYSTEM.
SYSTEM?
FOR EXILING...
CRIMINALS.
HUH...?
THE SECOND MOST SERIOUS PUNISHMENT FOR HEINOUS CRIMINALS IS...
BANISHING THEM TO THE LAND ABOVE.
SO LONG AS THEY DON'T INGEST AN ANTIDOTE, THEY WILL NEVER BE ABLE TO REGAIN HEIR FINS.
THEY HAVE NO OTHER CHOICE BUT TO SPEND THE REST OF THEIR DAYS WANDERING THE EARTH.

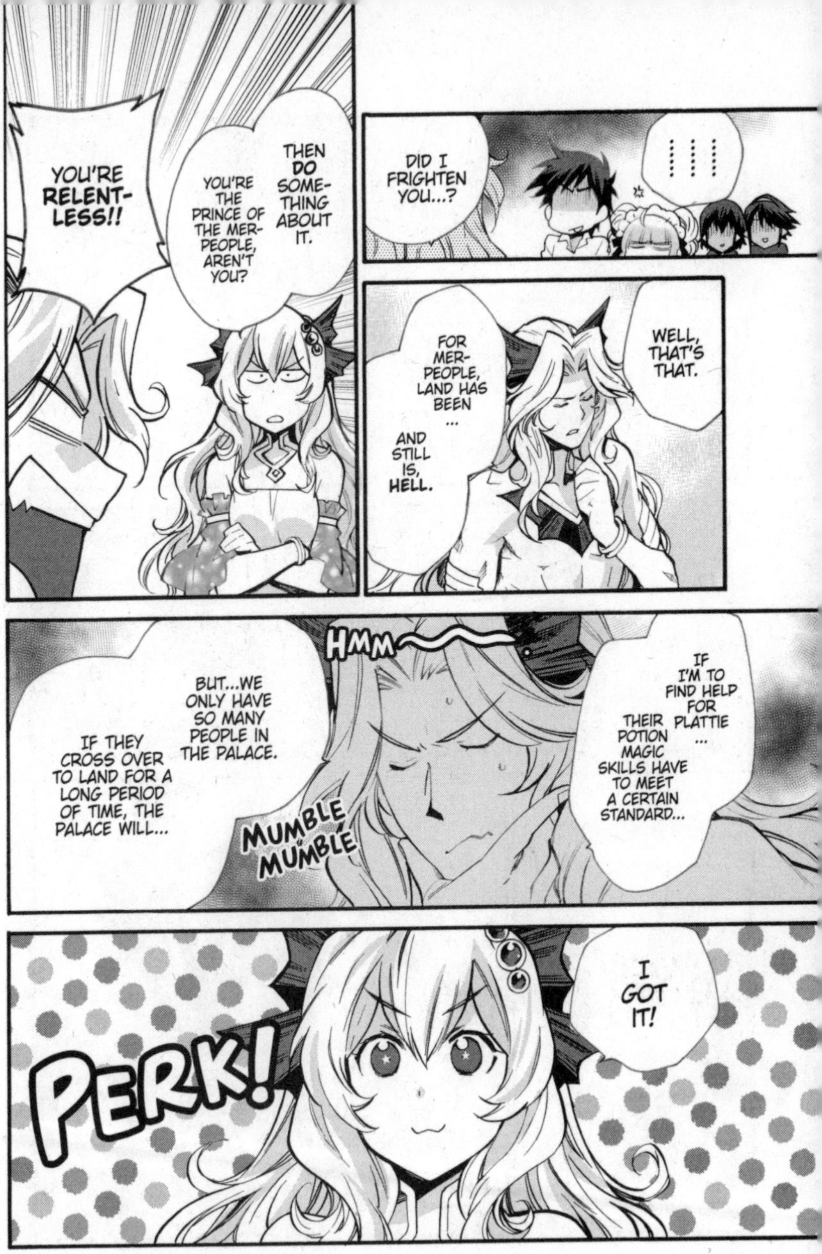

......
DID I FRIGHTEN YOU...?
WELL, THAT'S THAT.
FOR MER-PEOPLE, LAND HAS BEEN ...
AND STILL IS, HELL.
THEN DO SOMETHING ABOUT IT.
YOU'RE THE PRINCE OF THE MER-PEOPLE, AREN'T YOU?
YOU'RE RELENTLESS!!
HMM~
IF I'M TO FIND HELP FOR PLATTIE ...
THEIR POTION MAGIC SKILLS HAVE TO MEET A CERTAIN STANDARD...
BUT...WE ONLY HAVE SO MANY PEOPLE IN THE PALACE.
IF THEY CROSS OVER TO LAND FOR A LONG PERIOD OF TIME, THE PALACE WILL...
MUMBLE MUMBLE
I GOT IT!
PERK!

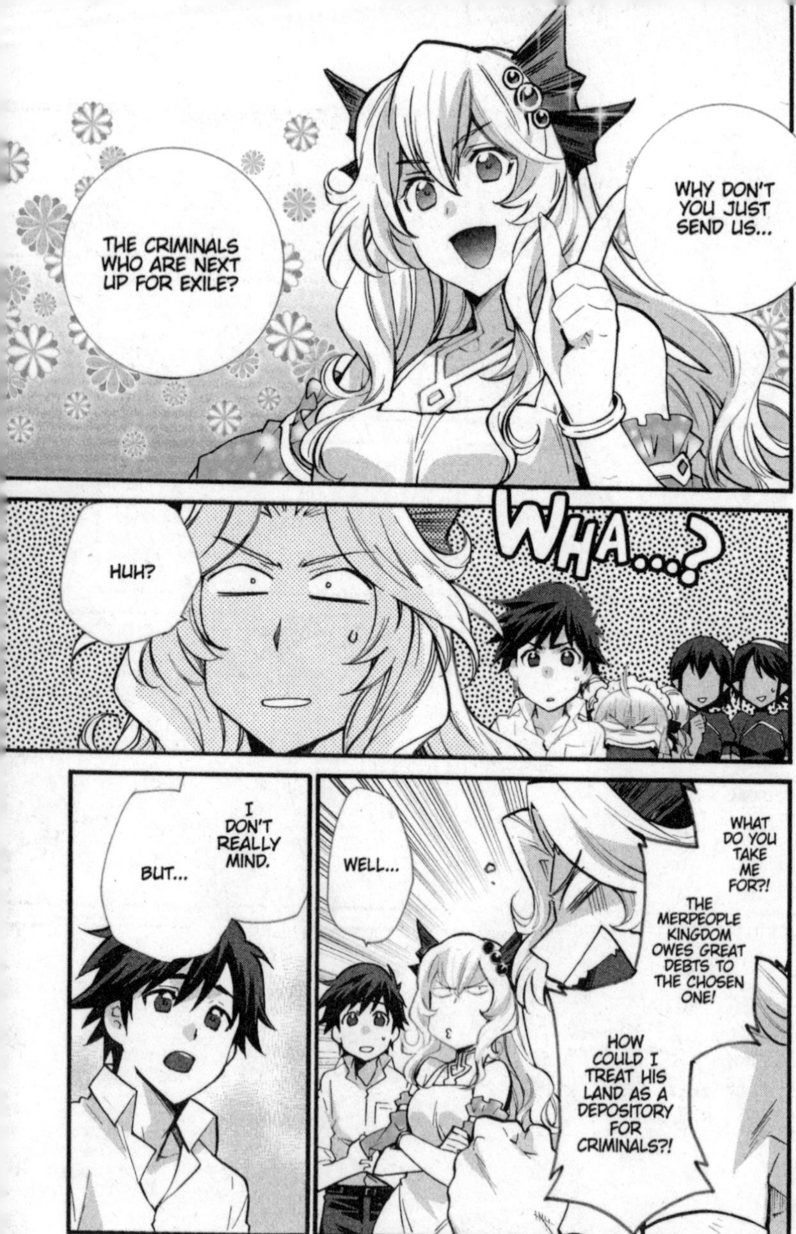
WHY DON'T YOU JUST SEND US...
THE CRIMINALS WHO ARE NEXT UP FOR EXILE?
WHA...?
HUH?
WHAT DO YOU TAKE ME FOR?!
THE MERPEOPLE KINGDOM OWES GREAT DEBTS TO THE CHOSEN ONE!
HOW COULD I TREAT HIS LAND AS A DEPOSITORY FOR CRIMINALS?!
WELL...
I DON'T REALLY MIND.
BUT...

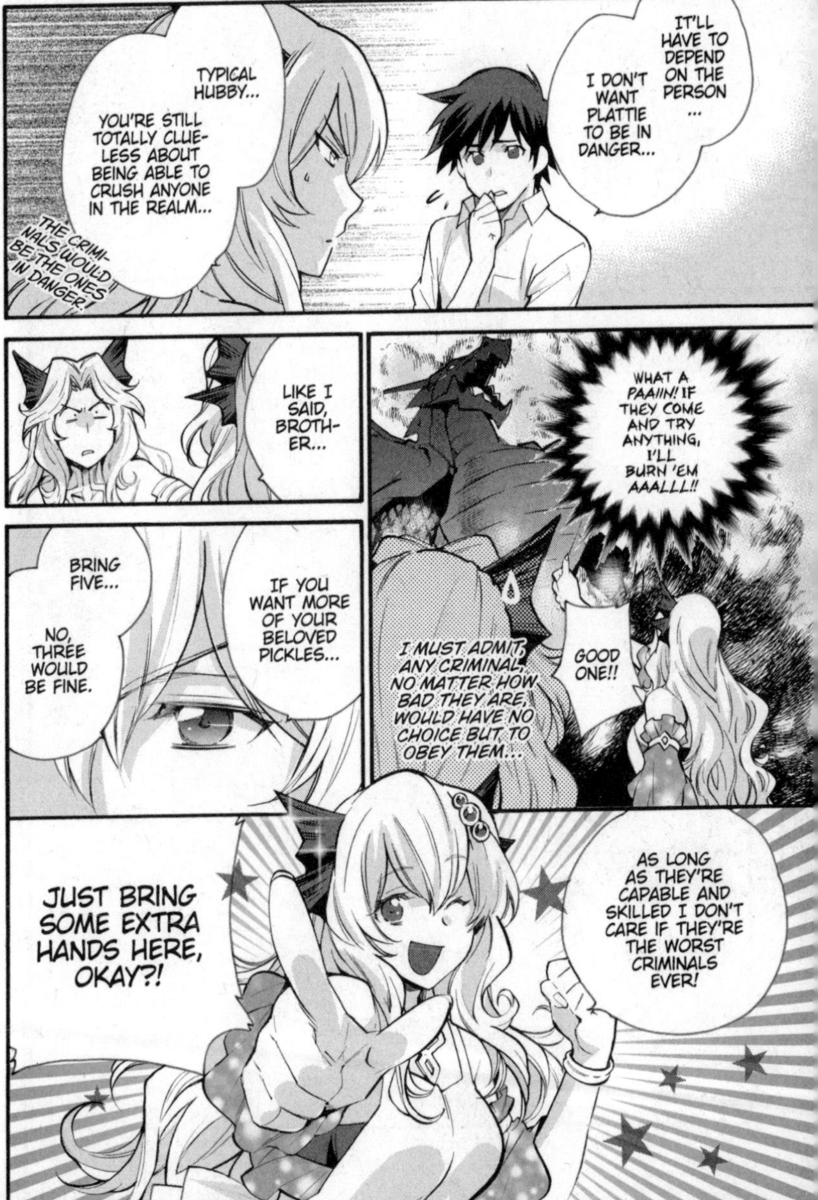

IT'LL HAVE TO DEPEND ON THE PERSON...
I DON'T WANT PLATTIE TO BE IN DANGER...
TYPICAL HUBBY...
YOU'RE STILL TOTALLY CLUE-LESS ABOUT BEING ABLE TO CRUSH ANYONE IN THE REALM...
THE CRIMI-NALS WOULD BE THE ONES IN DANGER!
WHAT A PAAIIN! IF THEY COME AND TRY ANYTHING, I'LL BURN 'EM AAALLL!!
GOOD ONE!!
I MUST ADMIT, ANY CRIMINAL, NO MATTER HOW BAD THEY ARE, WOULD HAVE NO CHOICE BUT TO OBEY THEM...
LIKE I SAID, BROTHER...
IF YOU WANT MORE OF YOUR BELOVED PICKLES...
BRING FIVE...
NO, THREE WOULD BE FINE.
AS LONG AS THEY'RE CAPABLE AND SKILLED I DON'T CARE IF THEY'RE THE WORST CRIMINALS EVER!
JUST BRING SOME EXTRA HANDS HERE, OKAY?!

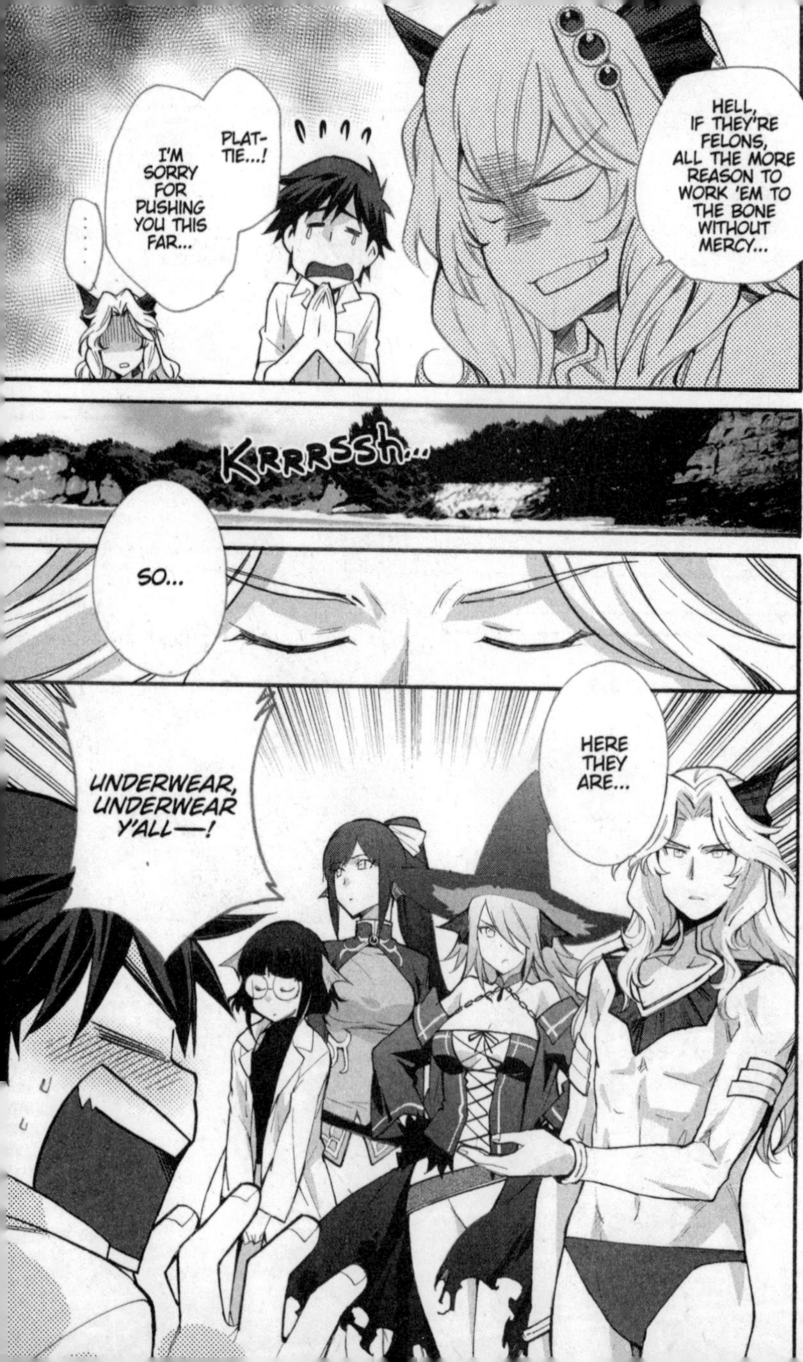
HELL, IF THEY'RE FELONS, ALL THE MORE REASON TO WORK 'EM TO THE BONE WITHOUT MERCY...
PLAT-TIE...!
I'M SORRY FOR PUSHING YOU THIS FAR...
....
KRRRSSh...
SO...
HERE THEY ARE...
UNDERWEAR, UNDERWEAR Y'ALL—!

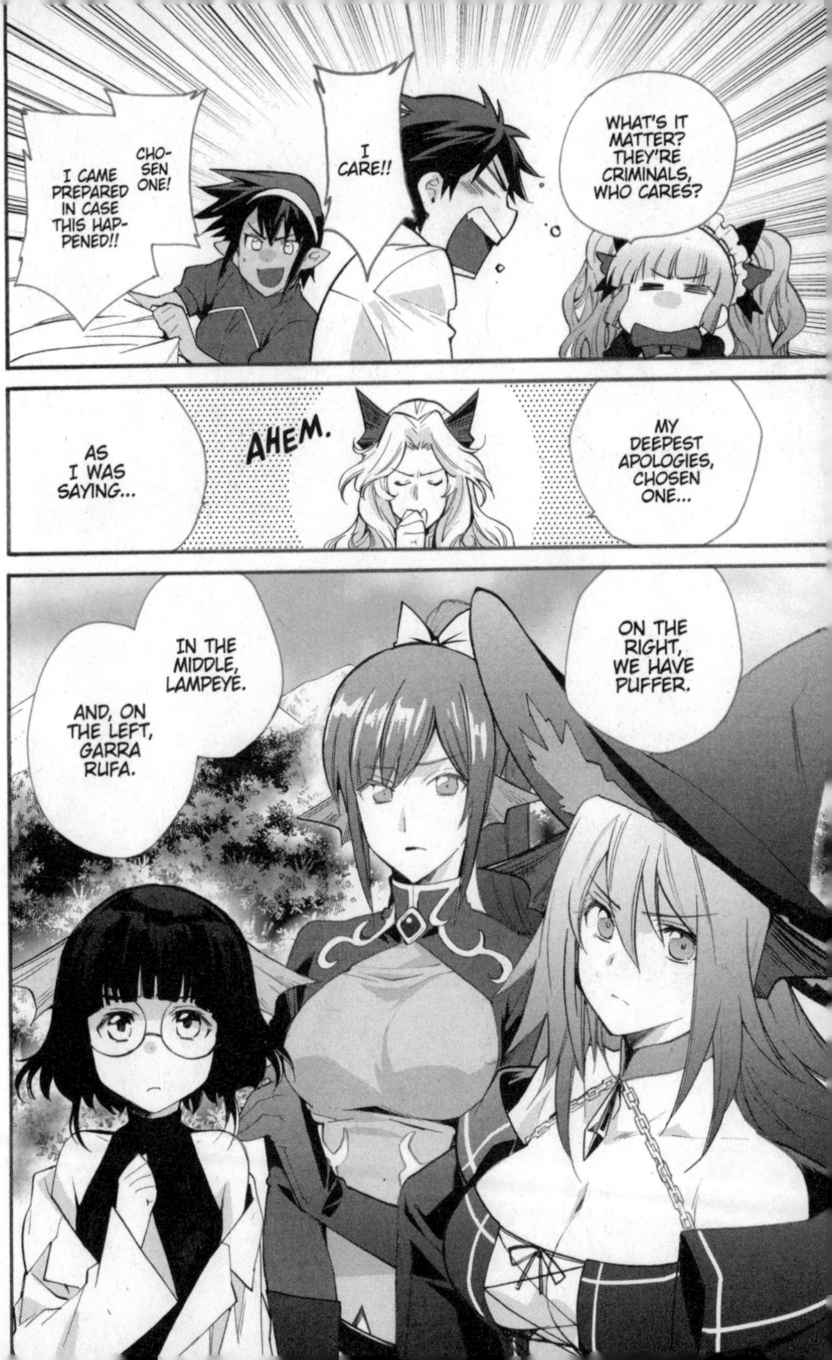
WHAT'S IT MATTER? THEY'RE CRIMINALS, WHO CARES?
I CARE!!
CHO-SEN ONE!
I CAME PREPARED IN CASE THIS HAP-PENED!!
MY DEEPEST APOLOGIES, CHOSEN ONE...
AHEM.
AS I WAS SAYING...
ON THE RIGHT, WE HAVE PUFFER.
IN THE MIDDLE, LAMPEYE.
AND, ON THE LEFT, GARRA RUFA.

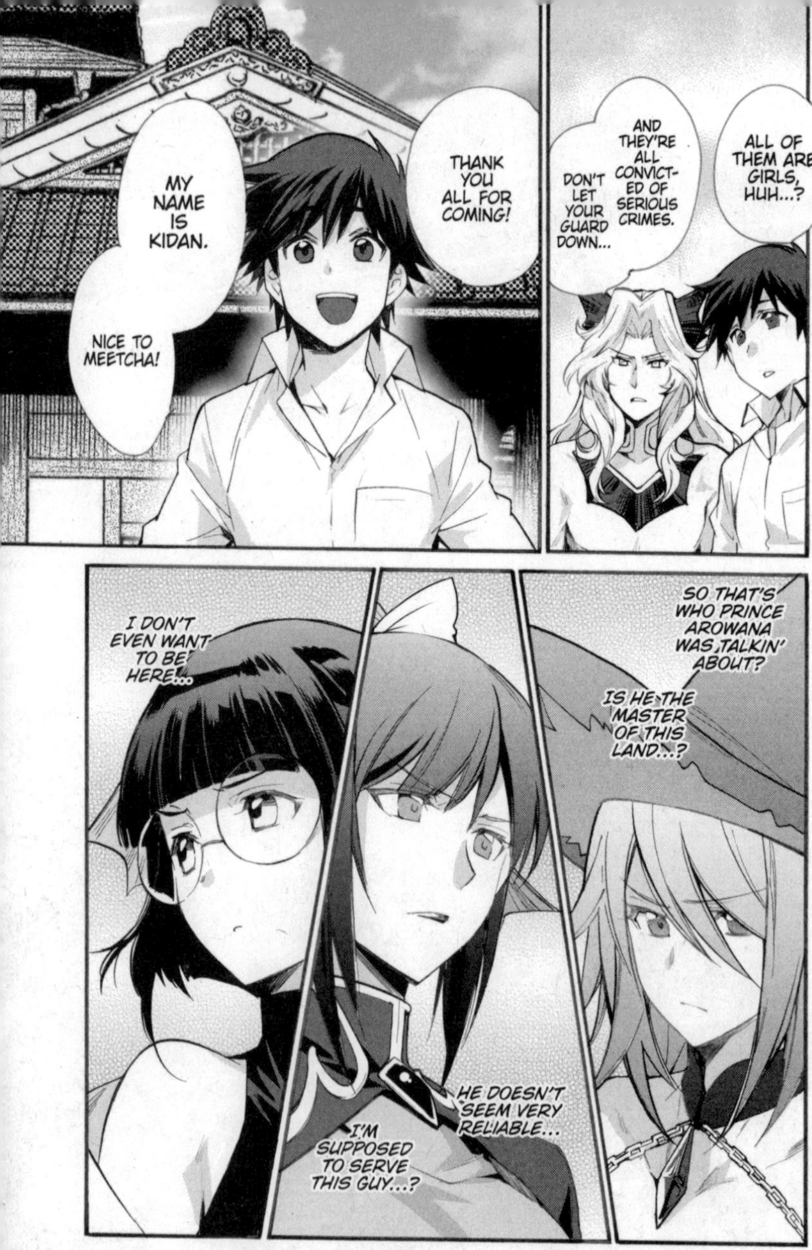
ALL OF THEM ARE GIRLS, HUH...?
AND THEY'RE ALL CONVICT-ED OF SERIOUS CRIMES.
DON'T LET YOUR GUARD DOWN...
THANK YOU ALL FOR COMING!
MY NAME IS KIDAN.
NICE TO MEETCHA!
SO THAT'S WHO PRINCE AROWANA WAS TALKIN' ABOUT?
IS HE THE MASTER OF THIS LAND...?
HE DOESN'T SEEM VERY RELIABLE...
I'M SUPPOSED TO SERVE THIS GUY...?
I DON'T EVEN WANT TO BE HERE...

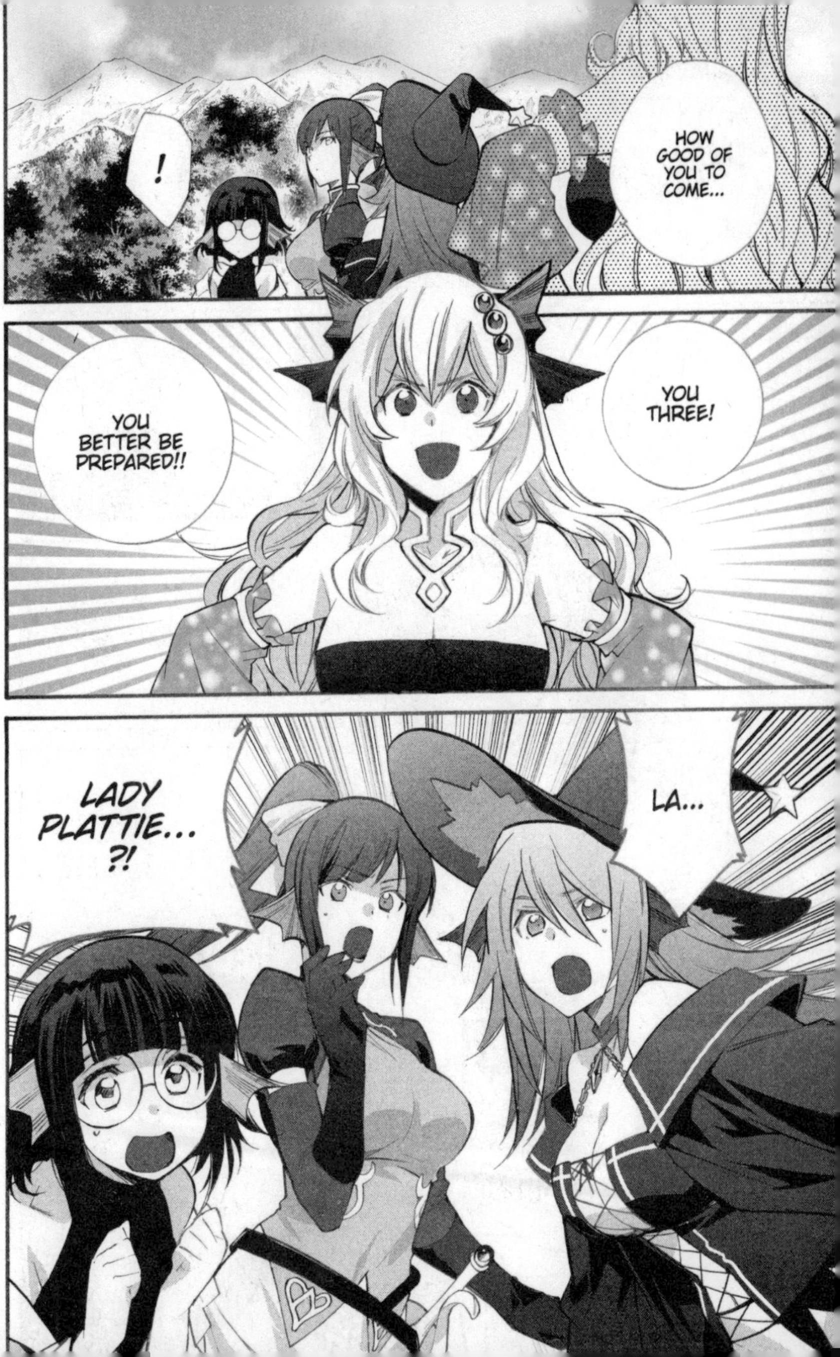
HOW GOOD OF YOU TO COME...
!
YOU THREE!
YOU BETTER BE PREPARED!!
LA...
LADY PLATTIE... ?!

CHAPTER 20

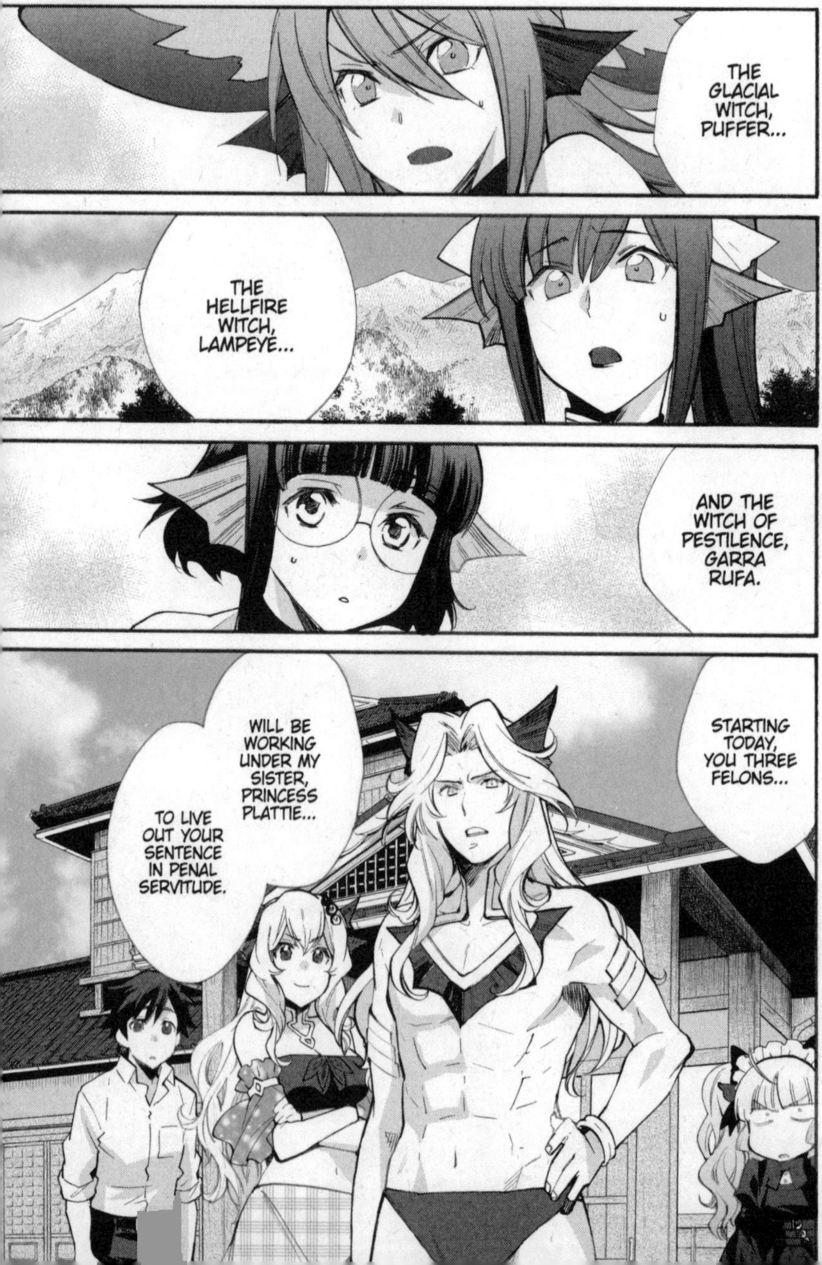
THE GLACIAL WITCH, PUFFER...
THE HELLFIRE WITCH, LAMPEYE...
AND THE WITCH OF PESTILENCE, GARRA RUFA.
STARTING TODAY, YOU THREE FELONS...
WILL BE WORKING UNDER MY SISTER, PRINCESS PLATTIE...
TO LIVE OUT YOUR SENTENCE IN PENAL SERVITUDE.

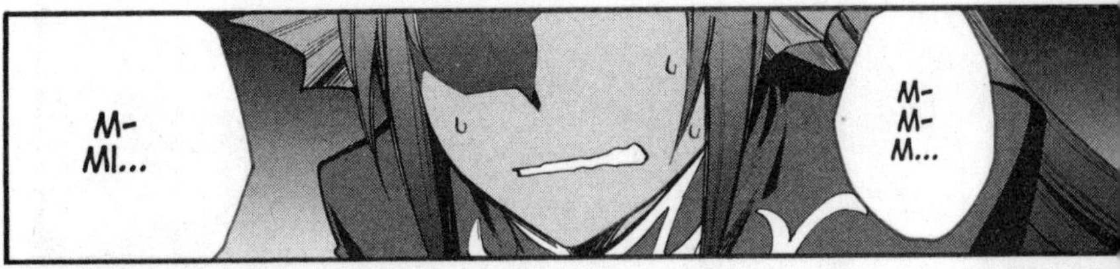
M-
M-
M...
M-
MI...

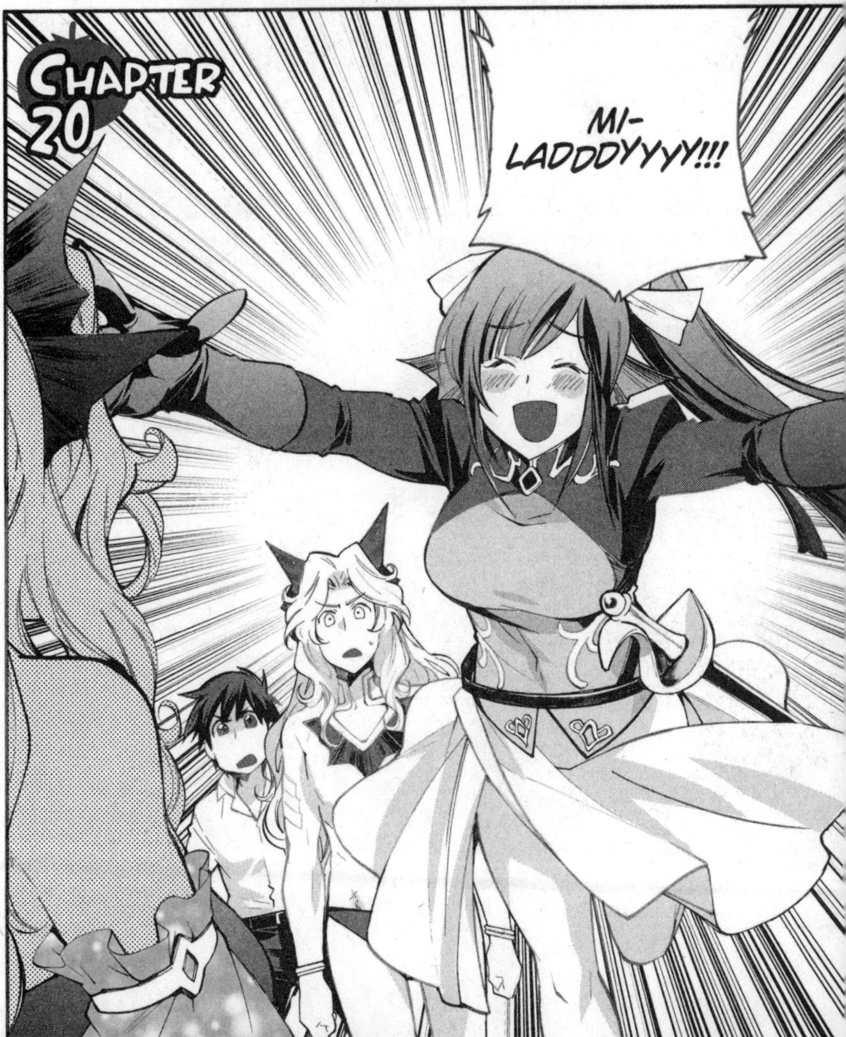
CHAPTER
20
MI-
LADDDYYYY!!!

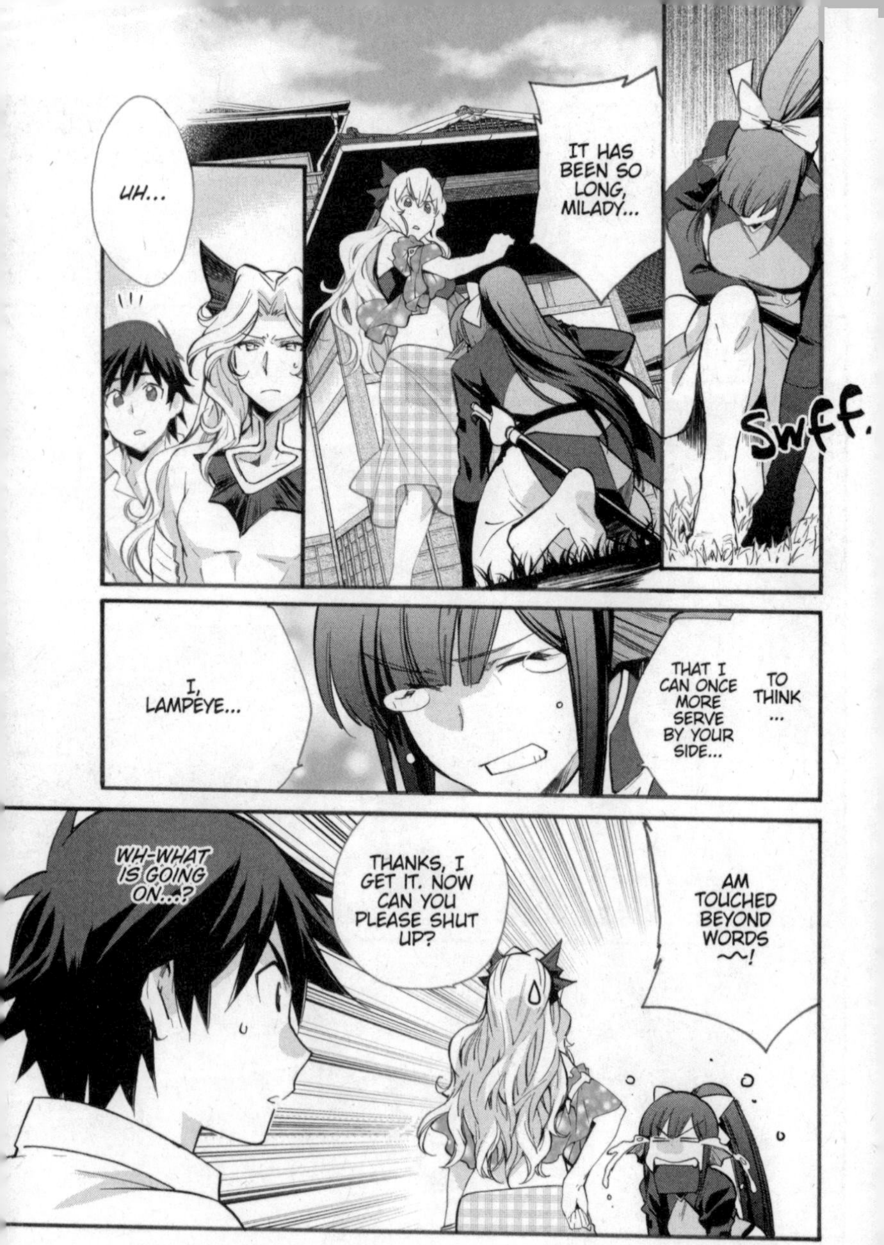
Swff.
IT HAS BEEN SO LONG, MILADY...
UH...
TO THINK ...
THAT I CAN ONCE MORE SERVE BY YOUR SIDE...
I, LAMPEYE...
AM TOUCHED BEYOND WORDS ~!
THANKS, I GET IT. NOW CAN YOU PLEASE SHUT UP?
WH-WHAT IS GOING ON...?

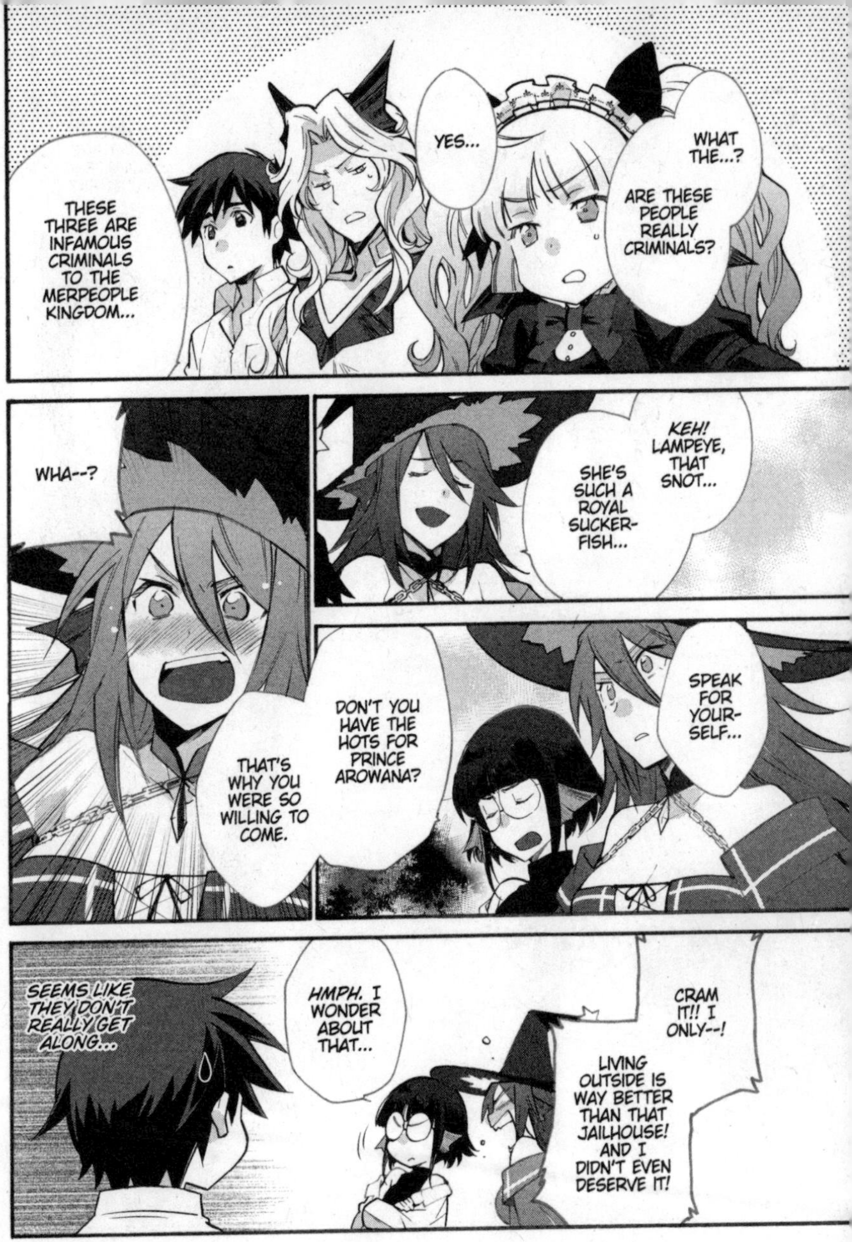
WHAT THE...?
ARE THESE PEOPLE REALLY CRIMINALS?
YES...
THESE THREE ARE INFAMOUS CRIMINALS TO THE MERPEOPLE KINGDOM...
KEH! LAMPEYE, THAT SNOT...
SHE'S SUCH A ROYAL SUCKER-FISH...
SPEAK FOR YOUR-SELF...
DON'T YOU HAVE THE HOTS FOR PRINCE AROWANA?
THAT'S WHY YOU WERE SO WILLING TO COME.
WHA--?
CRAM IT!! I ONLY--!
LIVING OUTSIDE IS WAY BETTER THAN THAT JAILHOUSE! AND I DIDN'T EVEN DESERVE IT!
HMPH. I WONDER ABOUT THAT...
SEEMS LIKE THEY DON'T REALLY GET ALONG...

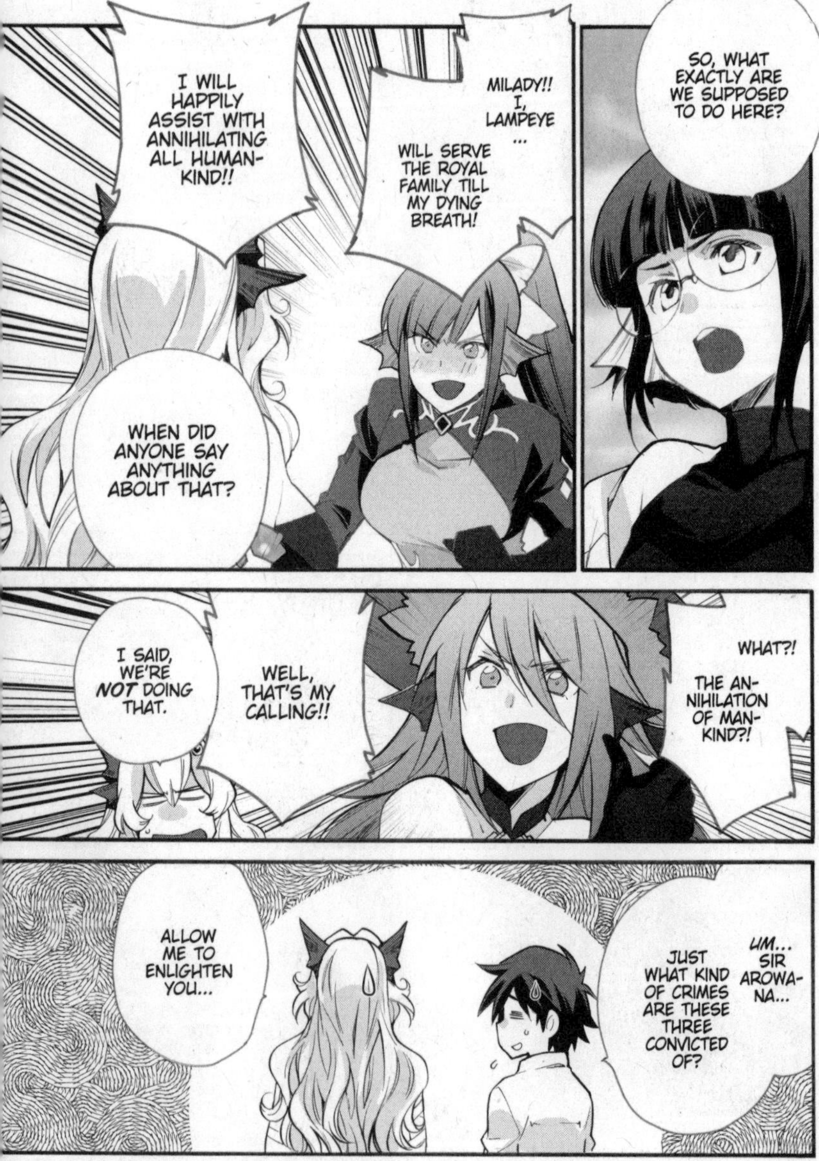
SO, WHAT EXACTLY ARE WE SUPPOSED TO DO HERE?
MILADY!! I, LAMPEYE ...
WILL SERVE THE ROYAL FAMILY TILL MY DYING BREATH!
I WILL HAPPILY ASSIST WITH ANNIHILATING ALL HUMANKIND!!
WHEN DID ANYONE SAY ANYTHING ABOUT THAT?
WHAT?!
THE ANNIHILATION OF MANKIND?!
WELL, THAT'S MY CALLING!!
I SAID, WE'RE **NOT** DOING THAT.
UM... SIR AROWANA...
JUST WHAT KIND OF CRIMES ARE THESE THREE CONVICTED OF?
ALLOW ME TO ENLIGHTEN YOU...

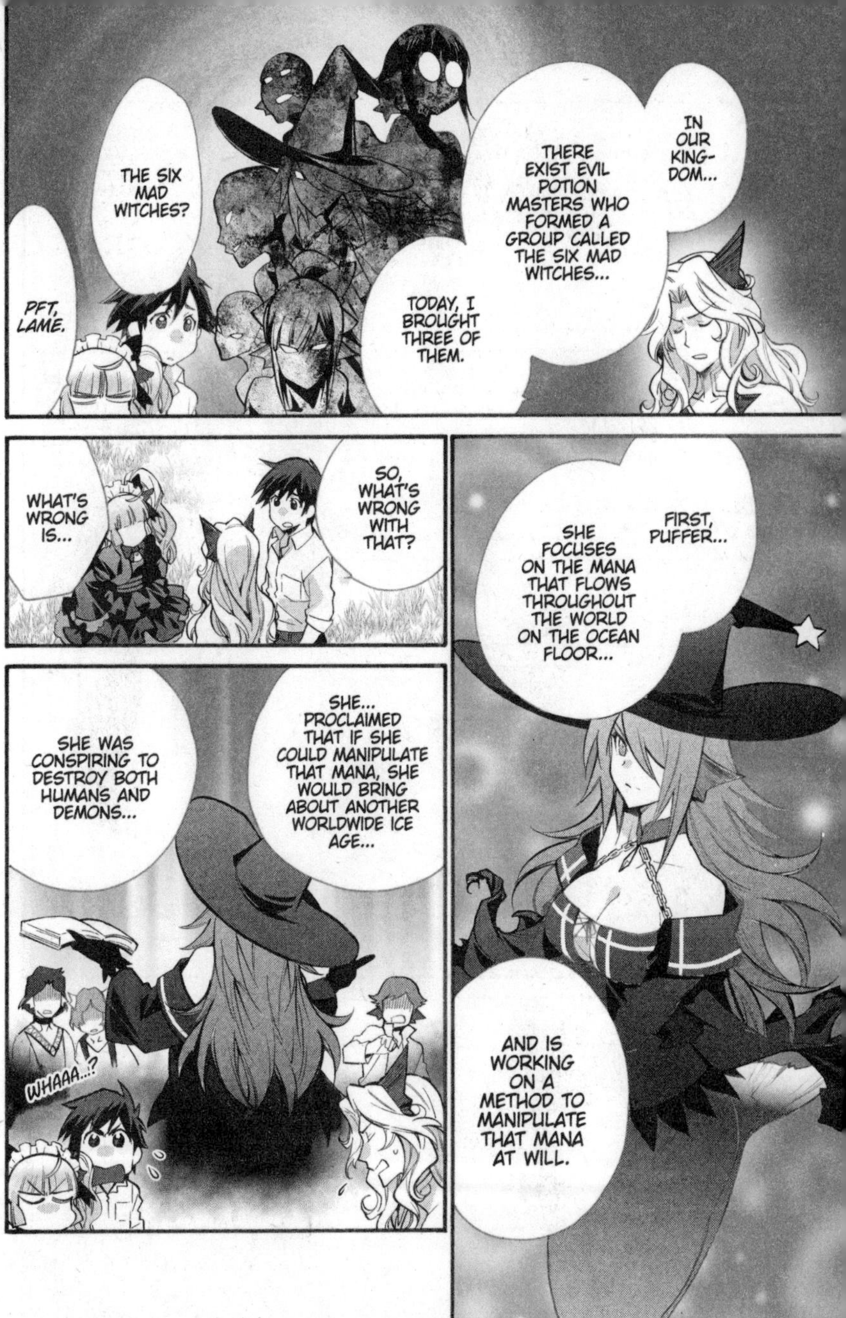
IN OUR KING-DOM...
THERE EXIST EVIL POTION MASTERS WHO FORMED A GROUP CALLED THE SIX MAD WITCHES...
TODAY, I BROUGHT THREE OF THEM.
THE SIX MAD WITCHES?
PFT, LAME.
FIRST, PUFFER...
SHE FOCUSES ON THE MANA THAT FLOWS THROUGHOUT THE WORLD ON THE OCEAN FLOOR...
AND IS WORKING ON A METHOD TO MANIPULATE THAT MANA AT WILL.
SO, WHAT'S WRONG WITH THAT?
WHAT'S WRONG IS...
SHE... PROCLAIMED THAT IF SHE COULD MANIPULATE THAT MANA, SHE WOULD BRING ABOUT ANOTHER WORLDWIDE ICE AGE...
SHE WAS CONSPIRING TO DESTROY BOTH HUMANS AND DEMONS...
WHAAA...?

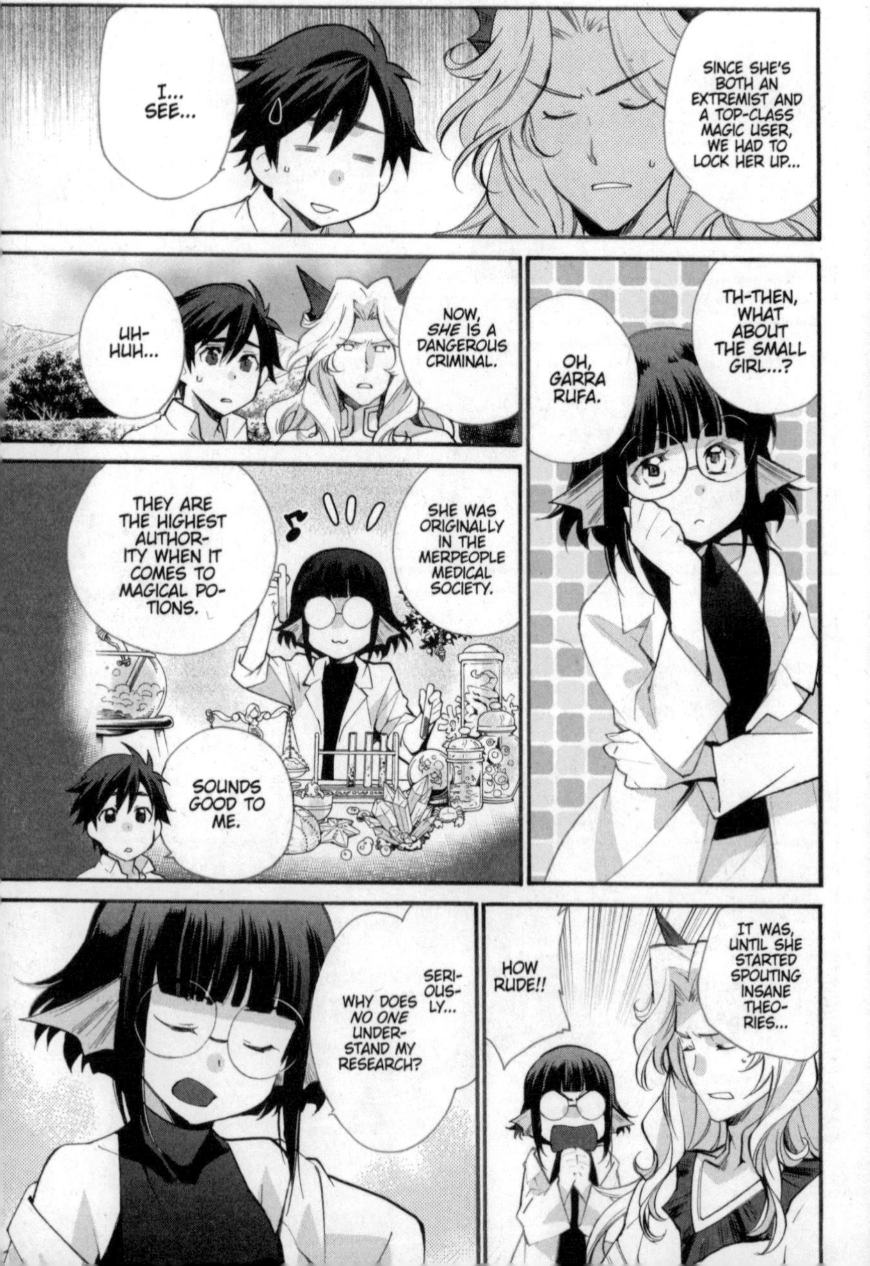
SINCE SHE'S BOTH AN EXTREMIST AND A TOP-CLASS MAGIC USER, WE HAD TO LOCK HER UP...
I... SEE...
TH-THEN, WHAT ABOUT THE SMALL GIRL...?
OH, GARRA RUFA.
NOW, *SHE* IS A DANGEROUS CRIMINAL.
UH-HUH...
SHE WAS ORIGINALLY IN THE MERPEOPLE MEDICAL SOCIETY.
THEY ARE THE HIGHEST AUTHOR-ITY WHEN IT COMES TO MAGICAL PO-TIONS.
SOUNDS GOOD TO ME.
IT WAS, UNTIL SHE STARTED SPOUTING INSANE THEO-RIES...
HOW RUDE!!
SERI-OUS-LY...
WHY DOES *NO ONE* UNDER-STAND MY RESEARCH?

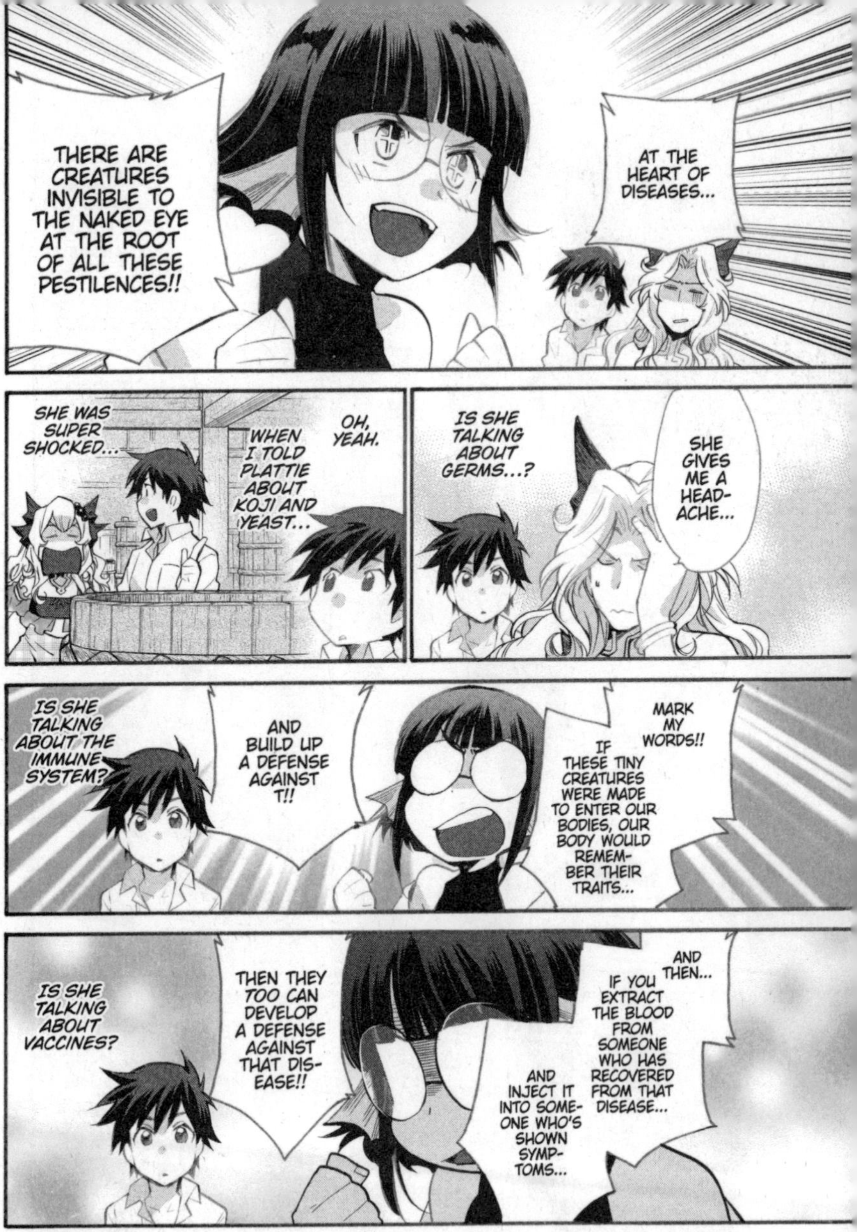
AT THE HEART OF DISEASES...
THERE ARE CREATURES INVISIBLE TO THE NAKED EYE AT THE ROOT OF ALL THESE PESTILENCES!!
SHE GIVES ME A HEADACHE...
IS SHE TALKING ABOUT GERMS...?
OH, YEAH.
WHEN I TOLD PLATTIE ABOUT KOJI AND YEAST...
SHE WAS SUPER SHOCKED...
MARK MY WORDS!!
IF THESE TINY CREATURES WERE MADE TO ENTER OUR BODIES, OUR BODY WOULD REMEMBER THEIR TRAITS...
AND BUILD UP A DEFENSE AGAINST T!!
IS SHE TALKING ABOUT THE IMMUNE SYSTEM?
AND THEN...
IF YOU EXTRACT THE BLOOD FROM SOMEONE WHO HAS RECOVERED FROM THAT DISEASE...
AND INJECT IT INTO SOMEONE WHO'S SHOWN SYMPTOMS...
THEN THEY TOO CAN DEVELOP A DEFENSE AGAINST THAT DISEASE!!
IS SHE TALKING ABOUT VACCINES?

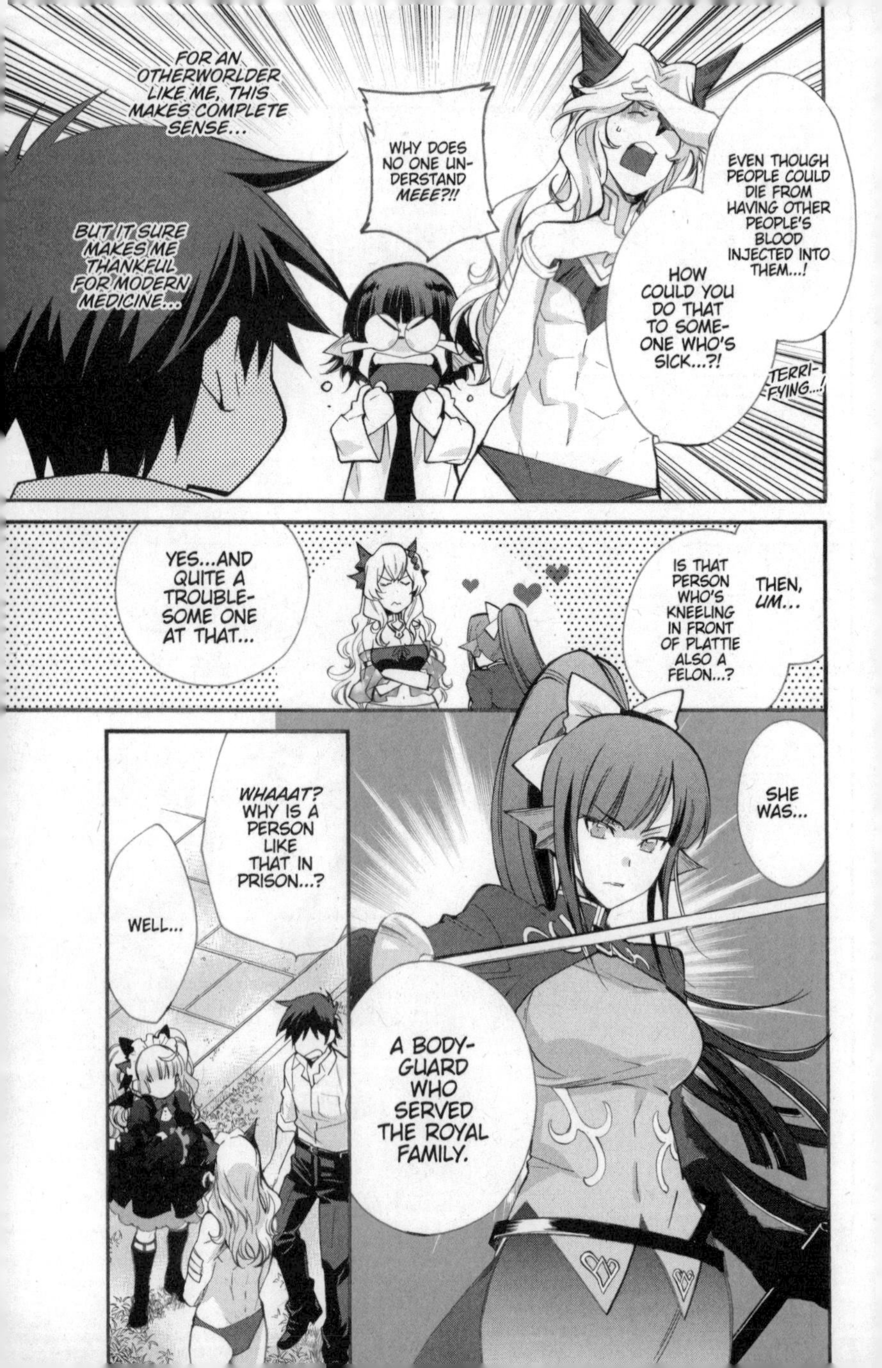
EVEN THOUGH PEOPLE COULD DIE FROM HAVING OTHER PEOPLE'S BLOOD INJECTED INTO THEM...!
HOW COULD YOU DO THAT TO SOME-ONE WHO'S SICK...?!
TERRI-FYING...!
WHY DOES NO ONE UN-DERSTAND MEEE?!!
FOR AN OTHERWORLDER LIKE ME, THIS MAKES COMPLETE SENSE...
BUT IT SURE MAKES ME THANKFUL FOR MODERN MEDICINE...
THEN, UM...
IS THAT PERSON WHO'S KNEELING IN FRONT OF PLATTIE ALSO A FELON...?
YES...AND QUITE A TROUBLE-SOME ONE AT THAT...
SHE WAS...
A BODY-GUARD WHO SERVED THE ROYAL FAMILY.
WHAAAT? WHY IS A PERSON LIKE THAT IN PRISON...?
WELL...

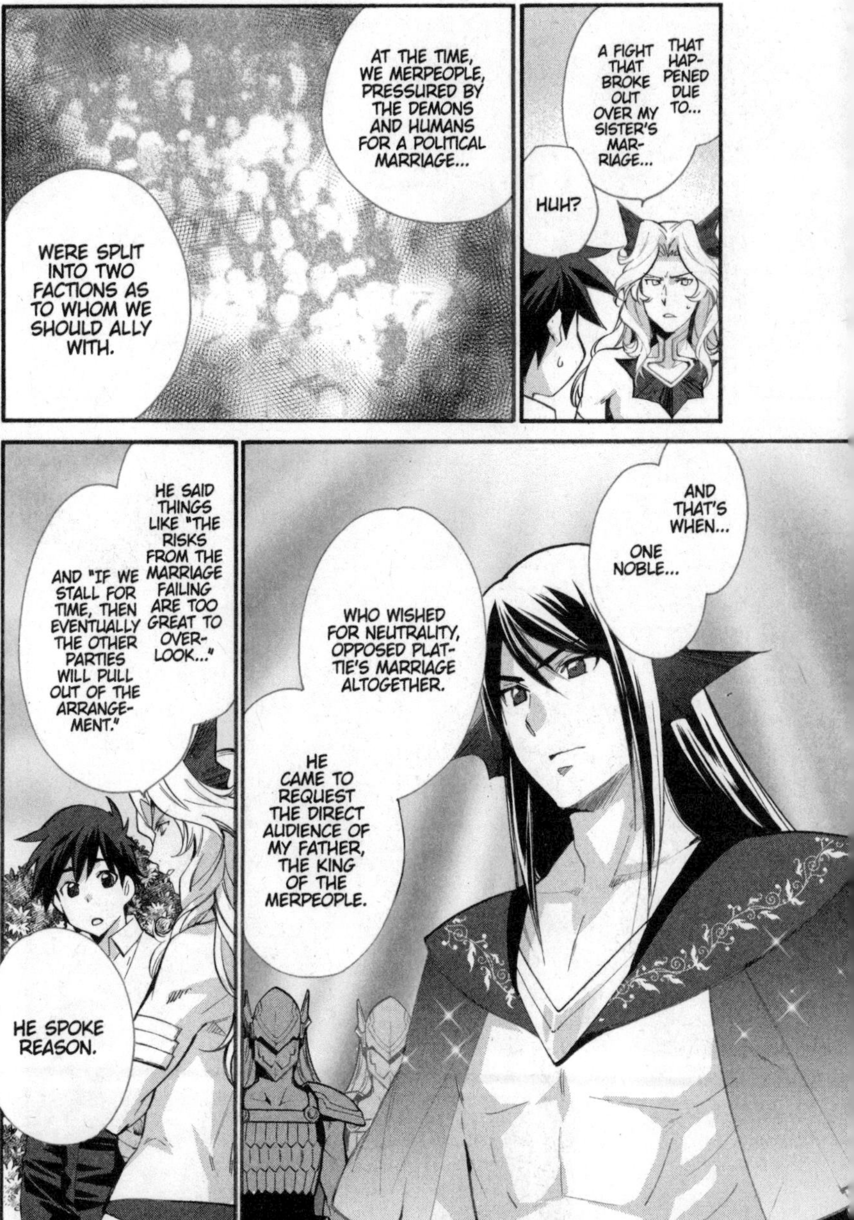
THAT HAP-PENED DUE TO...
A FIGHT THAT BROKE OUT OVER MY SISTER'S MAR-RIAGE...
HUH?
AT THE TIME, WE MERPEOPLE, PRESSURED BY THE DEMONS AND HUMANS FOR A POLITICAL MARRIAGE...
WERE SPLIT INTO TWO FACTIONS AS TO WHOM WE SHOULD ALLY WITH.
AND THAT'S WHEN...
ONE NOBLE...
WHO WISHED FOR NEUTRALITY, OPPOSED PLAT-TIE'S MARRIAGE ALTOGETHER.
HE CAME TO REQUEST THE DIRECT AUDIENCE OF MY FATHER, THE KING OF THE MERPEOPLE.
HE SAID THINGS LIKE "THE RISKS FROM THE MARRIAGE FAILING ARE TOO GREAT TO OVER-LOOK..."
AND "IF WE STALL FOR TIME, THEN EVENTUALLY THE OTHER PARTIES WILL PULL OUT OF THE ARRANGE-MENT."
HE SPOKE REASON.

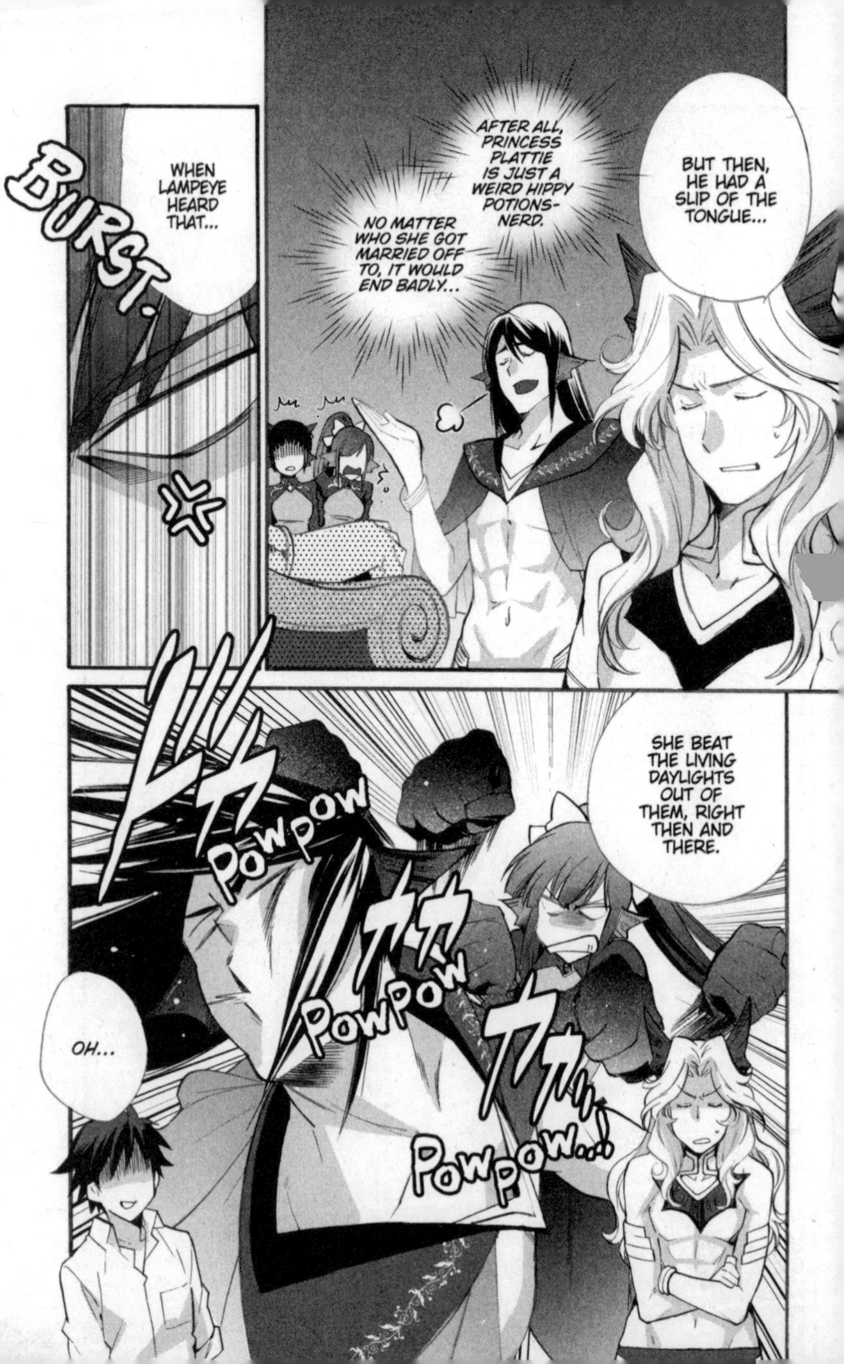

BUT THEN, HE HAD A SLIP OF THE TONGUE...
AFTER ALL, PRINCESS PLATTIE IS JUST A WEIRD HIPPY POTIONS-NERD.
NO MATTER WHO SHE GOT MARRIED OFF TO, IT WOULD END BADLY...
WHEN LAMPEYE HEARD THAT...
BURST.
SHE BEAT THE LIVING DAYLIGHTS OUT OF THEM, RIGHT THEN AND THERE.
POWPOW
POWPOW
POWPOW...!
OH...

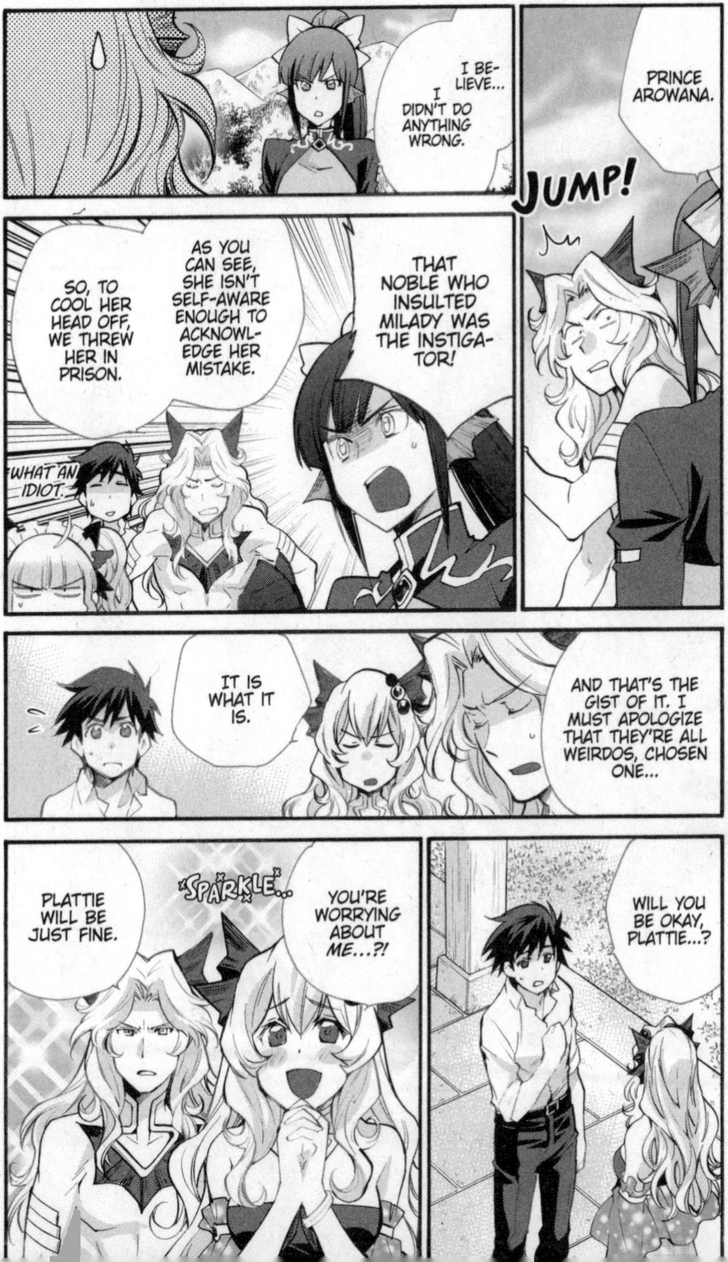
PRINCE AROWANA.
I BELIEVE... I DIDN'T DO ANYTHING WRONG.
JUMP!
THAT NOBLE WHO INSULTED MILADY WAS THE INSTIGATOR!
AS YOU CAN SEE, SHE ISN'T SELF-AWARE ENOUGH TO ACKNOWLEDGE HER MISTAKE.
SO, TO COOL HER HEAD OFF, WE THREW HER IN PRISON.
WHAT AN IDIOT.
AND THAT'S THE GIST OF IT. I MUST APOLOGIZE THAT THEY'RE ALL WEIRDOS, CHOSEN ONE...
IT IS WHAT IT IS.
WILL YOU BE OKAY, PLATTIE...?
YOU'RE WORRYING ABOUT ME...?!
SPARKLE...
PLATTIE WILL BE JUST FINE.

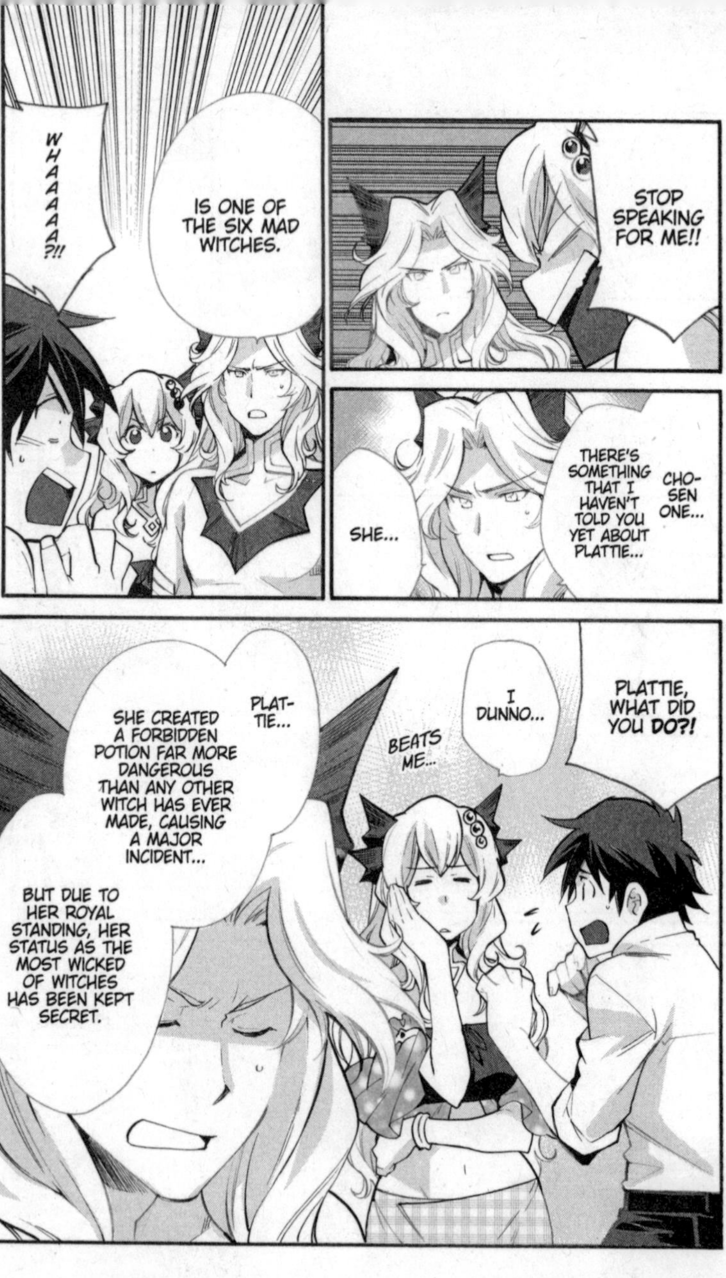
STOP SPEAKING FOR ME!!
CHO-SEN ONE...
THERE'S SOMETHING THAT I HAVEN'T TOLD YOU YET ABOUT PLATTIE...
SHE...
IS ONE OF THE SIX MAD WITCHES.
WHAAAAAA?!!
PLATTIE, WHAT DID YOU DO?!
I DUNNO...
BEATS ME...
PLAT-TIE...
SHE CREATED A FORBIDDEN POTION FAR MORE DANGEROUS THAN ANY OTHER WITCH HAS EVER MADE, CAUSING A MAJOR INCIDENT...
BUT DUE TO HER ROYAL STANDING, HER STATUS AS THE MOST WICKED OF WITCHES HAS BEEN KEPT SECRET.

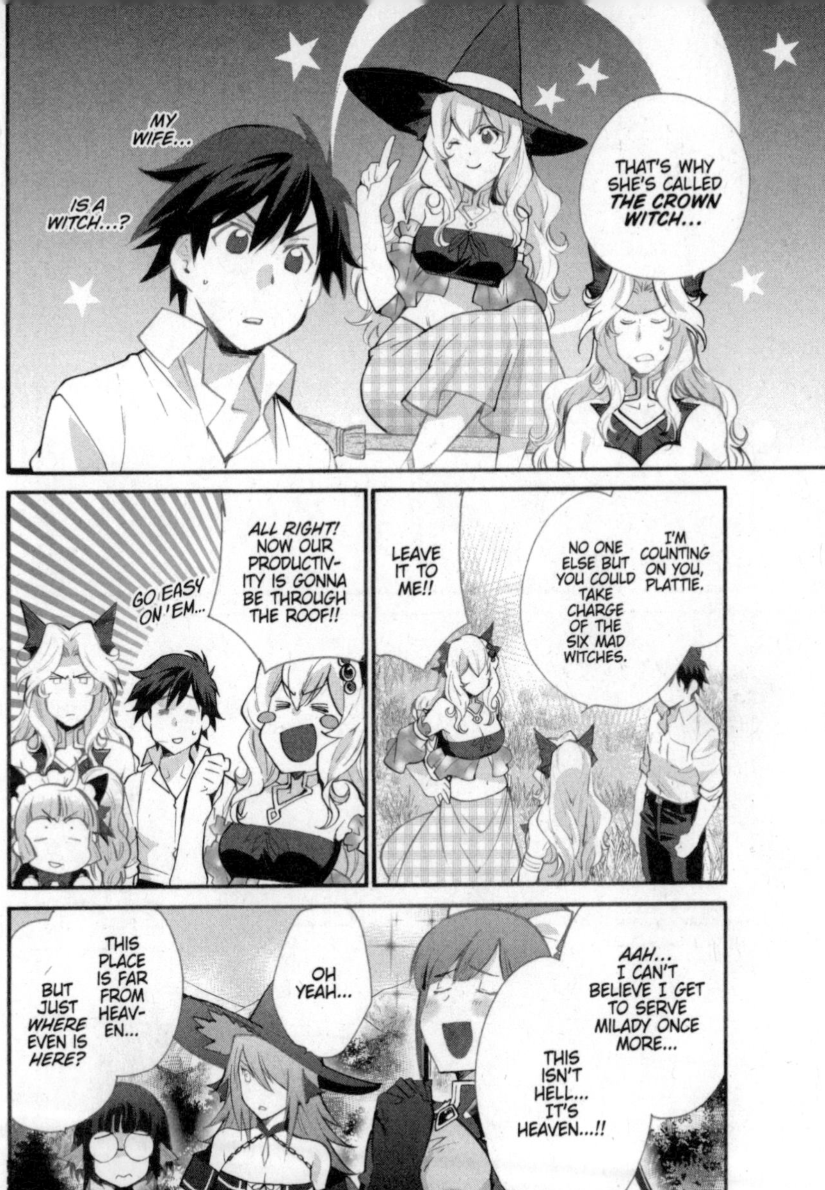
THAT'S WHY SHE'S CALLED *THE CROWN WITCH*...
MY WIFE...
IS A WITCH...?
I'M COUNTING ON YOU, PLATTIE.
NO ONE ELSE BUT YOU COULD TAKE CHARGE OF THE SIX MAD WITCHES.
LEAVE IT TO ME!!
ALL RIGHT! NOW OUR PRODUCTIVITY IS GONNA BE THROUGH THE ROOF!!
GO EASY ON 'EM...
AAH... I CAN'T BELIEVE I GET TO SERVE MILADY ONCE MORE...
THIS ISN'T HELL... IT'S HEAVEN...!!
OH YEAH...
THIS PLACE IS FAR FROM HEAVEN...
BUT JUST *WHERE* EVEN IS *HERE?*

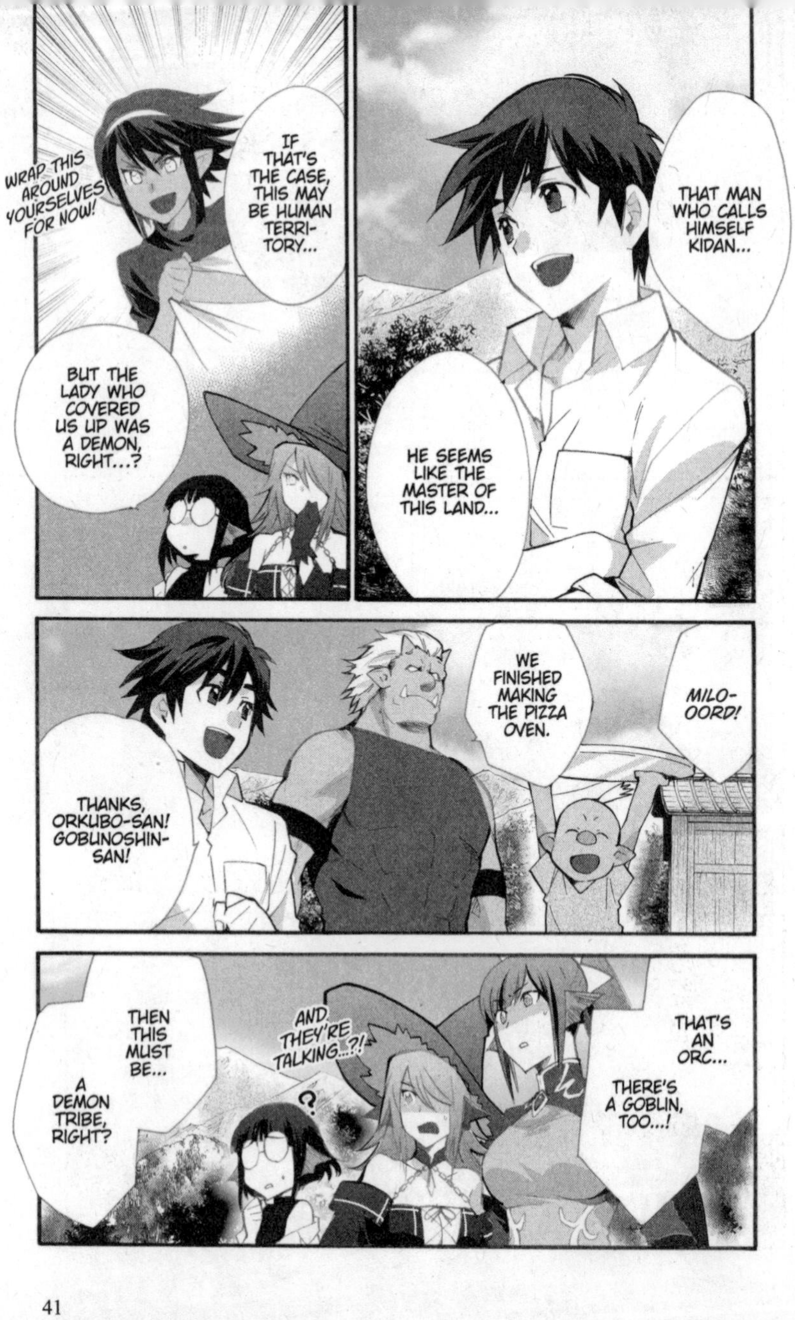
THAT MAN WHO CALLS HIMSELF KIDAN...
HE SEEMS LIKE THE MASTER OF THIS LAND...
IF THAT'S THE CASE, THIS MAY BE HUMAN TERRI-TORY...
WRAP THIS AROUND YOURSELVES FOR NOW!
BUT THE LADY WHO COVERED US UP WAS A DEMON, RIGHT...?
MILO-OORD!
WE FINISHED MAKING THE PIZZA OVEN.
THANKS, ORKUBO-SAN! GOBUNOSHIN-SAN!
THAT'S AN ORC...
THERE'S A GOBLIN, TOO...!
AND THEY'RE TALKING...?!
THEN THIS MUST BE...
A DEMON TRIBE, RIGHT?

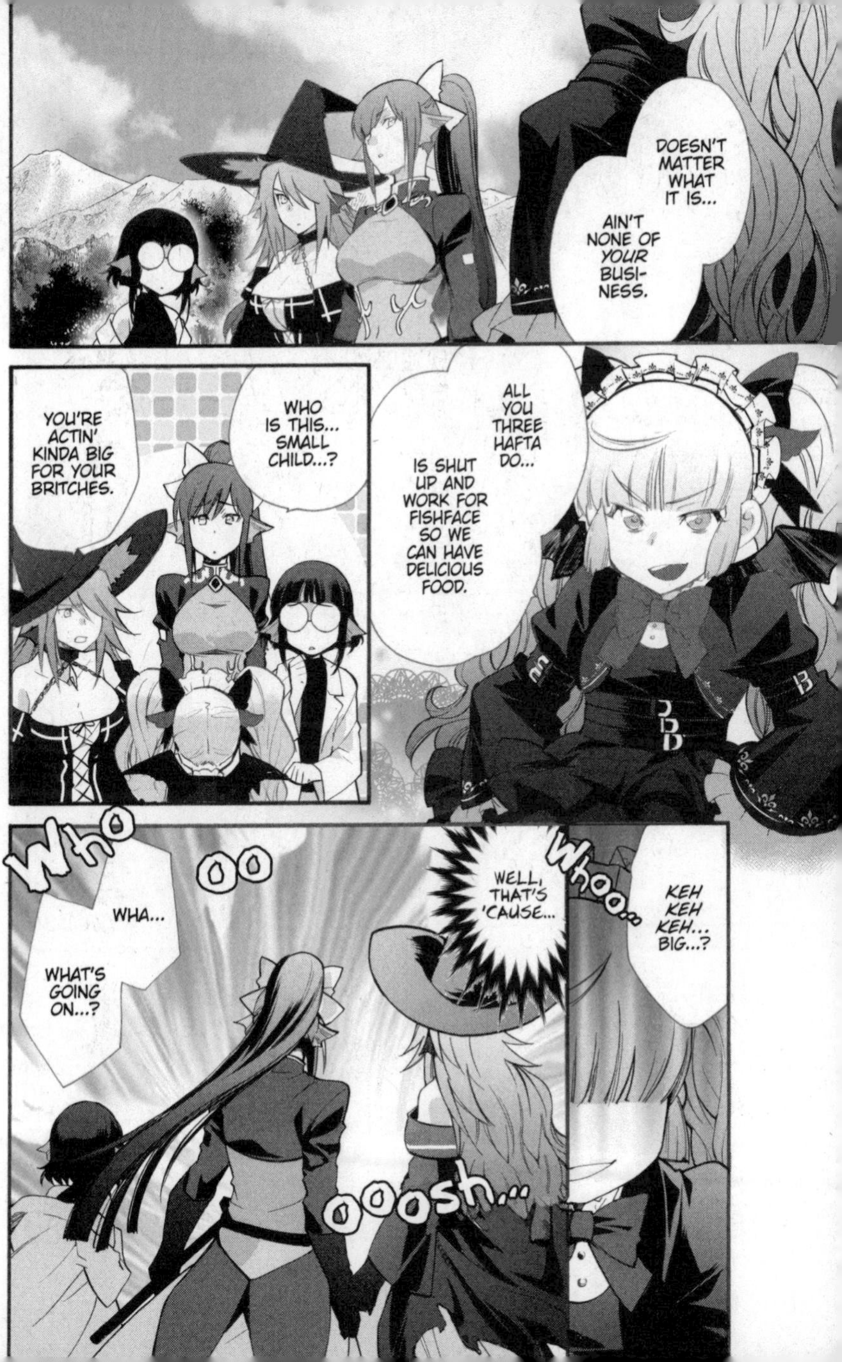
DOESN'T MATTER WHAT IT IS...
AIN'T NONE OF YOUR BUSI-NESS.
ALL YOU THREE HAFTA DO...
IS SHUT UP AND WORK FOR FISHFACE SO WE CAN HAVE DELICIOUS FOOD.
WHO IS THIS... SMALL CHILD...?
YOU'RE ACTIN' KINDA BIG FOR YOUR BRITCHES.
KEH KEH KEH... BIG...?
Whoo...
WELL, THAT'S 'CAUSE...
Whooo
WHA...
WHAT'S GOING ON...?
oooosh...

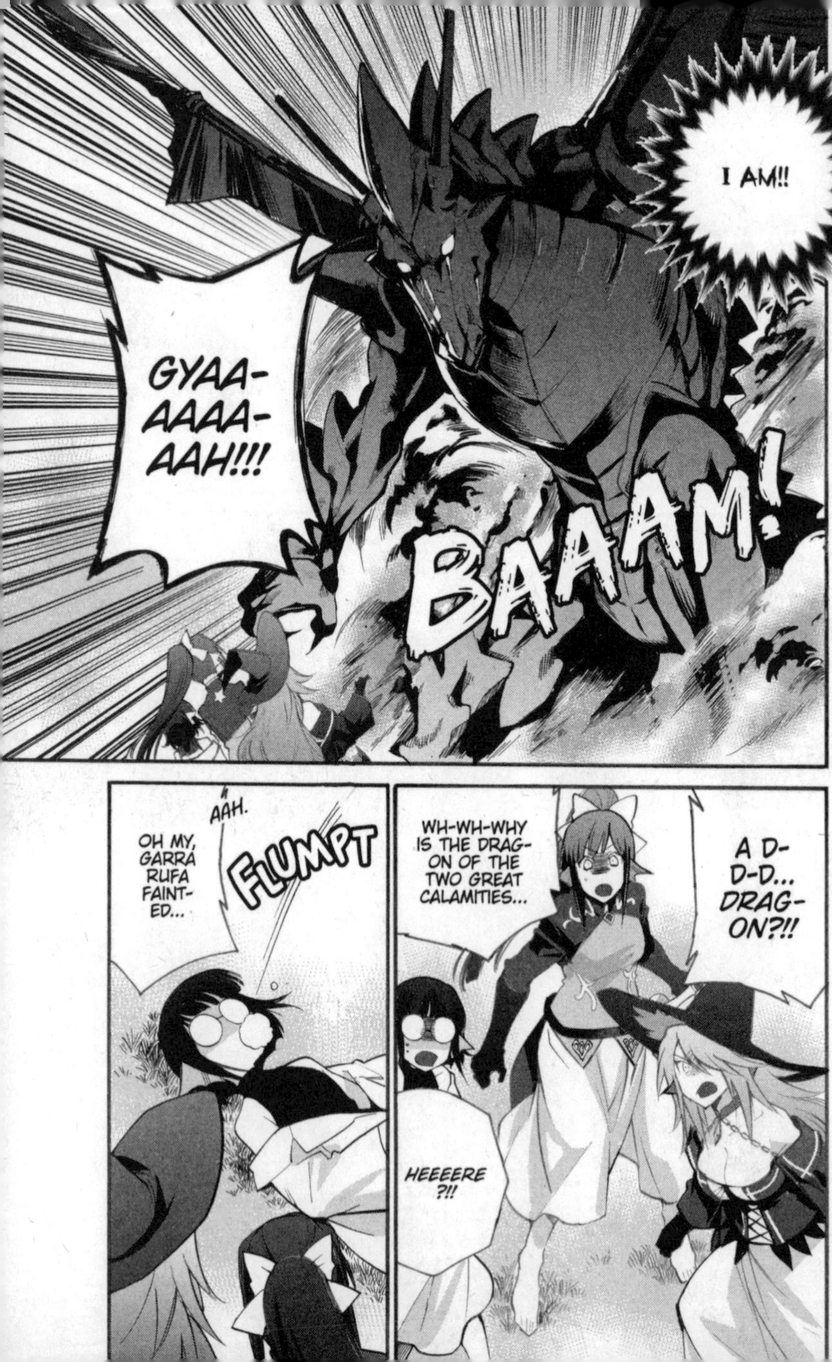
I AM!!
GYAA-
AAAA-
AAH!!!
BAAAM!
A D-
D-D...
DRAG-
ON?!!
WH-WH-WHY
IS THE DRAG-
ON OF THE
TWO GREAT
CALAMITIES...
HEEEERE
?!!
AAH.
FLUMPT
OH MY,
GARRA
RUFA
FAINT-
ED...

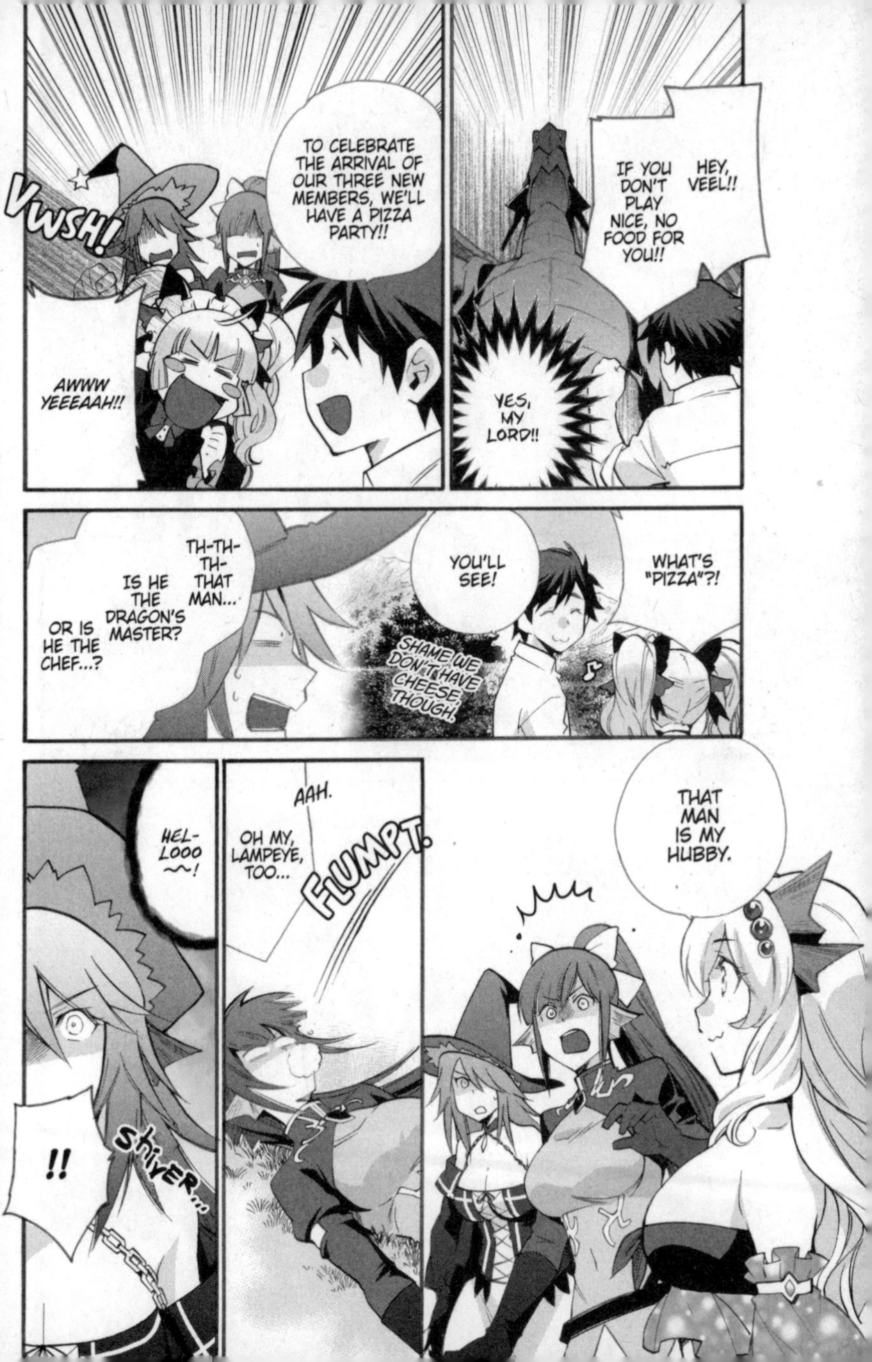
HEY, VEEL!!
IF YOU DON'T PLAY NICE, NO FOOD FOR YOU!!
YES, MY LORD!!
TO CELEBRATE THE ARRIVAL OF OUR THREE NEW MEMBERS, WE'LL HAVE A PIZZA PARTY!!
VWSH!
AWWW YEEEAAH!!
WHAT'S "PIZZA"?!
YOU'LL SEE!
SHAME WE DON'T HAVE CHEESE, THOUGH.
TH-TH-TH-THAT MAN...
IS HE THE DRAGON'S MASTER?
OR IS HE THE CHEF...?
THAT MAN IS MY HUBBY.
AAH.
OH MY, LAMPEYE, TOO...
FLUMPT.
HEL-LOOO ~!
!!
SHIVER...

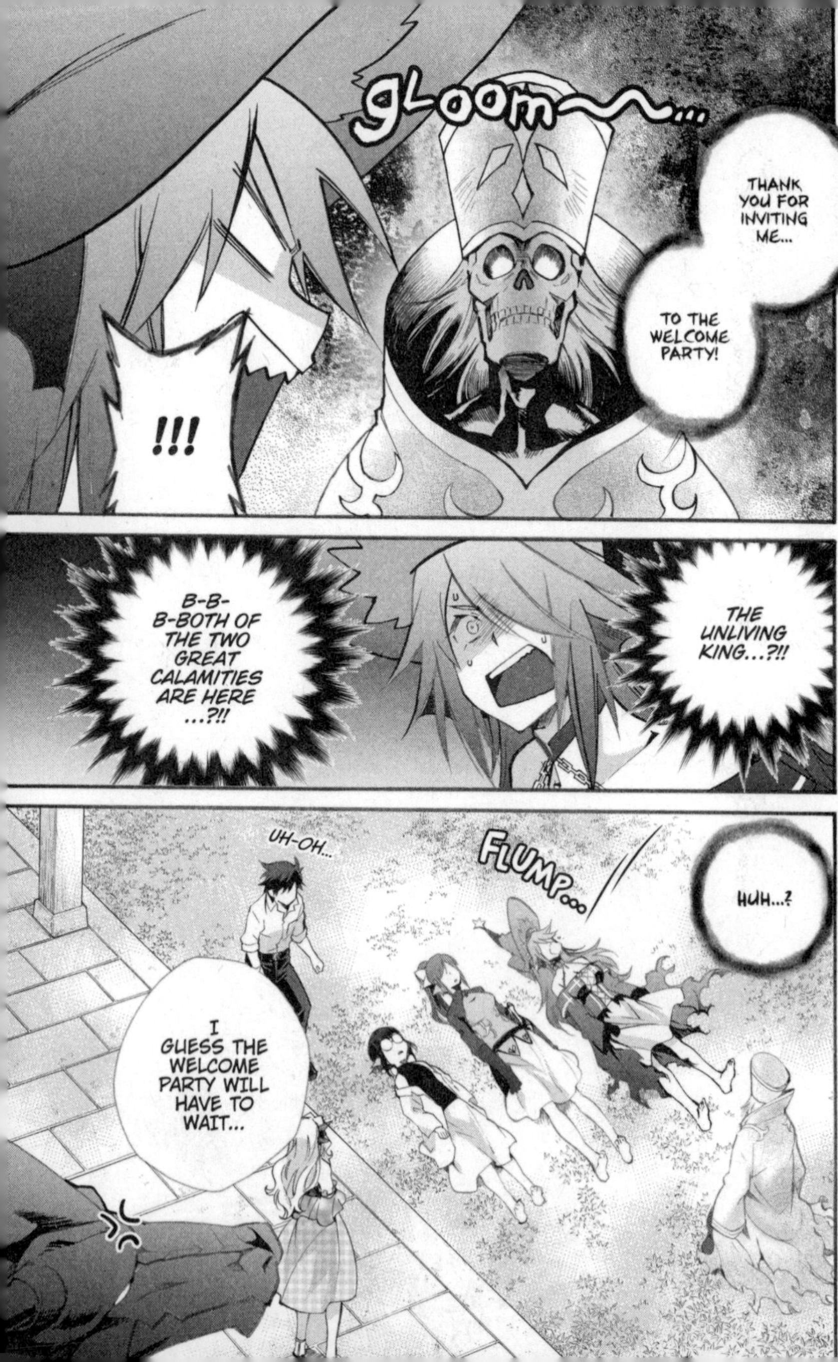
gLoom~~...
THANK YOU FOR INVITING ME...
TO THE WELCOME PARTY!
!!!
THE UNLIVING KING...?!!
B-B-B-BOTH OF THE TWO GREAT CALAMITIES ARE HERE ...?!!
HUH...?
FLUMP...
UH-OH...
I GUESS THE WELCOME PARTY WILL HAVE TO WAIT...

LET'S BUY THE LAND and CULTIVATE IT IN A DIFFERENT WORLD

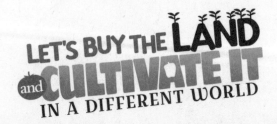

CHAPTER 21

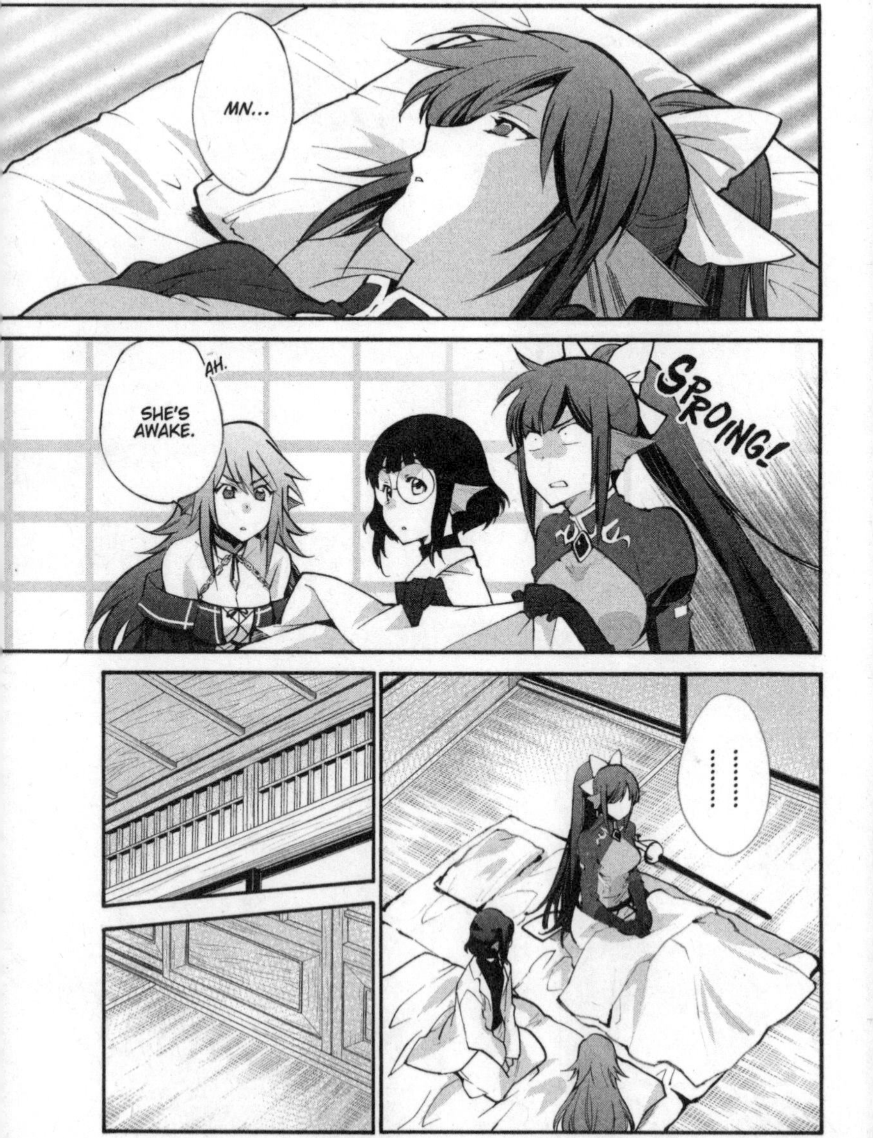
MN...
SPROING!
AH.
SHE'S AWAKE.
......

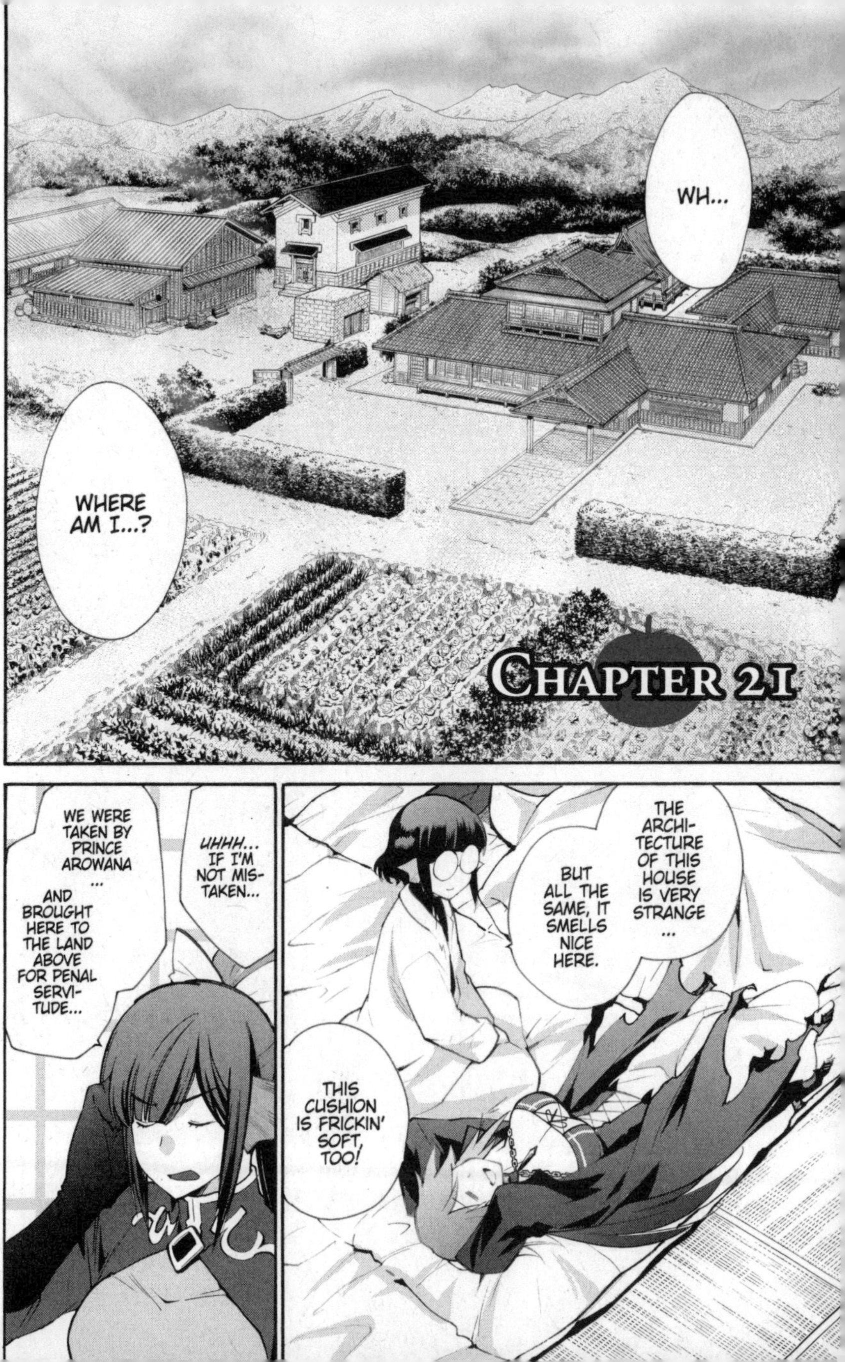
WH...
WHERE AM I...?
CHAPTER 21
THE ARCHITECTURE OF THIS HOUSE IS VERY STRANGE...
BUT ALL THE SAME, IT SMELLS NICE HERE.
THIS CUSHION IS FRICKIN' SOFT, TOO!
UHHH... IF I'M NOT MISTAKEN...
WE WERE TAKEN BY PRINCE AROWANA... AND BROUGHT HERE TO THE LAND ABOVE FOR PENAL SERVITUDE...

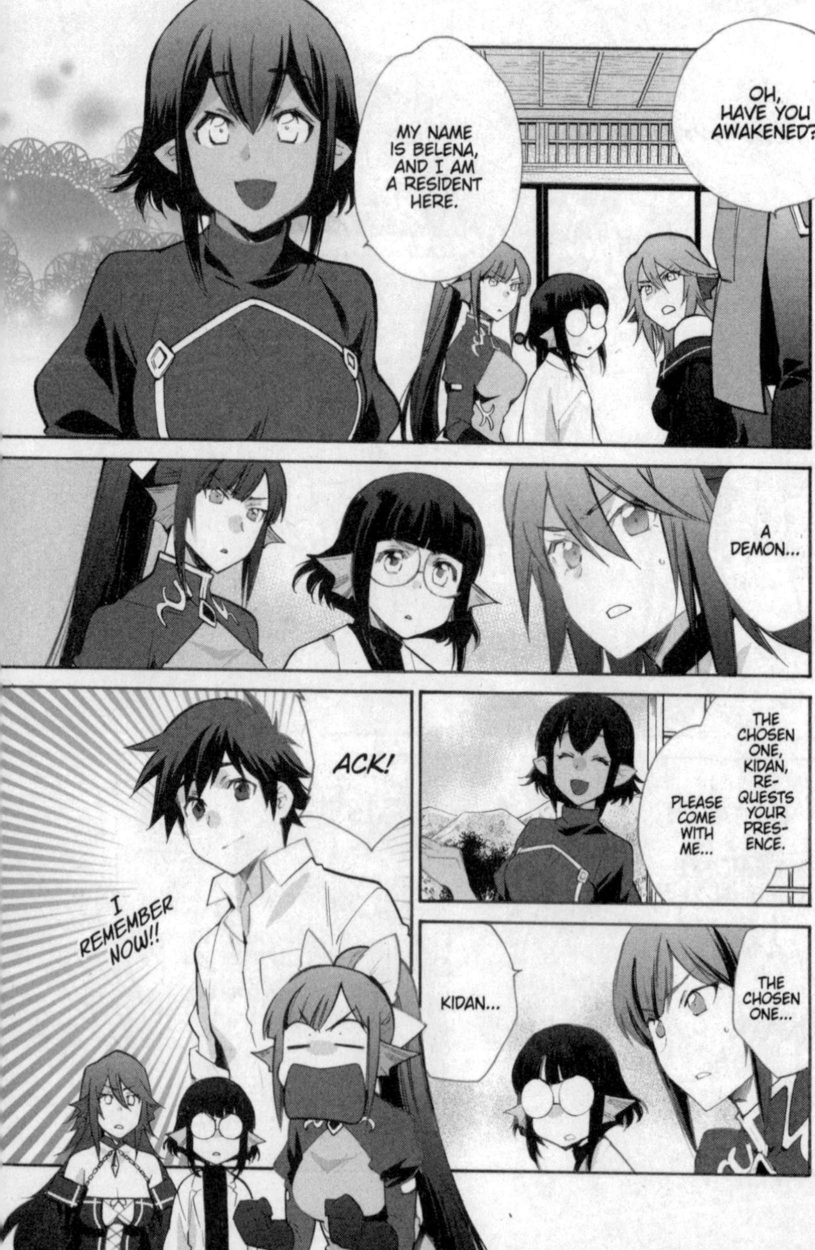
OH, HAVE YOU AWAKENED?
MY NAME IS BELENA, AND I AM A RESIDENT HERE.
A DEMON...
THE CHOSEN ONE, KIDAN, REQUESTS YOUR PRESENCE.
PLEASE COME WITH ME...
THE CHOSEN ONE...
KIDAN...
ACK!
I REMEMBER NOW!!

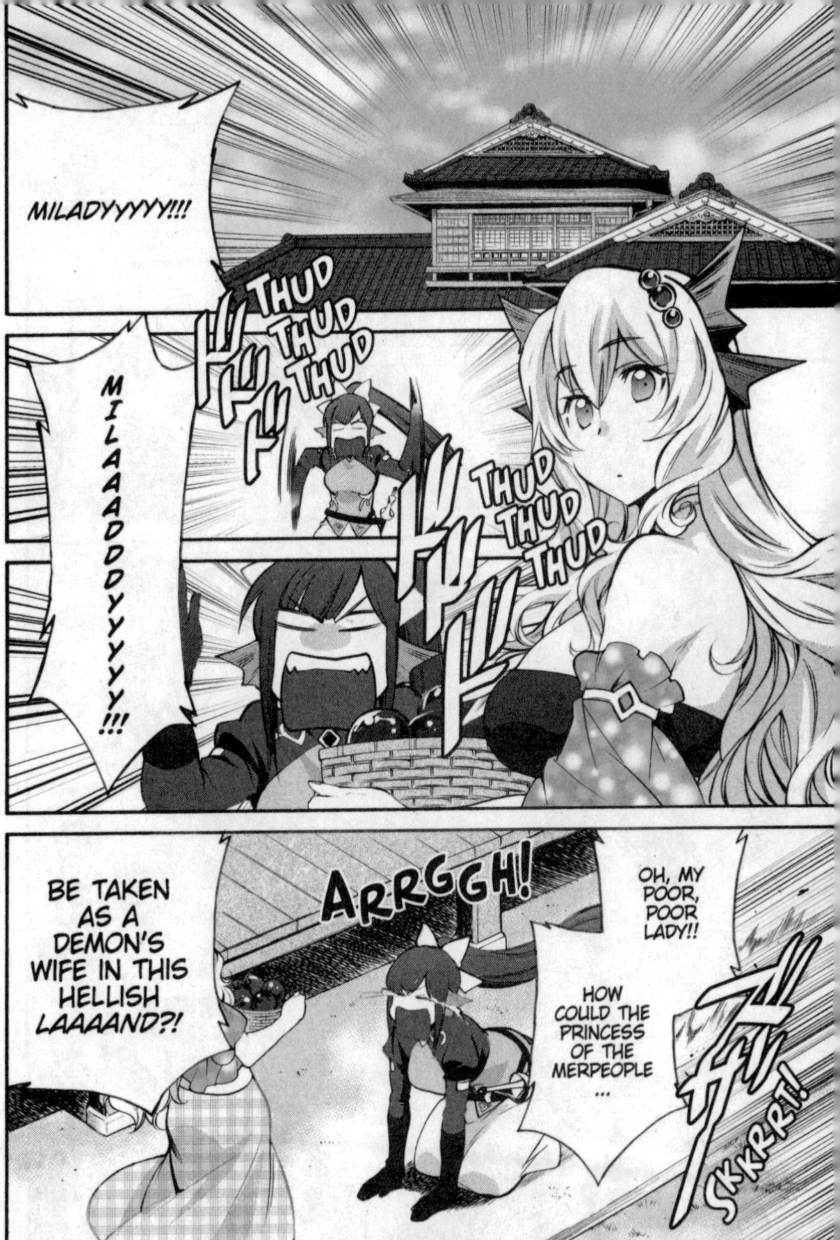
MILADYYYYY!!!
THUD THUD THUD
THUD THUD THUD
MILAAADDDYYYYY!!!
OH, MY POOR, POOR LADY!!
HOW COULD THE PRINCESS OF THE MERPEOPLE ...
SKKRT!
ARRGGH!
BE TAKEN AS A DEMON'S WIFE IN THIS HELLISH LAAAAND?!

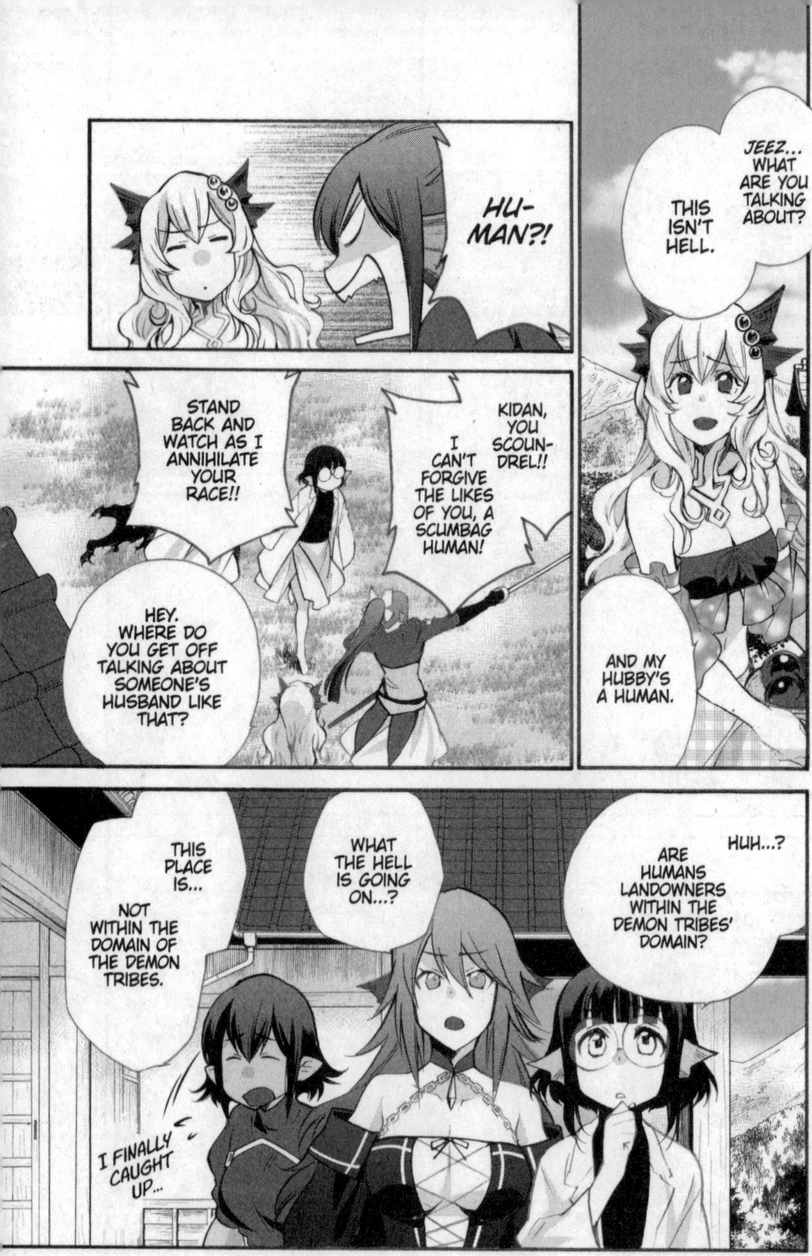
JEEZ... WHAT ARE YOU TALKING ABOUT?
THIS ISN'T HELL.
AND MY HUBBY'S A HUMAN.
HU-MAN?!
KIDAN, YOU SCOUN-DREL!!
I CAN'T FORGIVE THE LIKES OF YOU, A SCUMBAG HUMAN!
STAND BACK AND WATCH AS I ANNIHILATE YOUR RACE!!
HEY. WHERE DO YOU GET OFF TALKING ABOUT SOMEONE'S HUSBAND LIKE THAT?
HUH...?
ARE HUMANS LANDOWNERS WITHIN THE DEMON TRIBES' DOMAIN?
WHAT THE HELL IS GOING ON...?
THIS PLACE IS...
NOT WITHIN THE DOMAIN OF THE DEMON TRIBES.
I FINALLY CAUGHT UP...

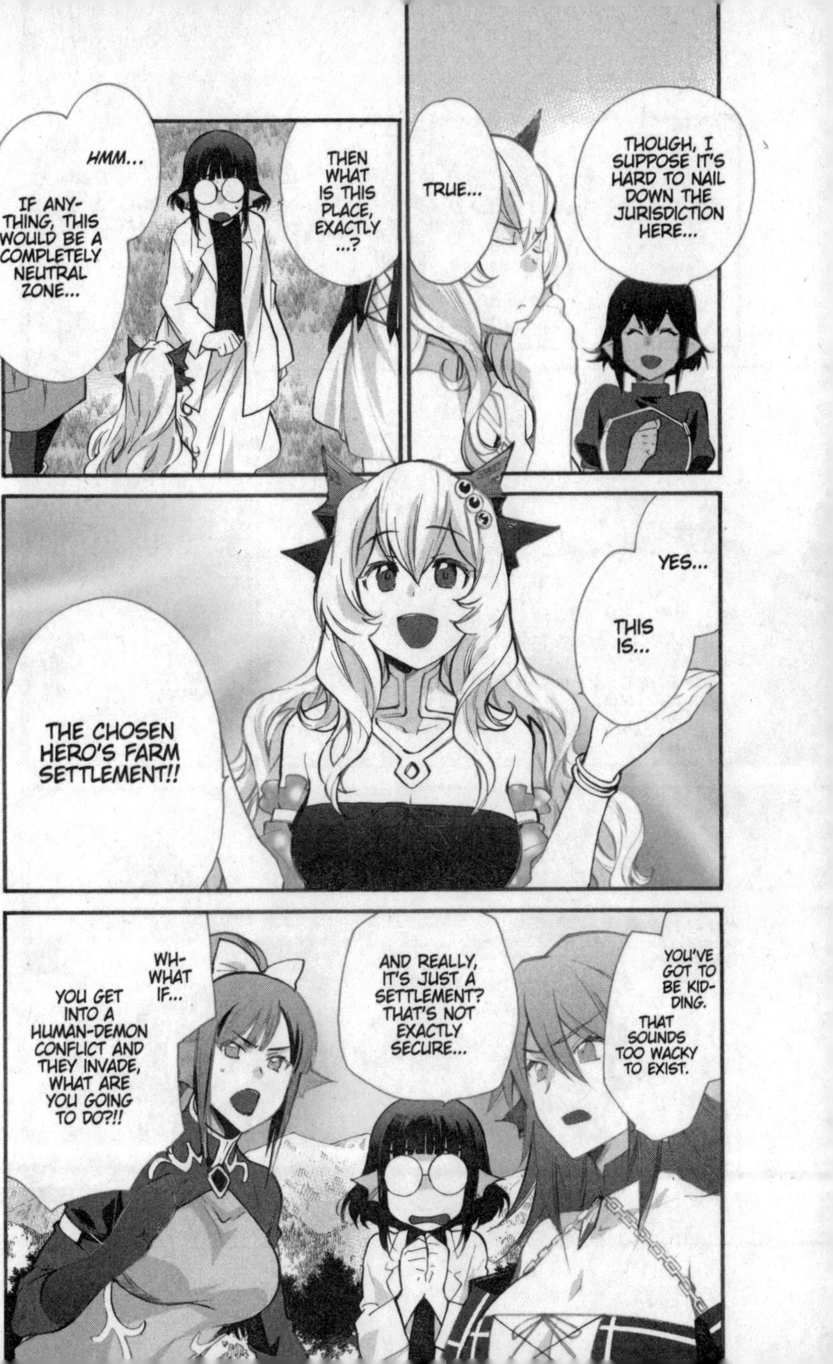
THOUGH, I SUPPOSE IT'S HARD TO NAIL DOWN THE JURISDICTION HERE...
TRUE...
THEN WHAT IS THIS PLACE, EXACTLY ...?
HMM...
IF ANYTHING, THIS WOULD BE A COMPLETELY NEUTRAL ZONE...
YES...
THIS IS...
THE CHOSEN HERO'S FARM SETTLEMENT!!
YOU'VE GOT TO BE KIDDING.
THAT SOUNDS TOO WACKY TO EXIST.
AND REALLY, IT'S JUST A SETTLEMENT? THAT'S NOT EXACTLY SECURE...
WH-WHAT IF...
YOU GET INTO A HUMAN-DEMON CONFLICT AND THEY INVADE, WHAT ARE YOU GOING TO DO?!!

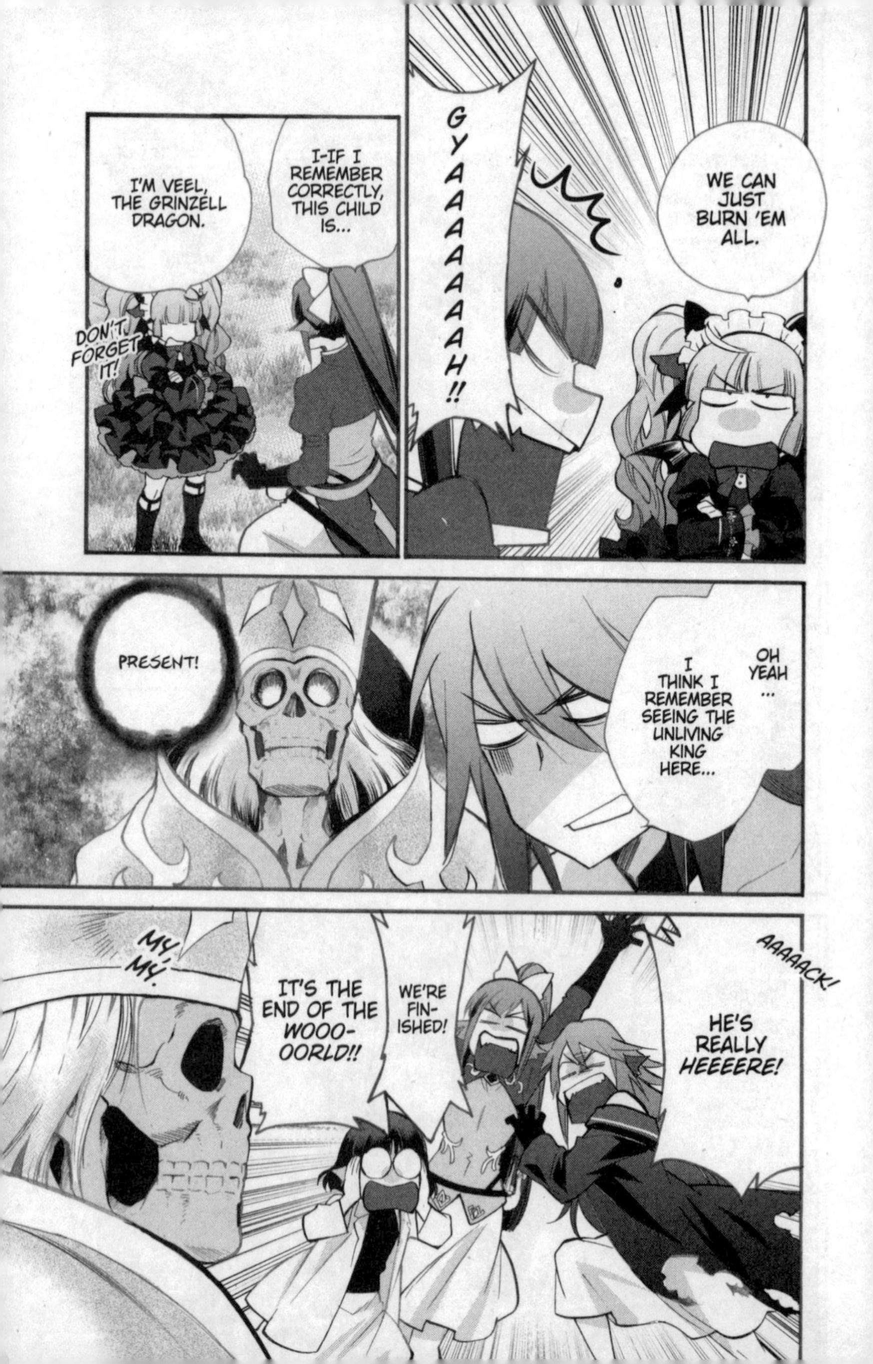
WE CAN JUST BURN 'EM ALL.
GYAAAAAAAH!!
I-IF I REMEMBER CORRECTLY, THIS CHILD IS...
I'M VEEL, THE GRINZELL DRAGON.
DON'T FORGET IT!
OH YEAH...
I THINK I REMEMBER SEEING THE UNLIVING KING HERE...
PRESENT!
AAAAACK!
HE'S REALLY HEEEERE!
WE'RE FIN-ISHED!
IT'S THE END OF THE WOOO-OORLD!!
MY, MY.

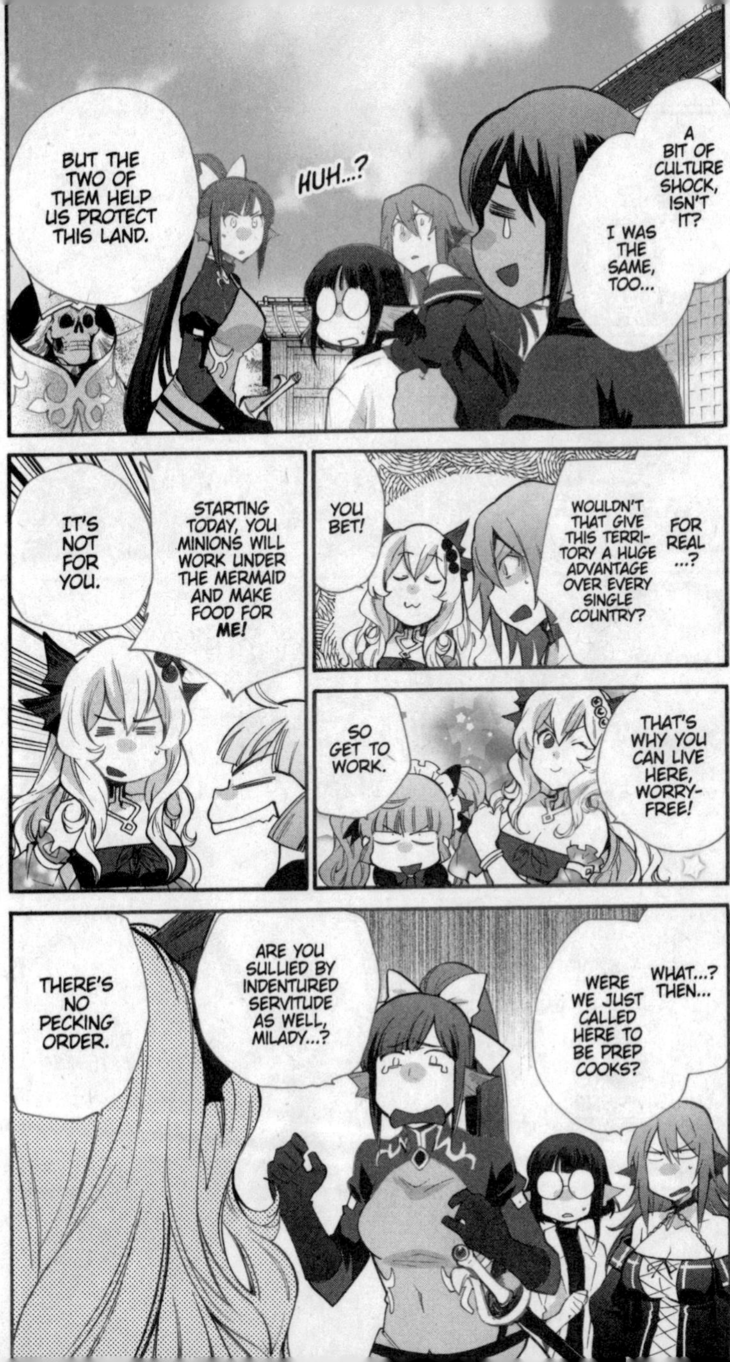
A BIT OF CULTURE SHOCK, ISN'T IT?
I WAS THE SAME, TOO...
HUH...?
BUT THE TWO OF THEM HELP US PROTECT THIS LAND.
FOR REAL...?
WOULDN'T THAT GIVE THIS TERRI-TORY A HUGE ADVANTAGE OVER EVERY SINGLE COUNTRY?
YOU BET!
THAT'S WHY YOU CAN LIVE HERE, WORRY-FREE!
SO GET TO WORK.
STARTING TODAY, YOU MINIONS WILL WORK UNDER THE MERMAID AND MAKE FOOD FOR ME!
IT'S NOT FOR YOU.
WHAT...? THEN...
WERE WE JUST CALLED HERE TO BE PREP COOKS?
ARE YOU SULLIED BY INDENTURED SERVITUDE AS WELL, MILADY...?
THERE'S NO PECKING ORDER.

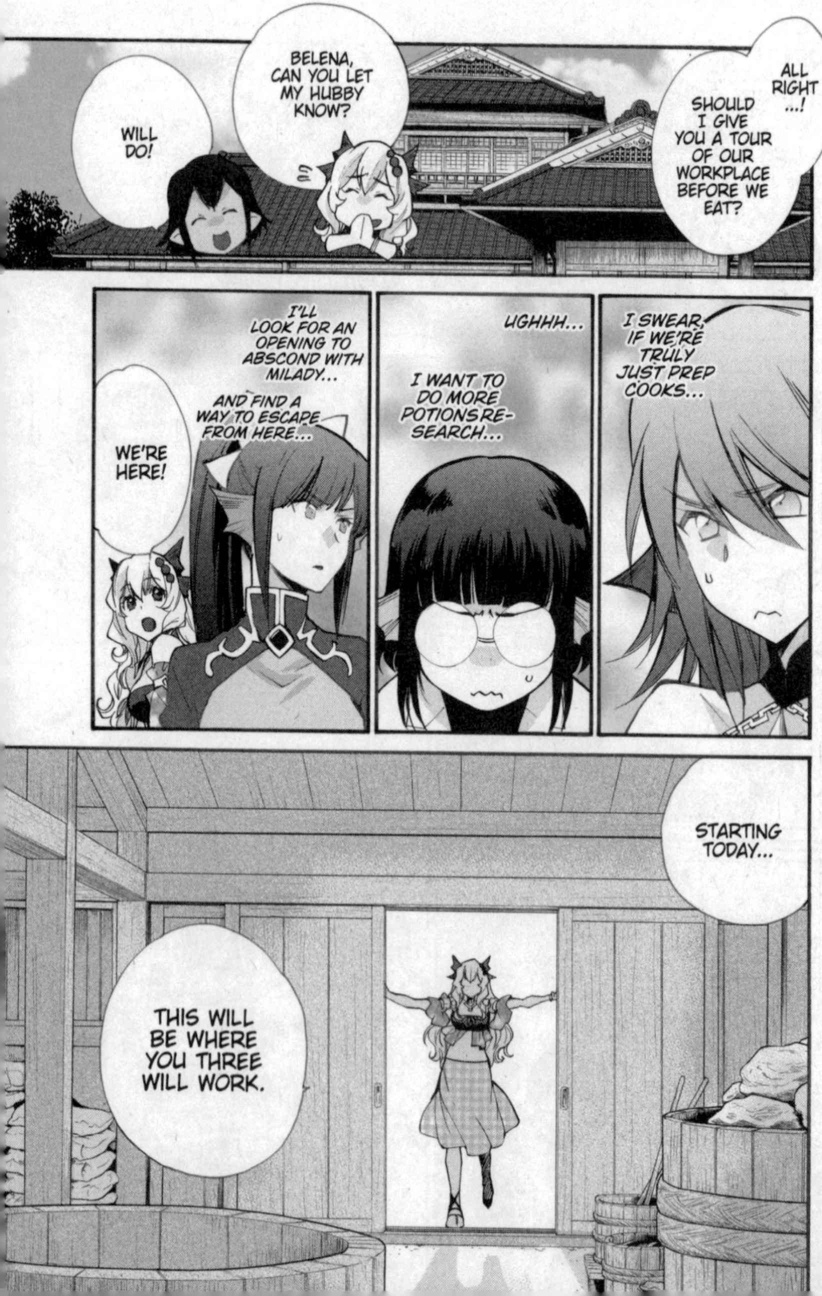
ALL RIGHT ...!
SHOULD I GIVE YOU A TOUR OF OUR WORKPLACE BEFORE WE EAT?
BELENA, CAN YOU LET MY HUBBY KNOW?
WILL DO!
I SWEAR, IF WE'RE TRULY JUST PREP COOKS...
UGHHH...
I WANT TO DO MORE POTIONS RE-SEARCH...
I'LL LOOK FOR AN OPENING TO ABSCOND WITH MILADY...
AND FIND A WAY TO ESCAPE FROM HERE...
WE'RE HERE!
STARTING TODAY...
THIS WILL BE WHERE YOU THREE WILL WORK.

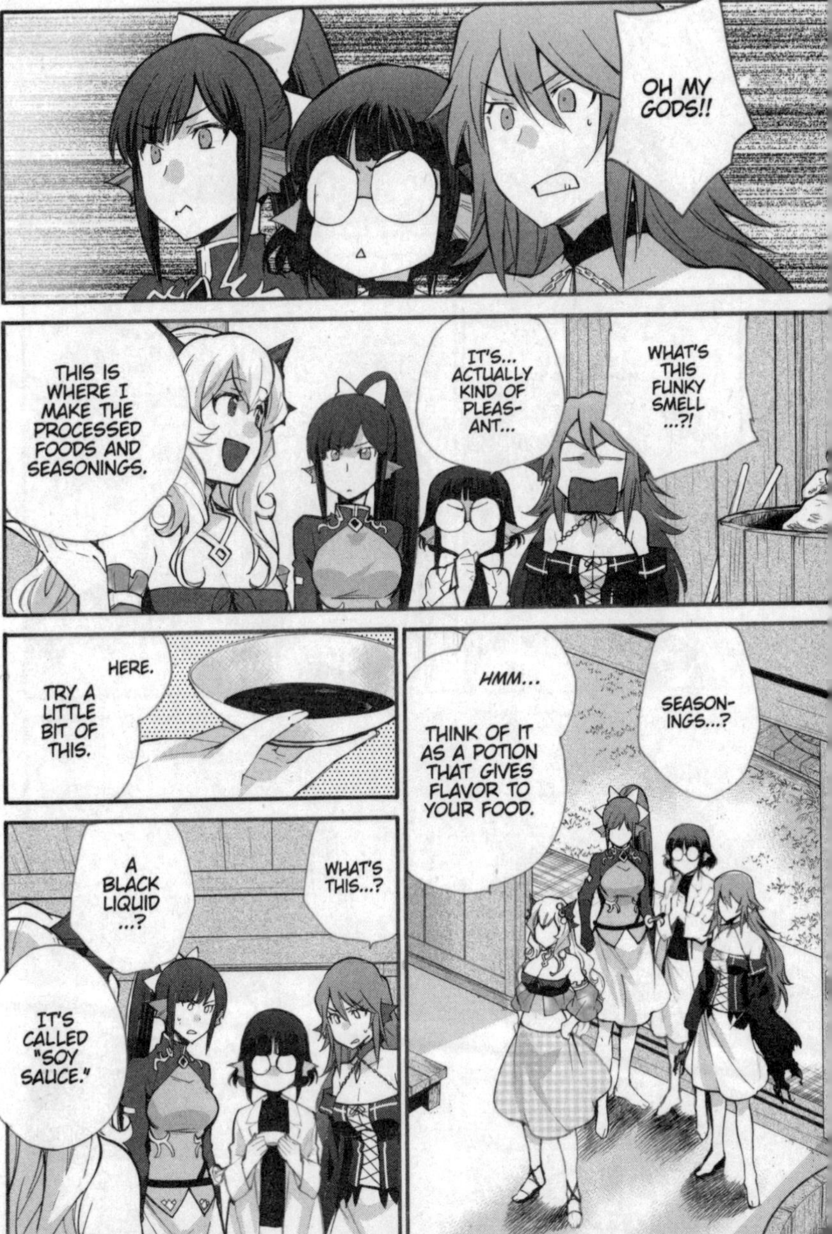
OH MY GODS!!
WHAT'S THIS FUNKY SMELL ...?!
IT'S... ACTUALLY KIND OF PLEAS-ANT...
THIS IS WHERE I MAKE THE PROCESSED FOODS AND SEASONINGS.
SEASON-INGS...?
HMM...
THINK OF IT AS A POTION THAT GIVES FLAVOR TO YOUR FOOD.
HERE.
TRY A LITTLE BIT OF THIS.
WHAT'S THIS...?
A BLACK LIQUID ...?
IT'S CALLED "SOY SAUCE."

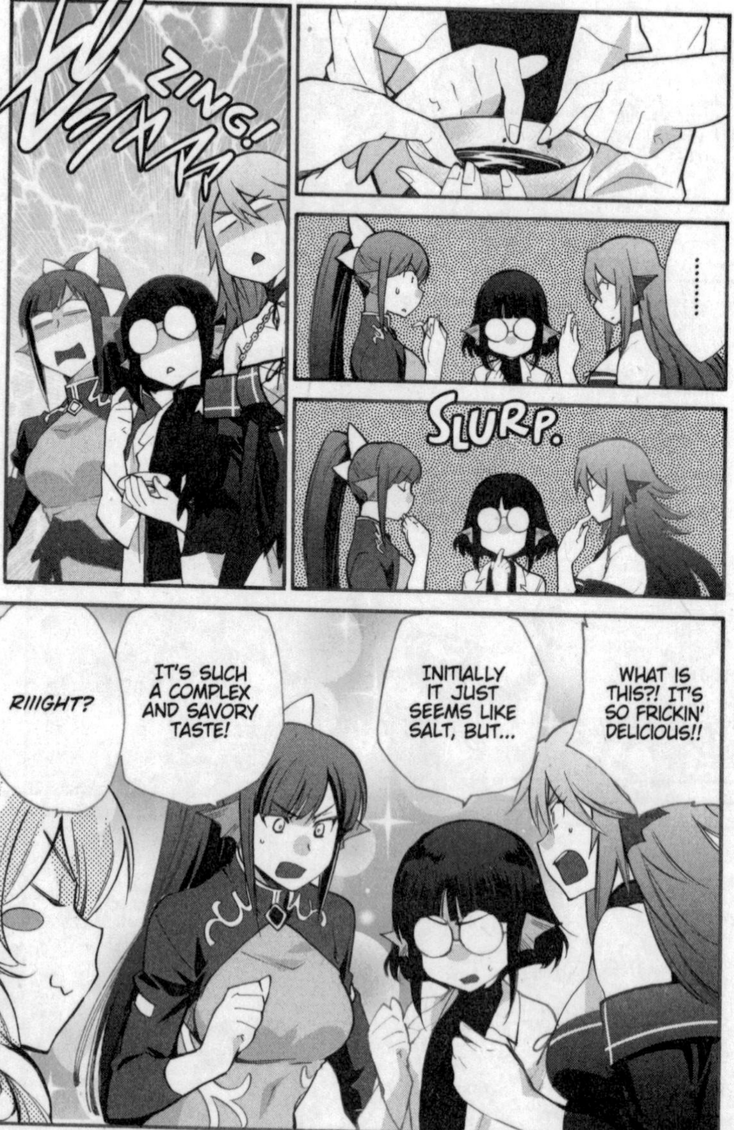
......
SLURP.
ZING!
WHAT IS THIS?! IT'S SO FRICKIN' DELICIOUS!!
INITIALLY IT JUST SEEMS LIKE SALT, BUT...
IT'S SUCH A COMPLEX AND SAVORY TASTE!
RIIIGHT?

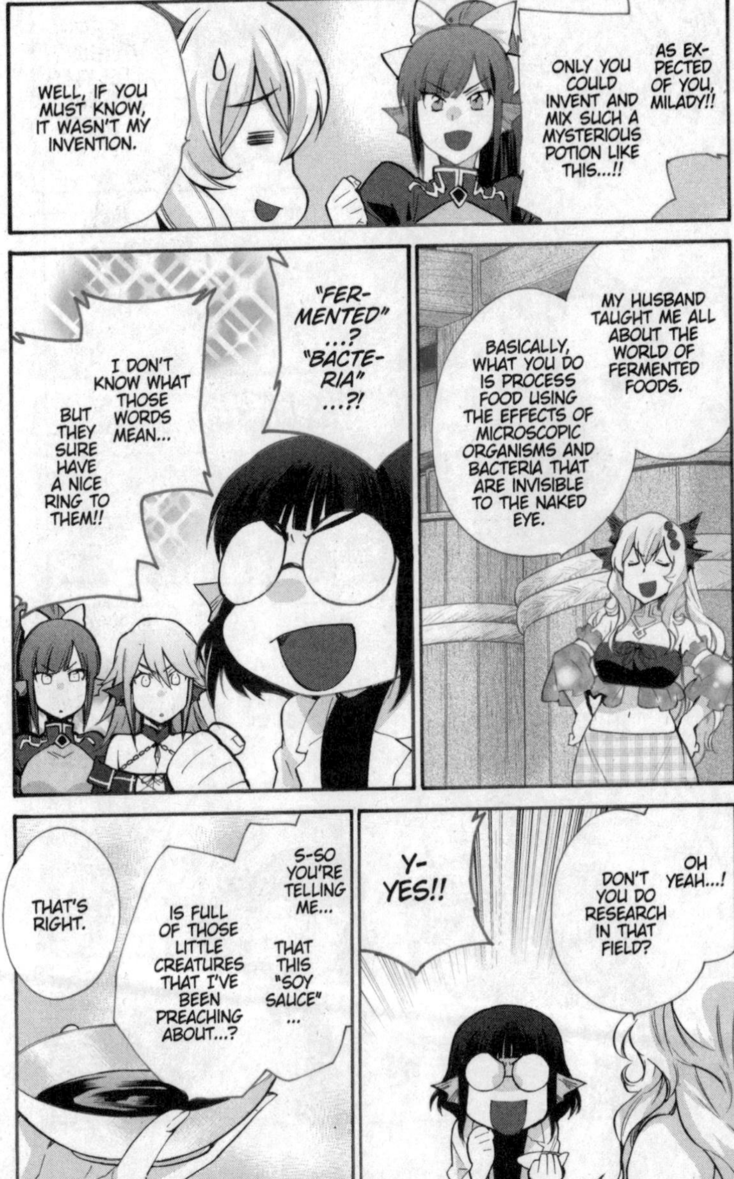
AS EXPECTED OF YOU, MILADY!!
ONLY YOU COULD INVENT AND MIX SUCH A MYSTERIOUS POTION LIKE THIS...!!
WELL, IF YOU MUST KNOW, IT WASN'T MY INVENTION.
MY HUSBAND TAUGHT ME ALL ABOUT THE WORLD OF FERMENTED FOODS.
BASICALLY, WHAT YOU DO IS PROCESS FOOD USING THE EFFECTS OF MICROSCOPIC ORGANISMS AND BACTERIA THAT ARE INVISIBLE TO THE NAKED EYE.
"FERMENTED"...? "BACTERIA"...?!
I DON'T KNOW WHAT THOSE WORDS MEAN...
BUT THEY SURE HAVE A NICE RING TO THEM!!
OH YEAH...!
DON'T YOU DO RESEARCH IN THAT FIELD?
Y-YES!!
S-SO YOU'RE TELLING ME...
THAT THIS "SOY SAUCE"...
IS FULL OF THOSE LITTLE CREATURES THAT I'VE BEEN PREACHING ABOUT...?
THAT'S RIGHT.

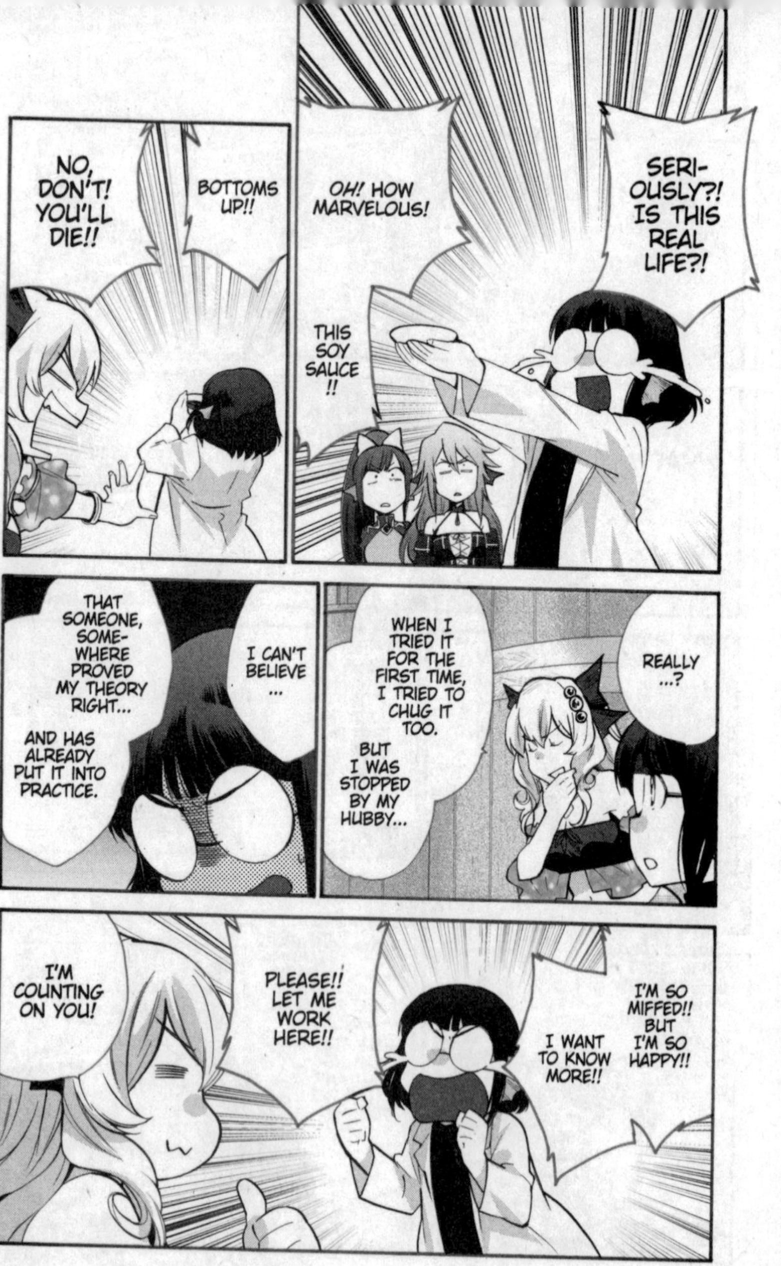
SERI-OUSLY?! IS THIS REAL LIFE?!
OH! HOW MARVELOUS!
THIS SOY SAUCE !!
BOTTOMS UP!!
NO, DON'T! YOU'LL DIE!!
REALLY ...?
WHEN I TRIED IT FOR THE FIRST TIME, I TRIED TO CHUG IT TOO.
BUT I WAS STOPPED BY MY HUBBY...
I CAN'T BELIEVE ...
THAT SOMEONE, SOME-WHERE PROVED MY THEORY RIGHT...
AND HAS ALREADY PUT IT INTO PRACTICE.
I'M SO MIFFED!! BUT I'M SO HAPPY!!
I WANT TO KNOW MORE!!
PLEASE!! LET ME WORK HERE!!
I'M COUNTING ON YOU!

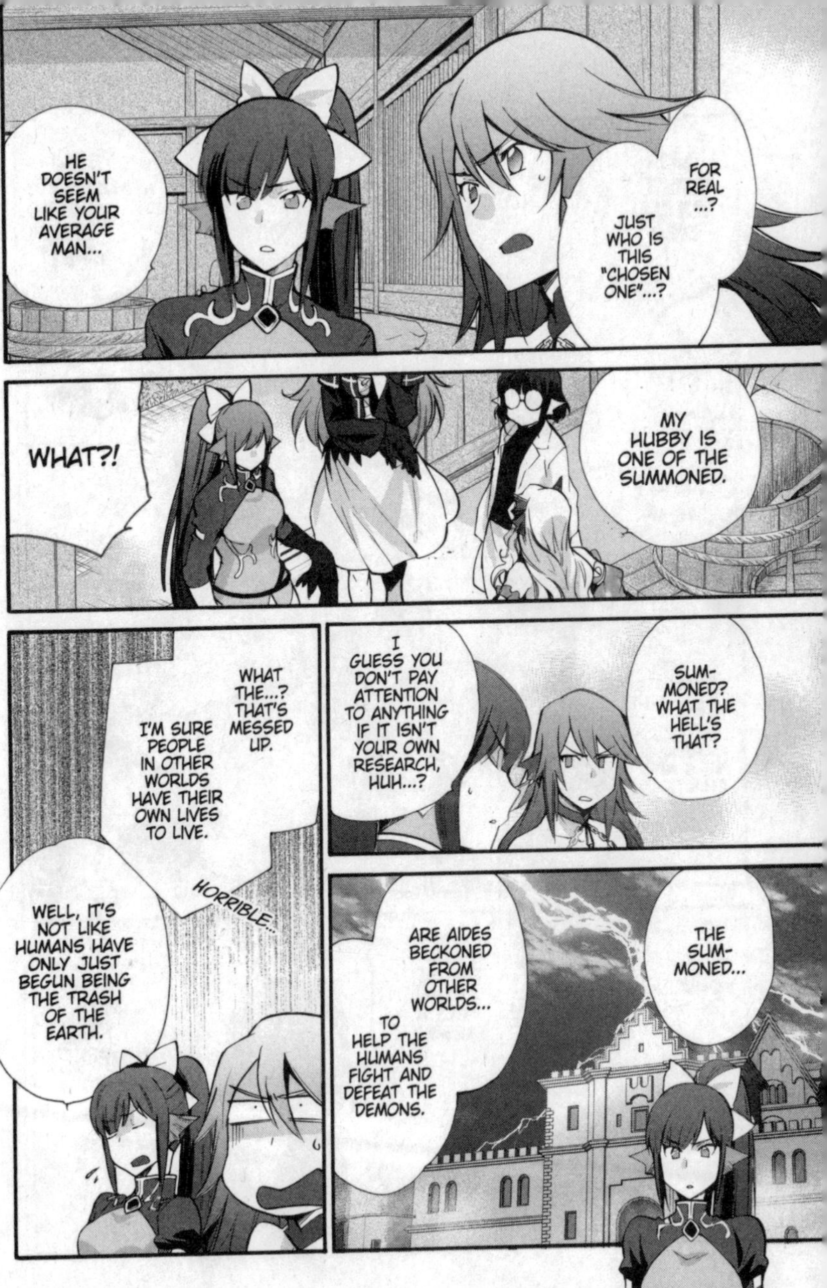
FOR REAL ...?
JUST WHO IS THIS "CHOSEN ONE"...?
HE DOESN'T SEEM LIKE YOUR AVERAGE MAN...
MY HUBBY IS ONE OF THE SUMMONED.
WHAT?!
SUM-MONED? WHAT THE HELL'S THAT?
I GUESS YOU DON'T PAY ATTENTION TO ANYTHING IF IT ISN'T YOUR OWN RESEARCH, HUH...?
THE SUM-MONED...
ARE AIDES BECKONED FROM OTHER WORLDS...
TO HELP THE HUMANS FIGHT AND DEFEAT THE DEMONS.
WHAT THE...? THAT'S MESSED UP.
I'M SURE PEOPLE IN OTHER WORLDS HAVE THEIR OWN LIVES TO LIVE.
HORRIBLE...
WELL, IT'S NOT LIKE HUMANS HAVE ONLY JUST BEGUN BEING THE TRASH OF THE EARTH.

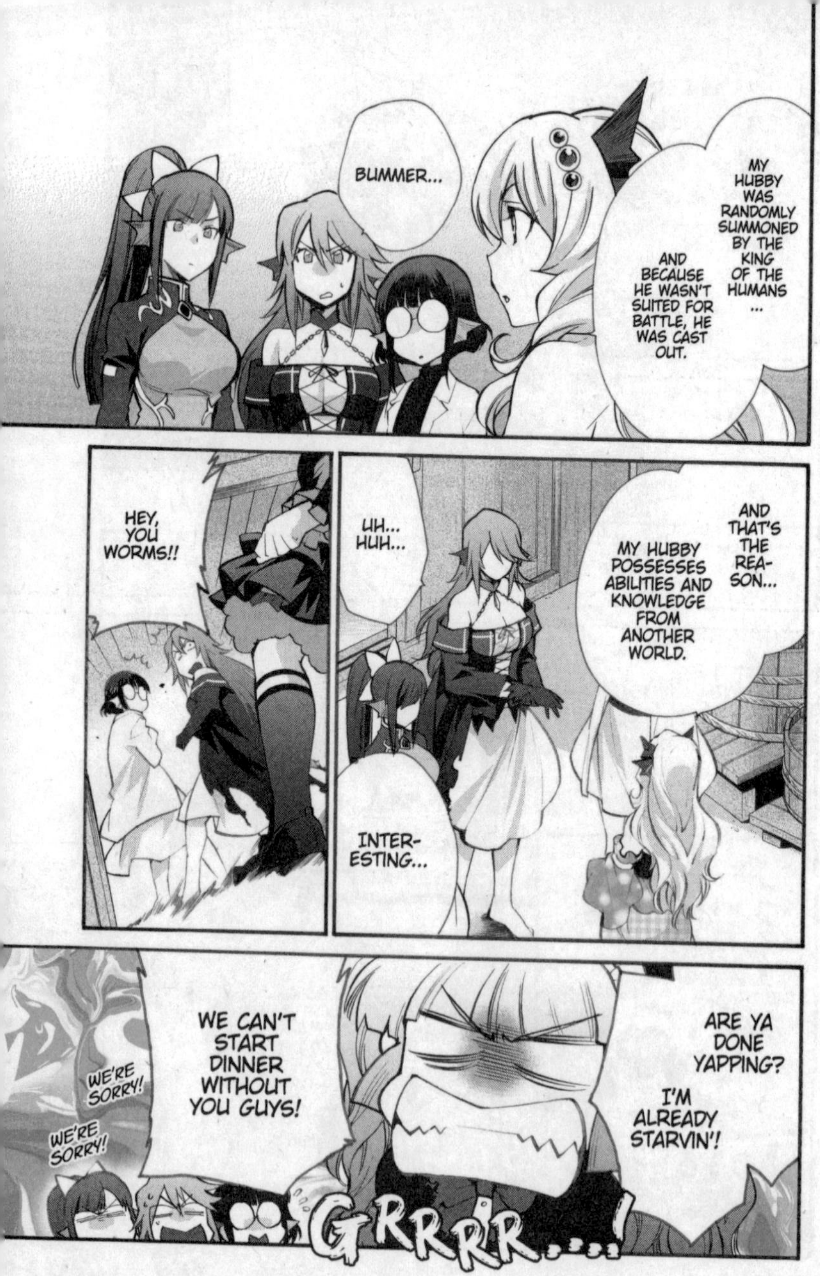
MY HUBBY WAS RANDOMLY SUMMONED BY THE KING OF THE HUMANS ...
AND BECAUSE HE WASN'T SUITED FOR BATTLE, HE WAS CAST OUT.
BUMMER...
AND THAT'S THE REA-SON...
MY HUBBY POSSESSES ABILITIES AND KNOWLEDGE FROM ANOTHER WORLD.
UH... HUH...
INTER-ESTING...
HEY, YOU WORMS!!
ARE YA DONE YAPPING?
I'M ALREADY STARVIN'!
WE CAN'T START DINNER WITHOUT YOU GUYS!
WE'RE SORRY!
WE'RE SORRY!
GRRRR...!

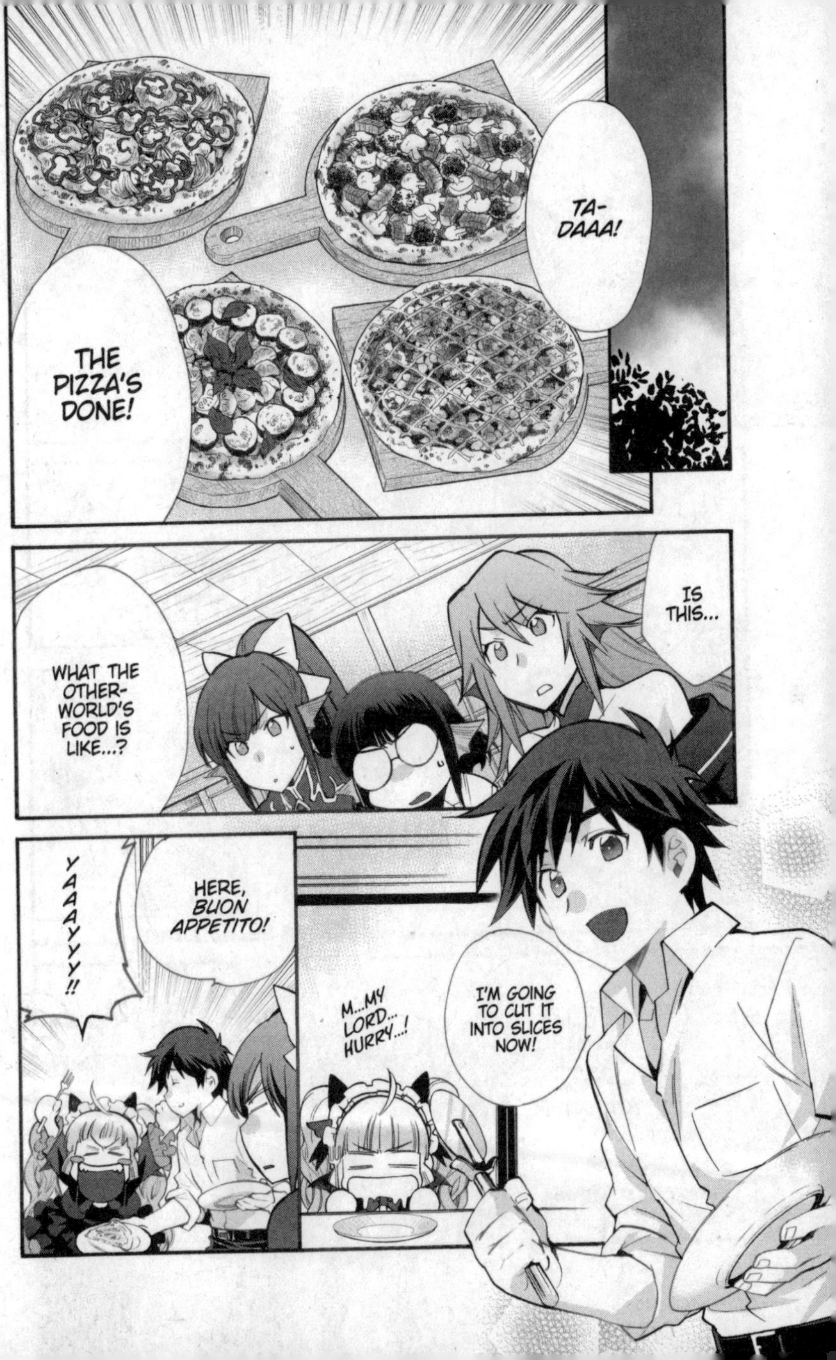
TA-DAAA!
THE PIZZA'S DONE!
IS THIS...
WHAT THE OTHER-WORLD'S FOOD IS LIKE...?
I'M GOING TO CUT IT INTO SLICES NOW!
M...MY LORD... HURRY...!
HERE, BUON APPETITO!
YAAAAYYY!!

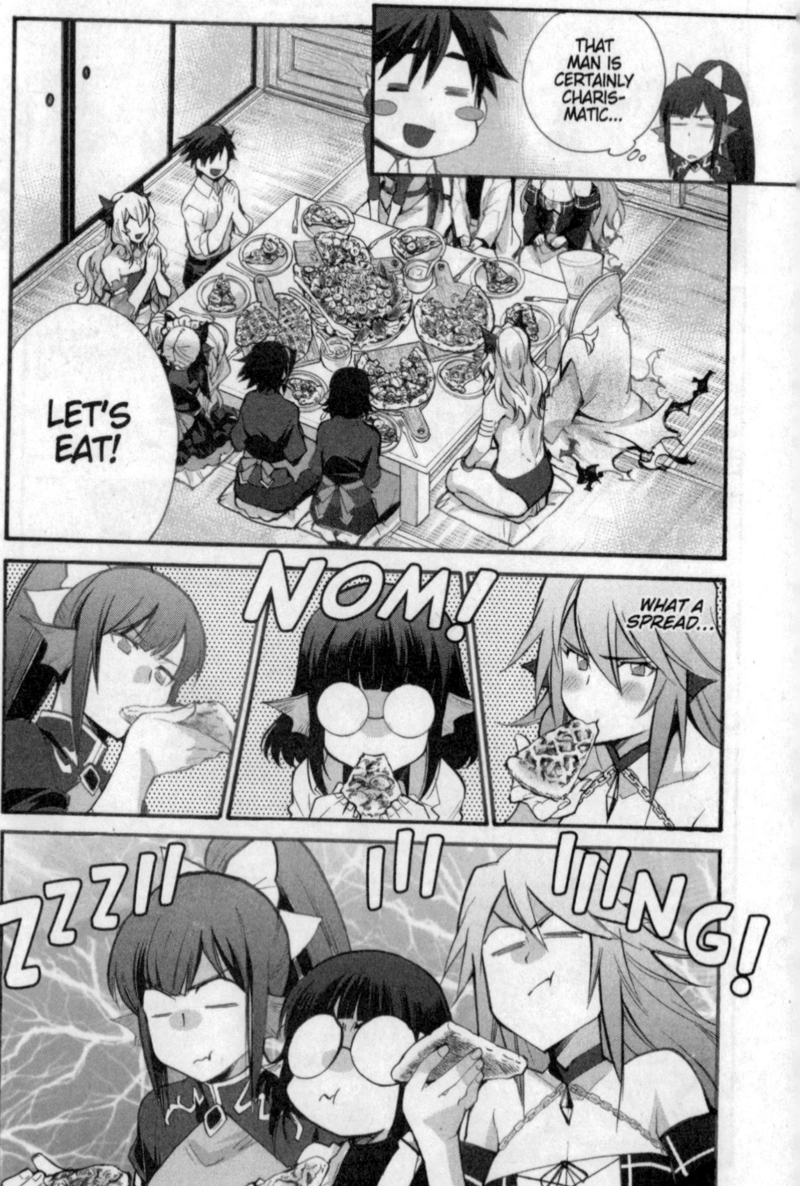
THAT MAN IS CERTAINLY CHARIS-MATIC...
LET'S EAT!
WHAT A SPREAD...
NOM!
ZZZII III IIING!

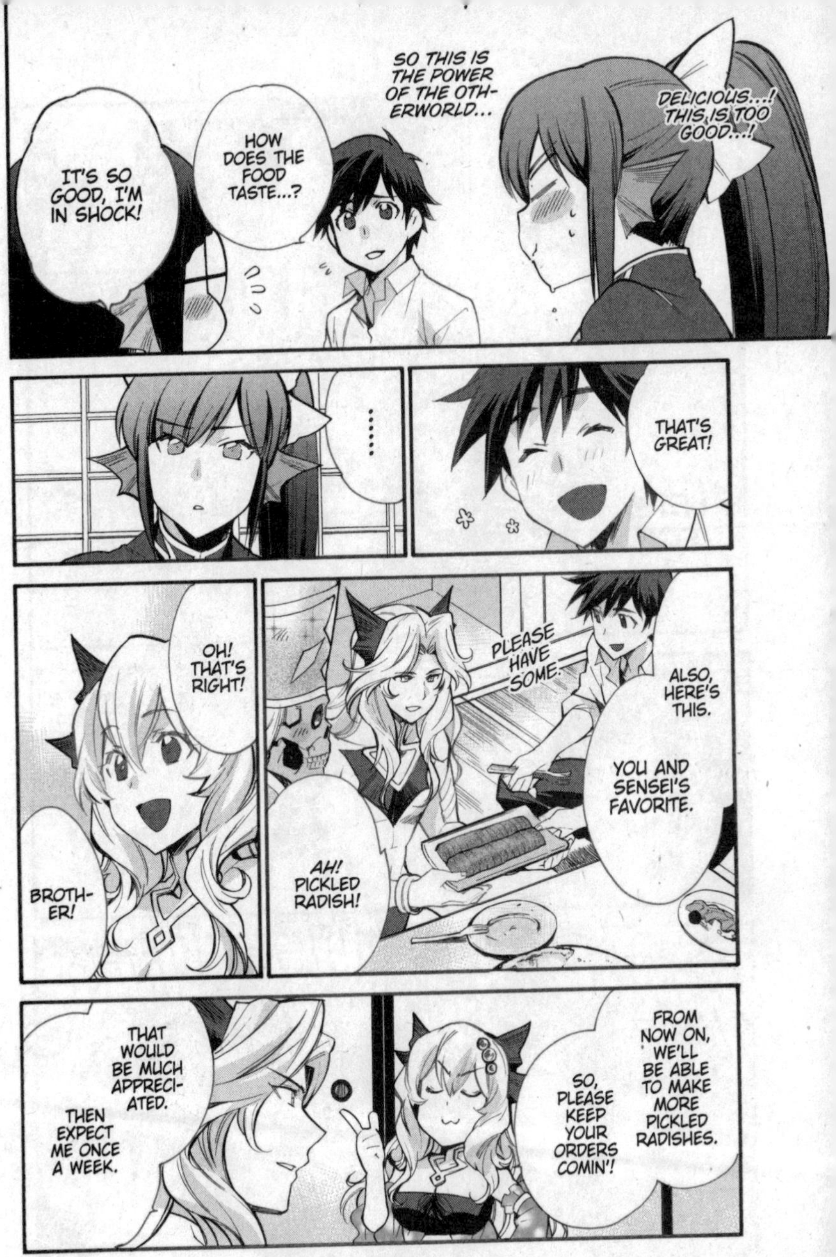
DELICIOUS...! THIS IS TOO GOOD...!
SO THIS IS THE POWER OF THE OTHER-ERWORLD...
HOW DOES THE FOOD TASTE...?
IT'S SO GOOD, I'M IN SHOCK!
THAT'S GREAT!
......
ALSO, HERE'S THIS.
PLEASE HAVE SOME.
YOU AND SENSEI'S FAVORITE.
AH! PICKLED RADISH!
OH! THAT'S RIGHT!
BROTH-ER!
FROM NOW ON, WE'LL BE ABLE TO MAKE MORE PICKLED RADISHES.
SO, PLEASE KEEP YOUR ORDERS COMIN'!
THAT WOULD BE MUCH APPRECI-ATED.
THEN EXPECT ME ONCE A WEEK.

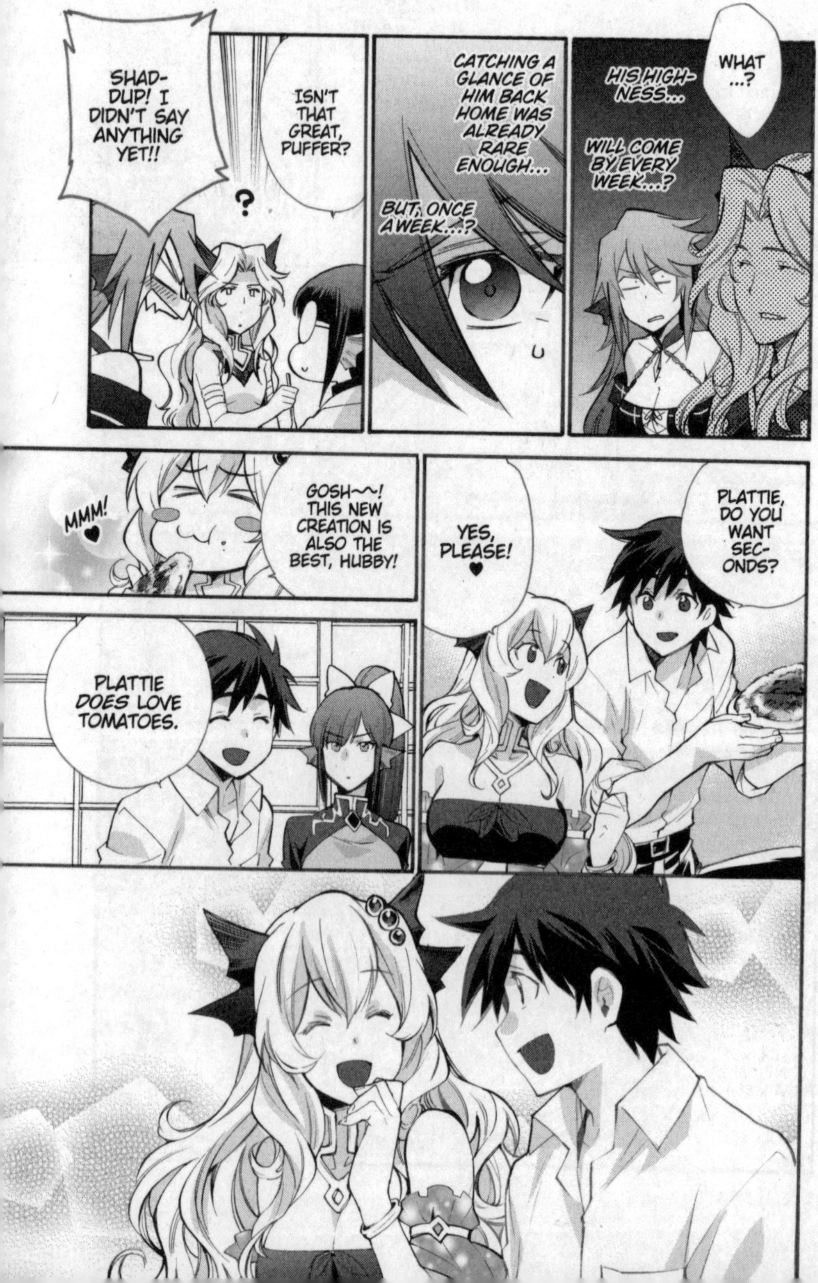

WHAT ...?
HIS HIGH-NESS...
WILL COME BY EVERY WEEK...?
CATCHING A GLANCE OF HIM BACK HOME WAS ALREADY RARE ENOUGH...
BUT, ONCE A WEEK...?
ISN'T THAT GREAT, PUFFER?
?
SHAD-DUP! I DIDN'T SAY ANYTHING YET!!
PLATTIE, DO YOU WANT SEC-ONDS?
YES, PLEASE! ♥
GOSH~~! THIS NEW CREATION IS ALSO THE BEST, HUBBY!
MMM! ♥
PLATTIE DOES LOVE TOMATOES.

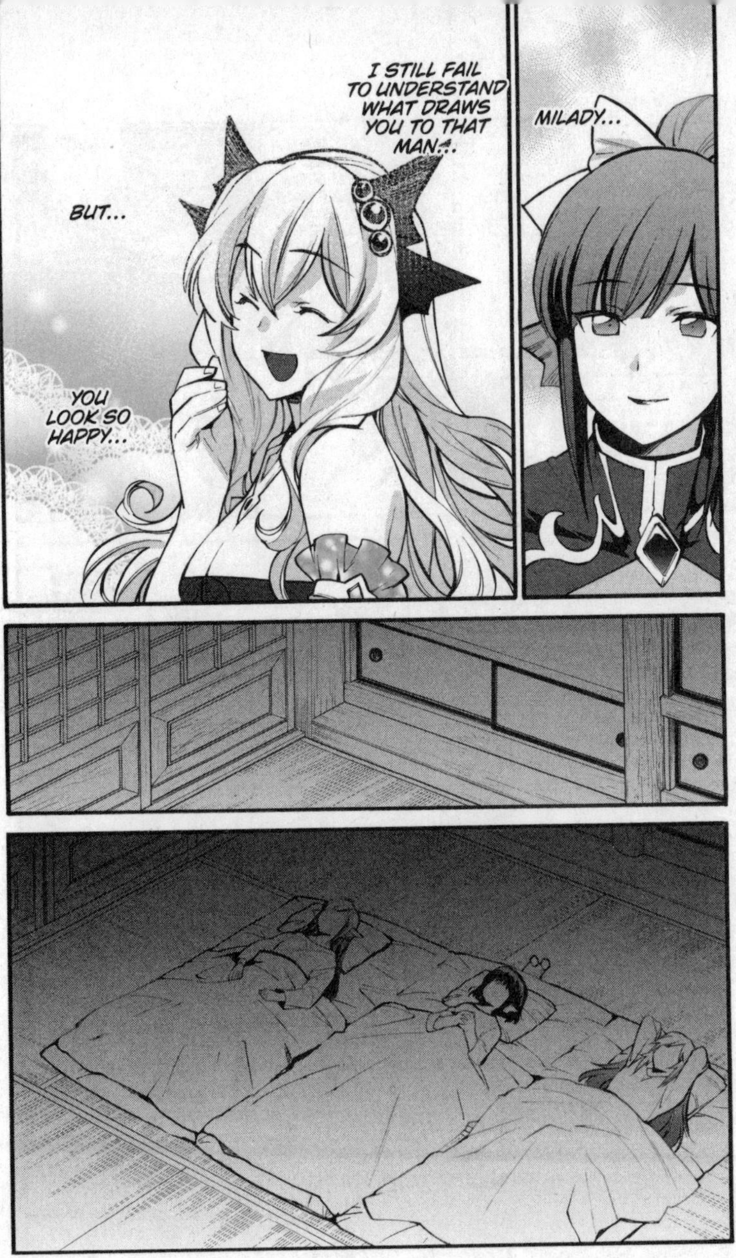
MILADY...
I STILL FAIL TO UNDERSTAND WHAT DRAWS YOU TO THAT MAN...
BUT...
YOU LOOK SO HAPPY...

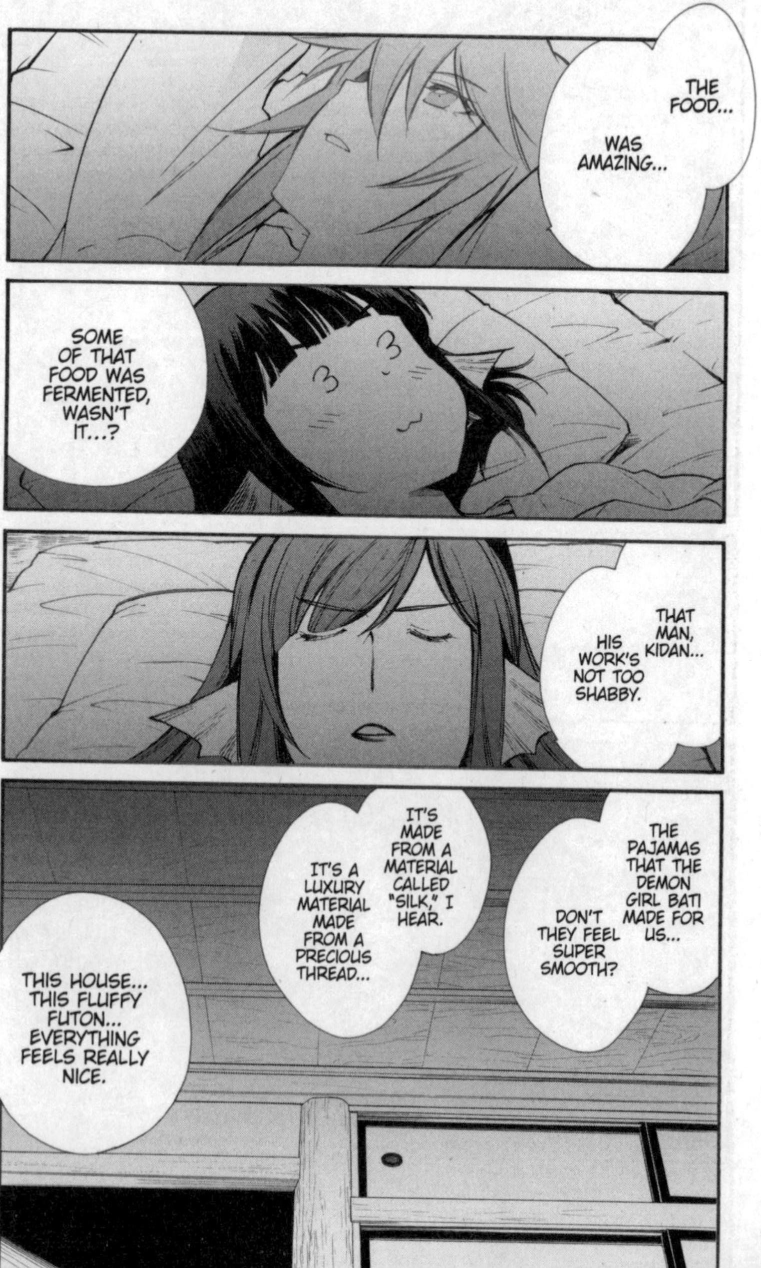
THE FOOD... WAS AMAZING...
SOME OF THAT FOOD WAS FERMENTED, WASN'T IT...?
THAT MAN, KIDAN... HIS WORK'S NOT TOO SHABBY.
THE PAJAMAS THAT THE DEMON GIRL BATI MADE FOR US... DON'T THEY FEEL SUPER SMOOTH?
IT'S MADE FROM A MATERIAL CALLED "SILK," I HEAR. IT'S A LUXURY MATERIAL MADE FROM A PRECIOUS THREAD...
THIS HOUSE... THIS FLUFFY FUTON... EVERYTHING FEELS REALLY NICE.

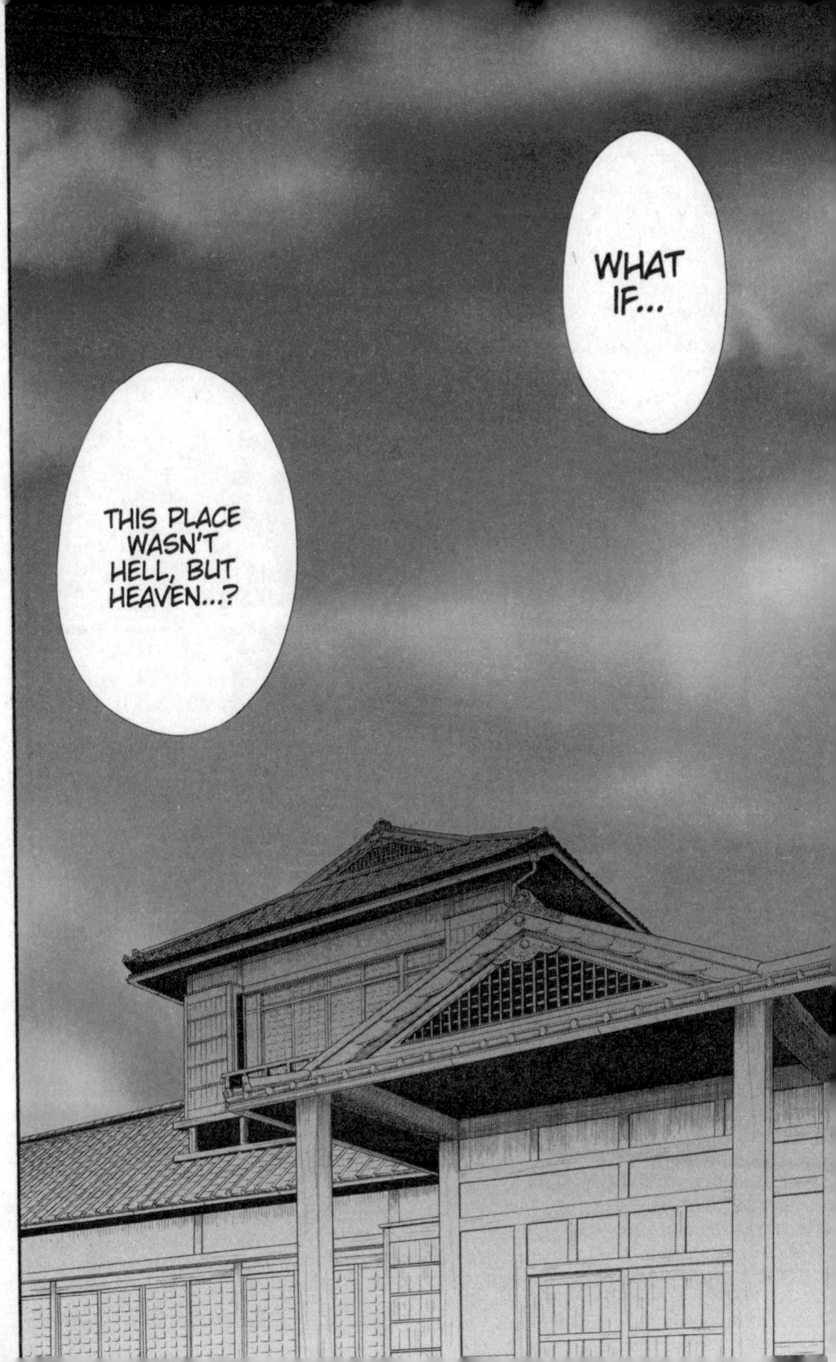
WHAT IF...
THIS PLACE WASN'T HELL, BUT HEAVEN...?

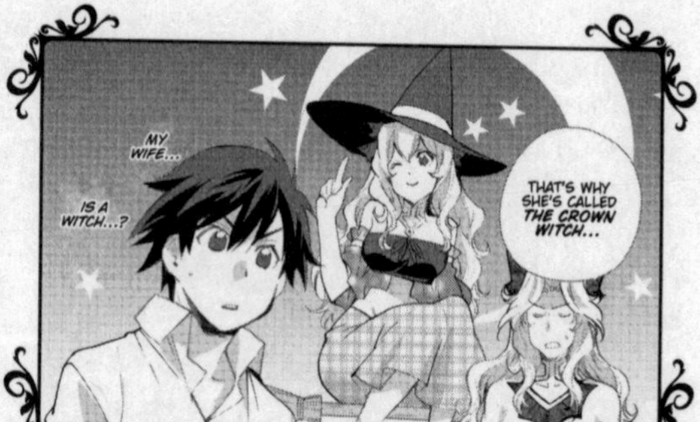
THAT'S WHY SHE'S CALLED THE CROWN WITCH...
MY WIFE...
IS A WITCH...?

LET'S BUY THE LAND and CULTIVATE IT IN A DIFFERENT WORLD

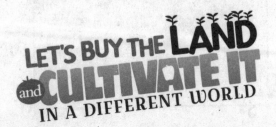

Chapter 22

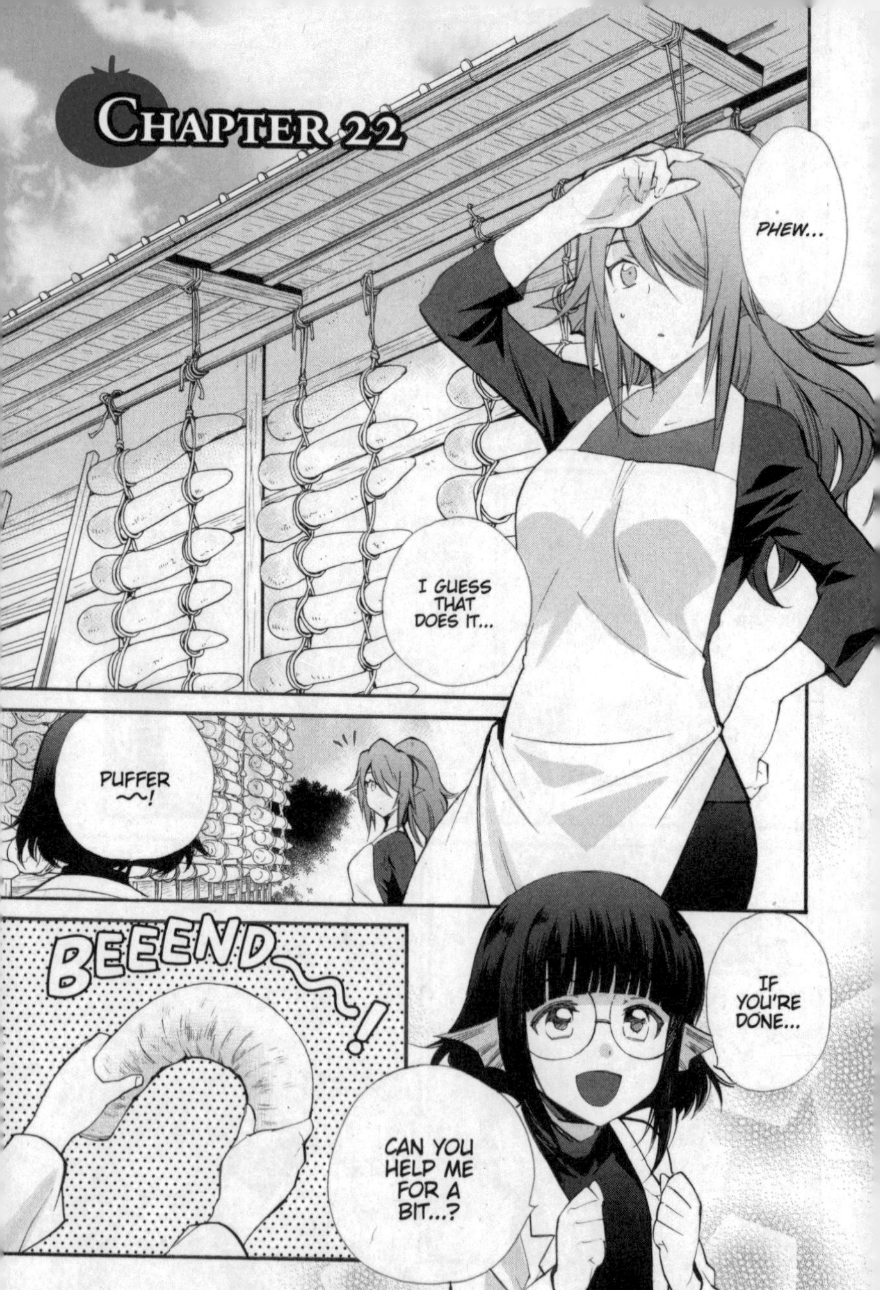
PHEW...
I GUESS THAT DOES IT...
PUFFER ~~!
IF YOU'RE DONE...
CAN YOU HELP ME FOR A BIT...?
BEEEND~~!

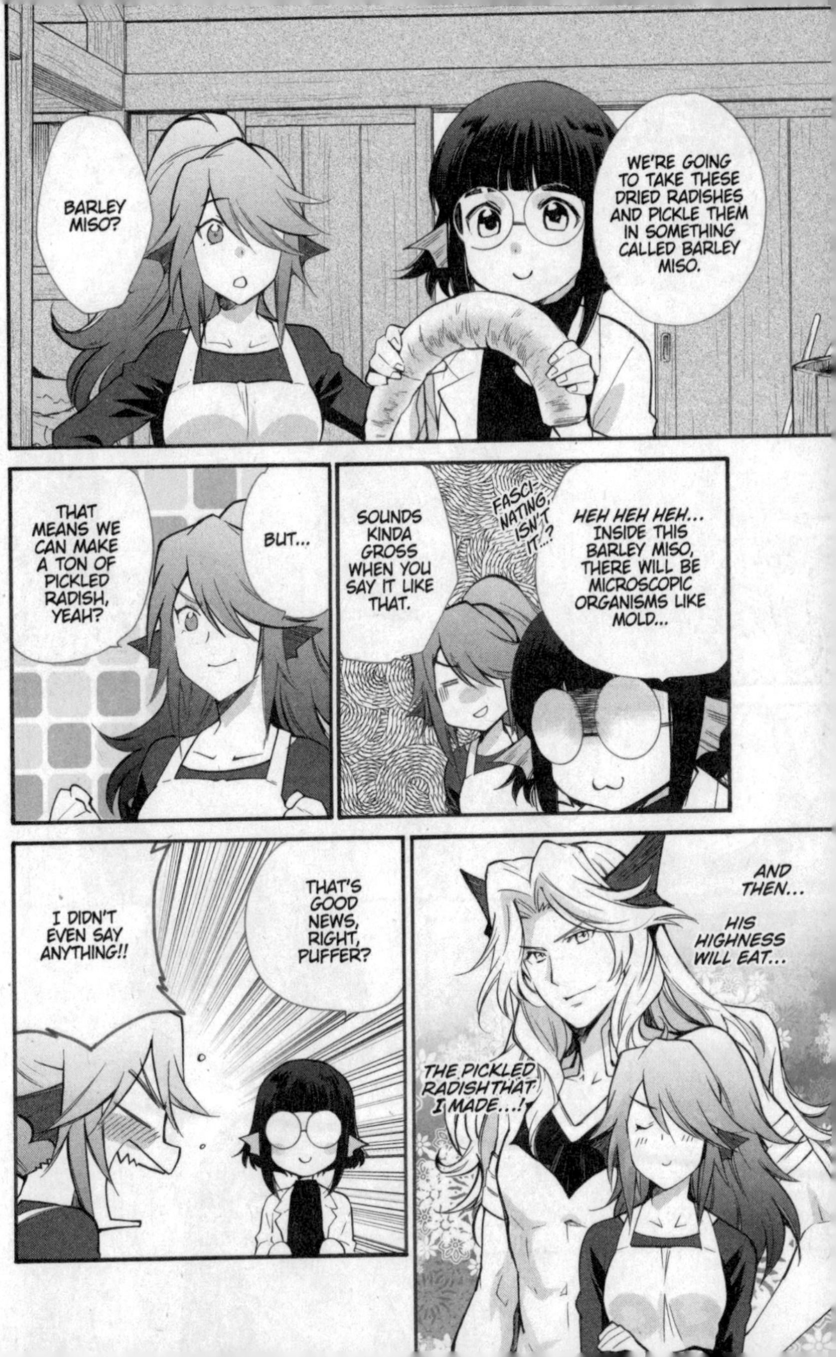
WE'RE GOING TO TAKE THESE DRIED RADISHES AND PICKLE THEM IN SOMETHING CALLED BARLEY MISO.
BARLEY MISO?
HEH HEH HEH... INSIDE THIS BARLEY MISO, THERE WILL BE MICROSCOPIC ORGANISMS LIKE MOLD...
FASCI-NATING, ISN'T IT...?
SOUNDS KINDA GROSS WHEN YOU SAY IT LIKE THAT.
BUT...
THAT MEANS WE CAN MAKE A TON OF PICKLED RADISH, YEAH?
AND THEN...
HIS HIGHNESS WILL EAT...
THE PICKLED RADISH THAT I MADE...!
THAT'S GOOD NEWS, RIGHT, PUFFER?
I DIDN'T EVEN SAY ANYTHING!!

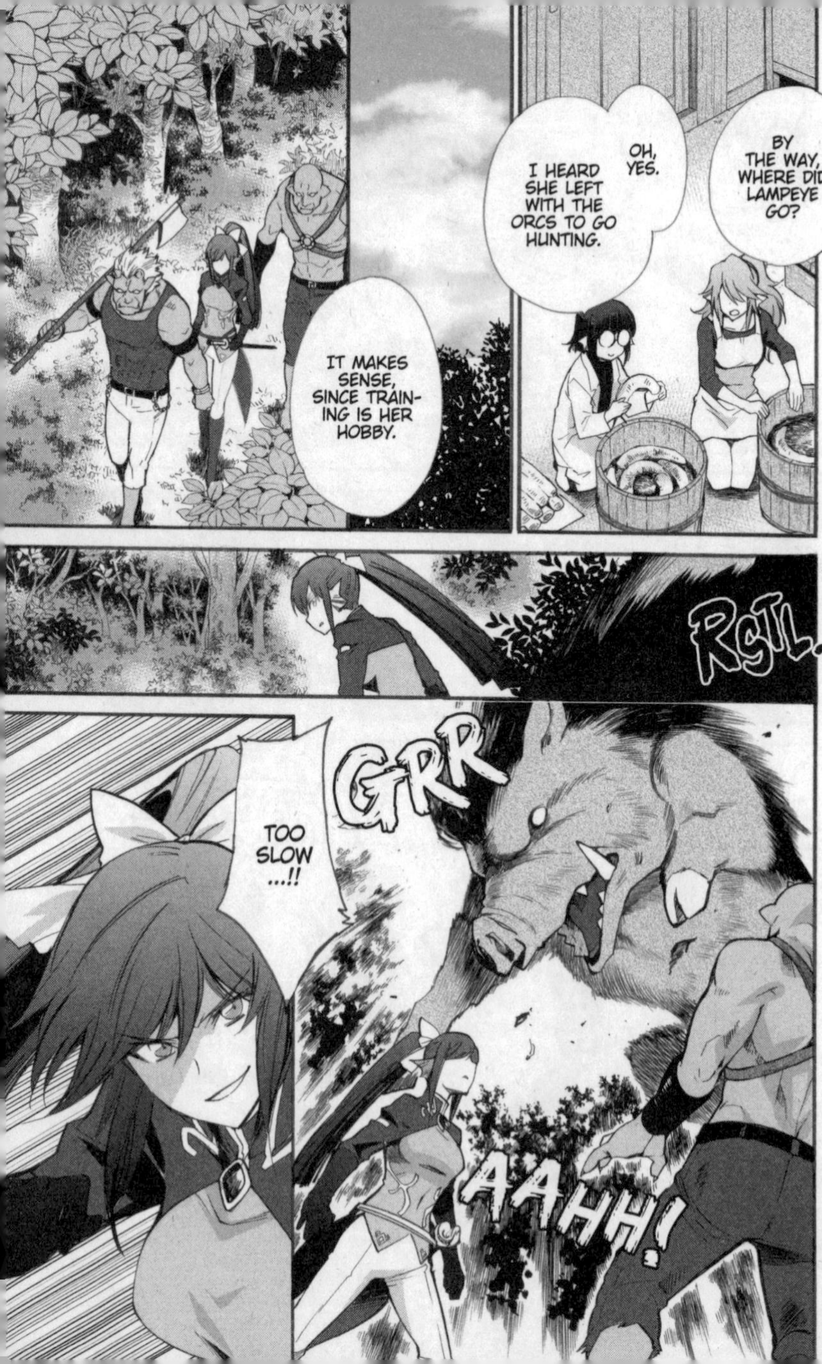
BY THE WAY, WHERE DID LAMPEYE GO?
OH, YES.
I HEARD SHE LEFT WITH THE ORCS TO GO HUNTING.
IT MAKES SENSE, SINCE TRAIN-ING IS HER HOBBY.
RSTL.
GRR
TOO SLOW ...!!
AAHH!

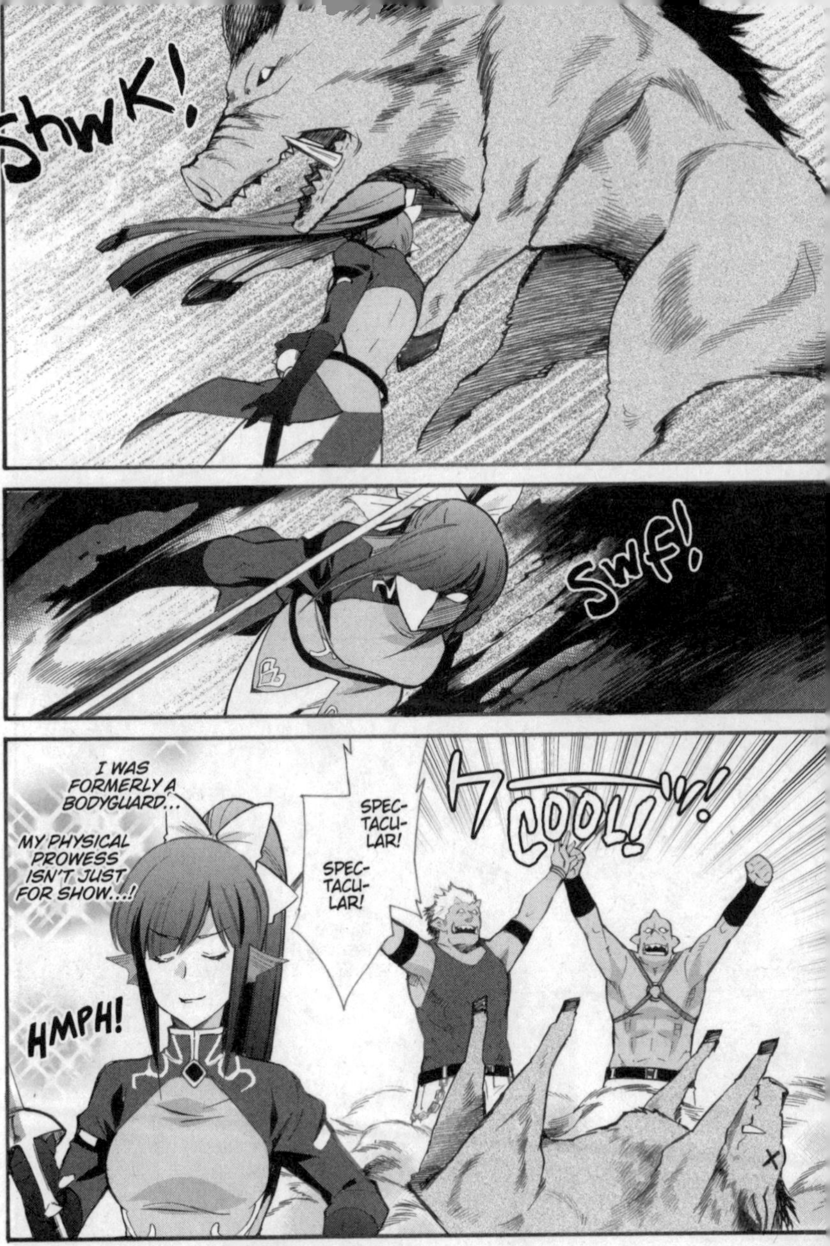
SHWK!
SWF!
COOL!
SPEC-TACU-LAR!
SPEC-TACU-LAR!
I WAS FORMERLY A BODYGUARD...
MY PHYSICAL PROWESS ISN'T JUST FOR SHOW...!
HMPH!

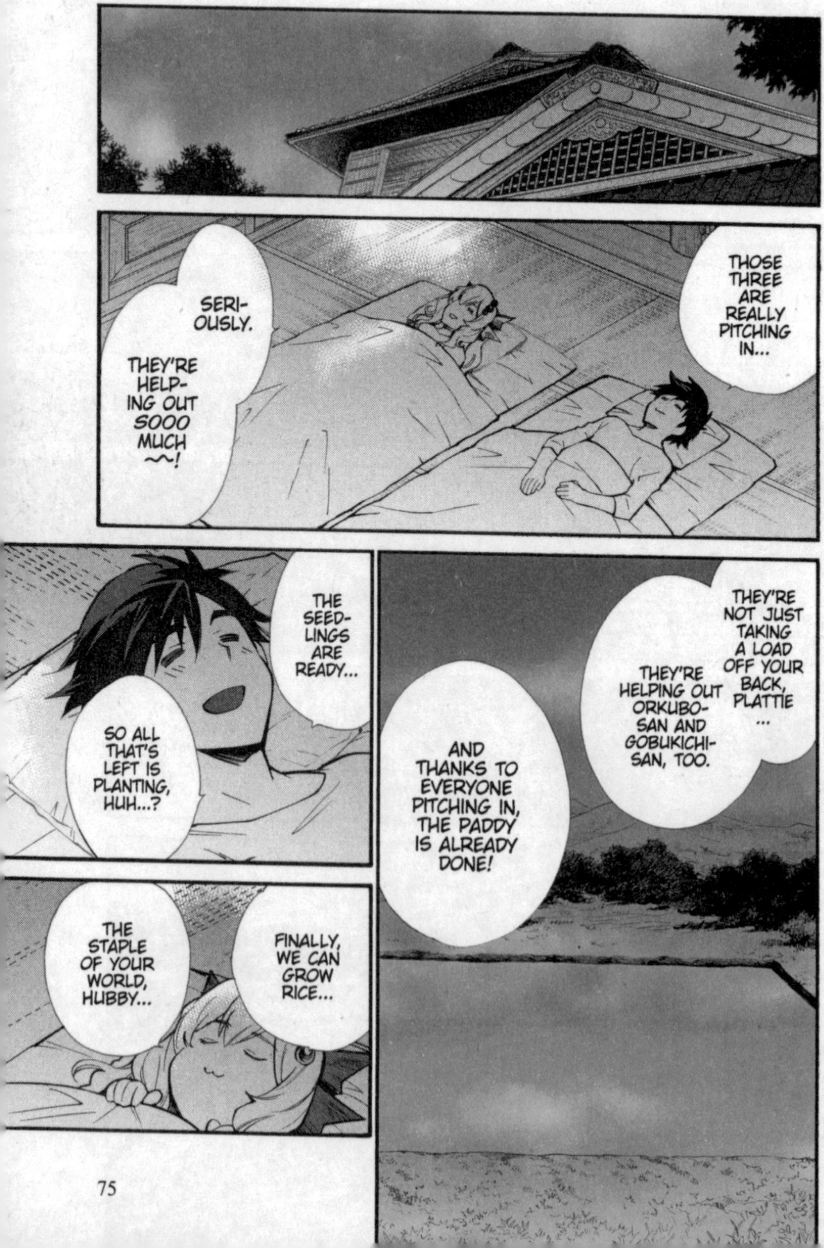
THOSE THREE ARE REALLY PITCHING IN...
SERIOUSLY.
THEY'RE HELPING OUT SOOO MUCH ~!
THEY'RE NOT JUST TAKING A LOAD OFF YOUR BACK, PLATTIE...
THEY'RE HELPING OUT ORKUBO-SAN AND GOBUKICHI-SAN, TOO.
AND THANKS TO EVERYONE PITCHING IN, THE PADDY IS ALREADY DONE!
THE SEEDLINGS ARE READY...
SO ALL THAT'S LEFT IS PLANTING, HUH...?
FINALLY, WE CAN GROW RICE...
THE STAPLE OF YOUR WORLD, HUBBY...

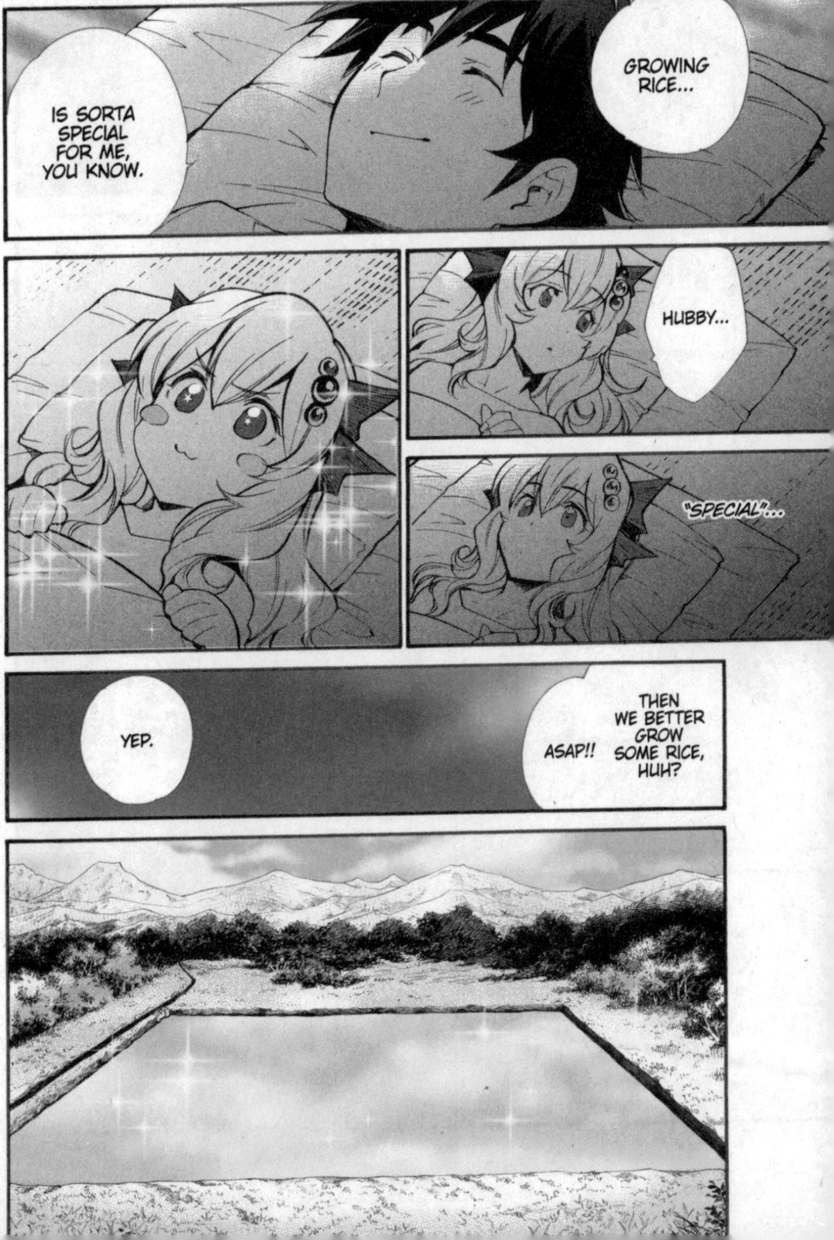
GROWING RICE...
IS SORTA SPECIAL FOR ME, YOU KNOW.
HUBBY...
"SPECIAL"...
THEN WE BETTER GROW SOME RICE, HUH?
ASAP!!
YEP.

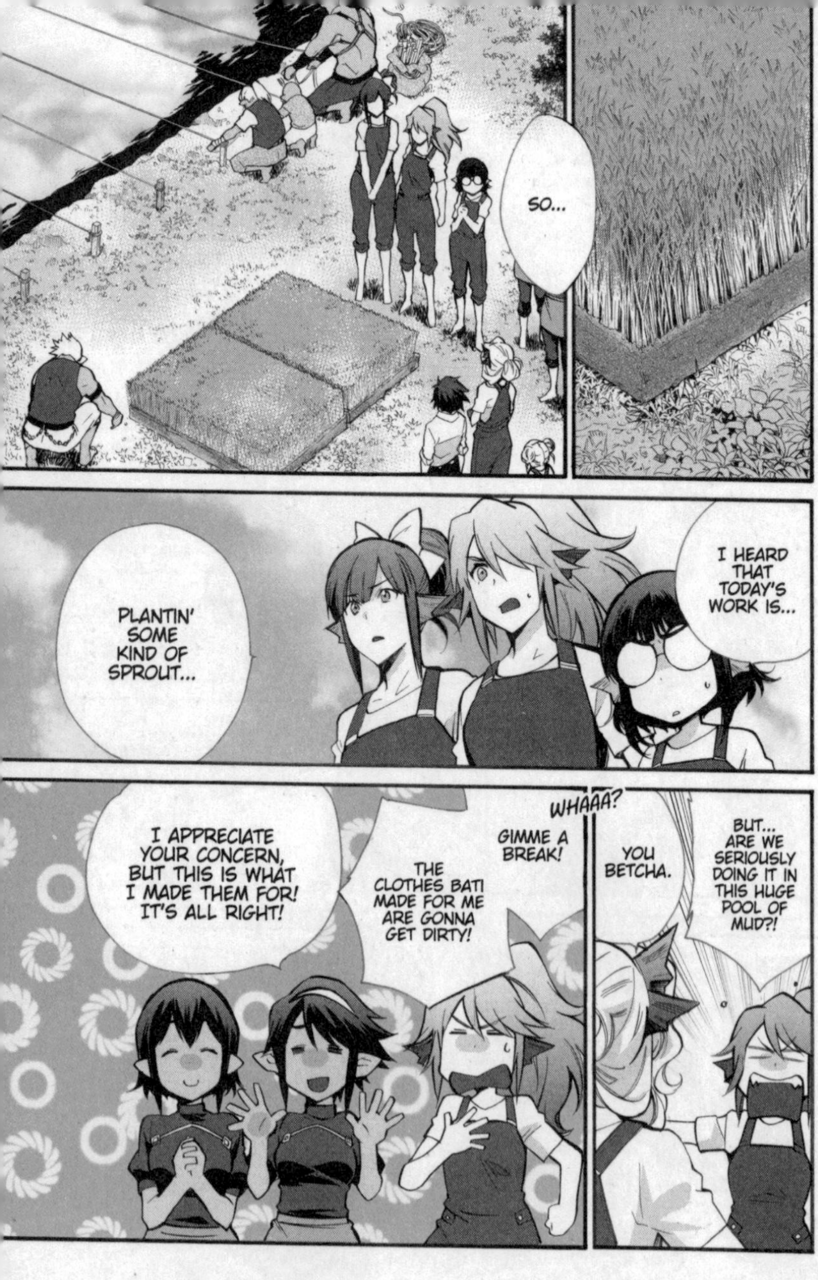
SO...
I HEARD THAT TODAY'S WORK IS...
PLANTIN' SOME KIND OF SPROUT...
BUT... ARE WE SERIOUSLY DOING IT IN THIS HUGE POOL OF MUD?!
YOU BETCHA.
WHAAA?
GIMME A BREAK!
THE CLOTHES BATI MADE FOR ME ARE GONNA GET DIRTY!
I APPRECIATE YOUR CONCERN, BUT THIS IS WHAT I MADE THEM FOR! IT'S ALL RIGHT!

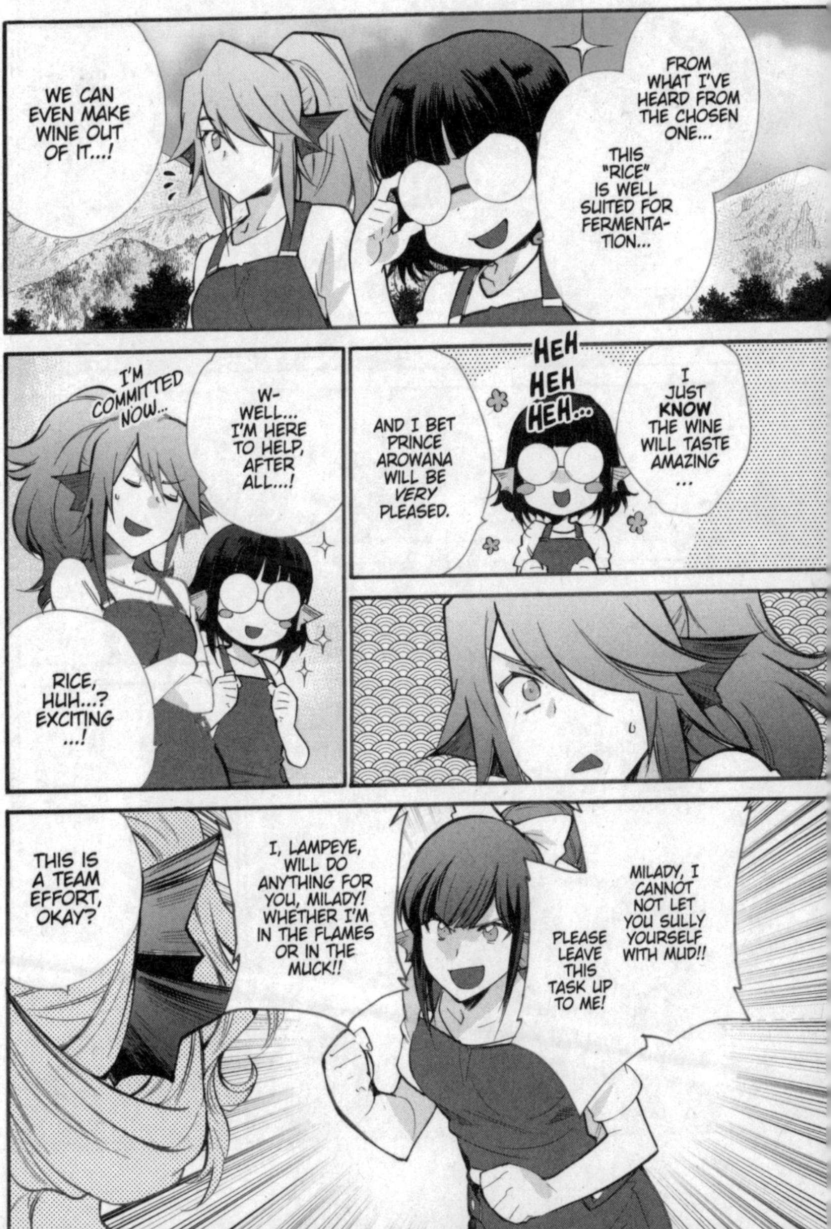
FROM WHAT I'VE HEARD FROM THE CHOSEN ONE...
THIS "RICE" IS WELL SUITED FOR FERMENTATION...
WE CAN EVEN MAKE WINE OUT OF IT...!
I JUST **KNOW** THE WINE WILL TASTE AMAZING ...
HEH HEH HEH...
AND I BET PRINCE AROWANA WILL BE *VERY* PLEASED.
W-WELL... I'M HERE TO HELP, AFTER ALL...!
I'M COMMITTED NOW...
RICE, HUH...? EXCITING ...!
MILADY, I CANNOT NOT LET YOU SULLY YOURSELF WITH MUD!!
PLEASE LEAVE THIS TASK UP TO ME!
I, LAMPEYE, WILL DO ANYTHING FOR YOU, MILADY! WHETHER I'M IN THE FLAMES OR IN THE MUCK!!
THIS IS A TEAM EFFORT, OKAY?

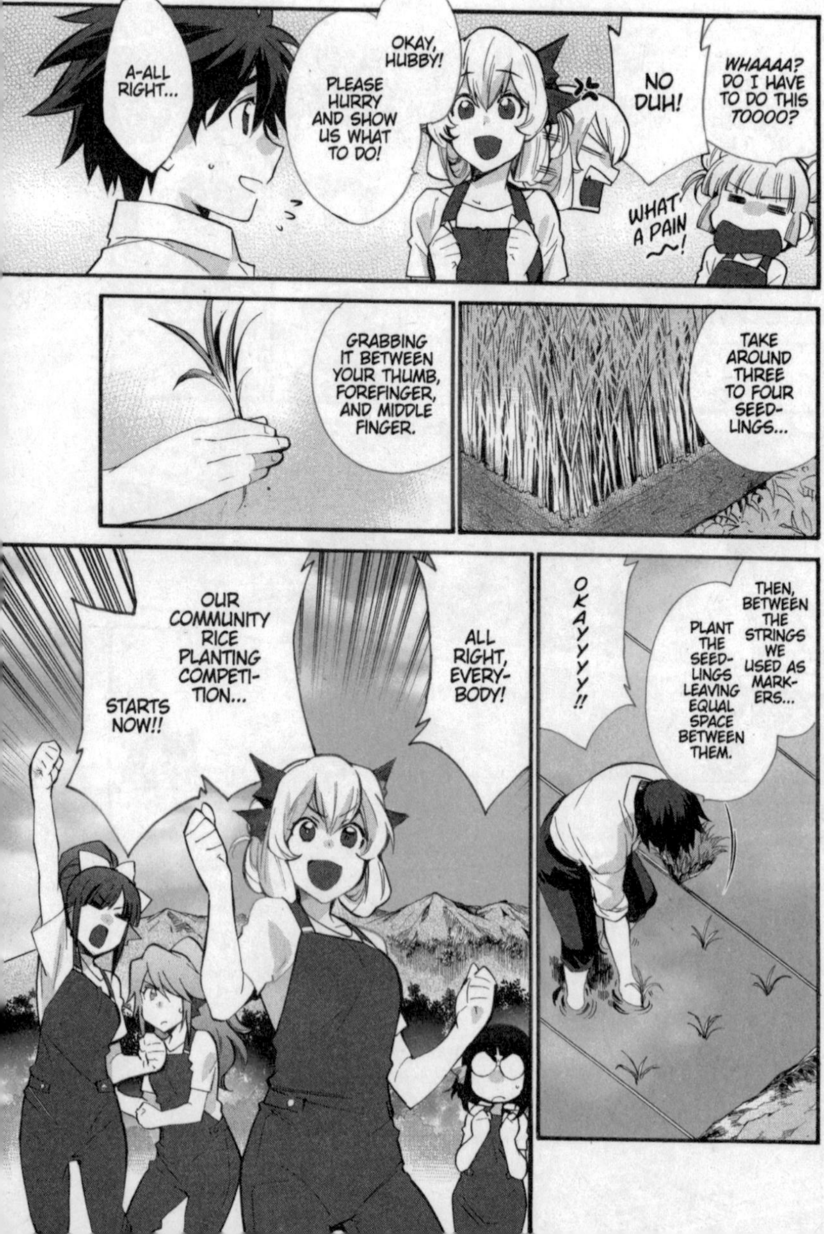
WHAAAA? DO I HAVE TO DO THIS TOOOO?
NO DUH!
WHAT A PAIN ~!
OKAY, HUBBY! PLEASE HURRY AND SHOW US WHAT TO DO!
A-ALL RIGHT...
TAKE AROUND THREE TO FOUR SEED-LINGS...
GRABBING IT BETWEEN YOUR THUMB, FOREFINGER, AND MIDDLE FINGER.
THEN, BETWEEN THE STRINGS WE USED AS MARK-ERS...
PLANT THE SEED-LINGS LEAVING EQUAL SPACE BETWEEN THEM.
OKAYYYY!!
ALL RIGHT, EVERY-BODY!
OUR COMMUNITY RICE PLANTING COMPETI-TION...
STARTS NOW!!

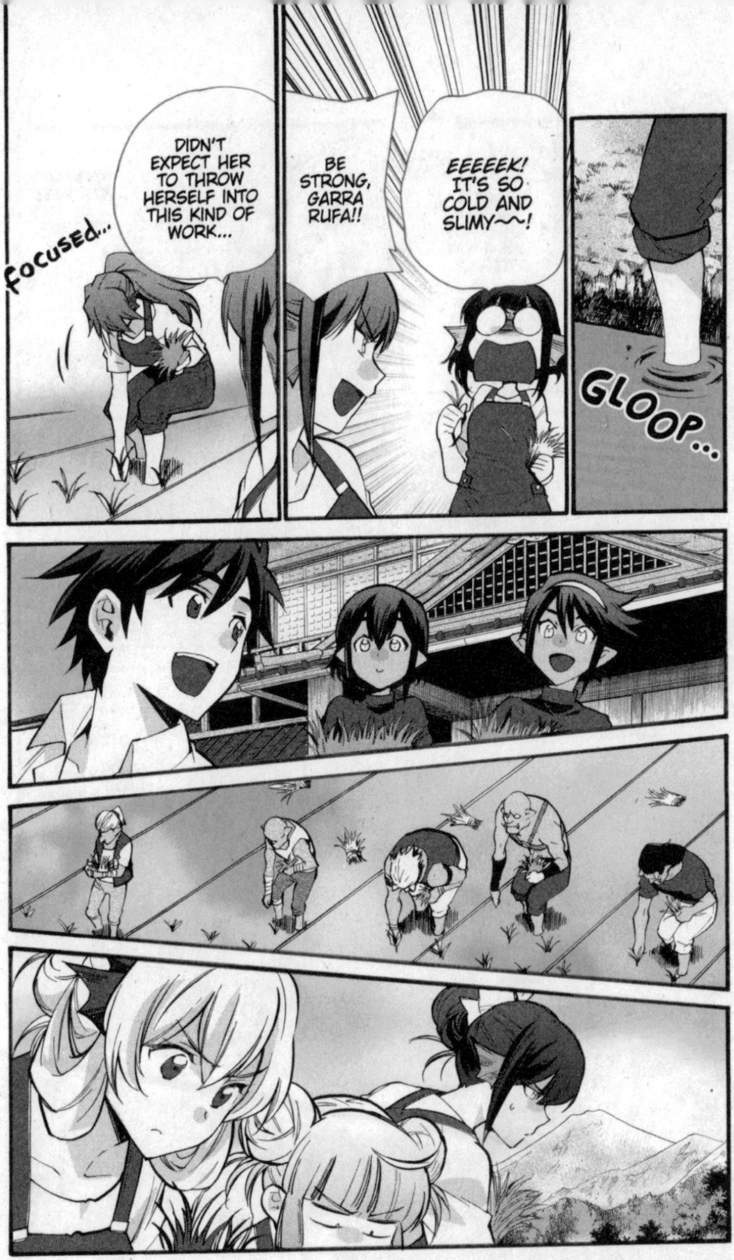
GLOOP...
EEEEEK! IT'S SO COLD AND SLIMY~~!
BE STRONG, GARRA RUFA!!
DIDN'T EXPECT HER TO THROW HERSELF INTO THIS KIND OF WORK...
Focused...

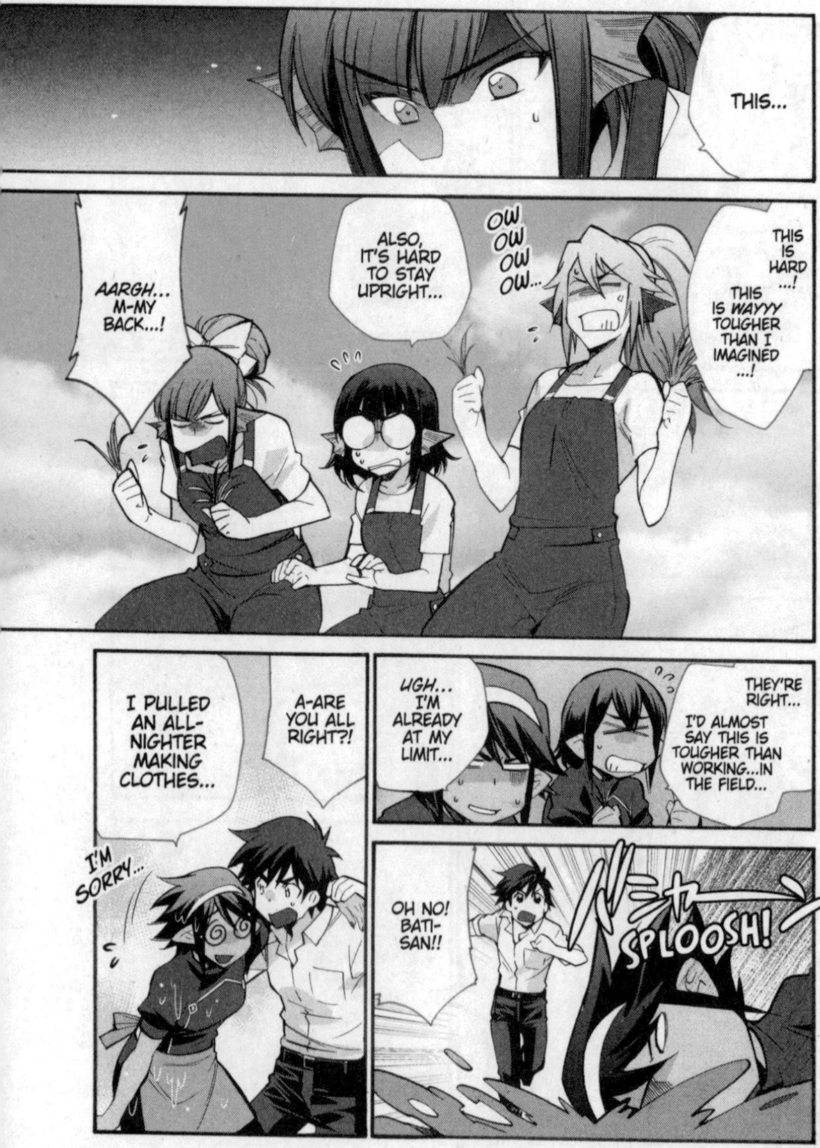
THIS...
THIS IS HARD...! THIS IS WAYYY TOUGHER THAN I IMAGINED...!
OW OW OW OW...
ALSO, IT'S HARD TO STAY UPRIGHT...
AARGH... M-MY BACK...!
THEY'RE RIGHT... I'D ALMOST SAY THIS IS TOUGHER THAN WORKING...IN THE FIELD...
UGH... I'M ALREADY AT MY LIMIT...
SPLOOSH!
OH NO! BATI-SAN!!
A-ARE YOU ALL RIGHT?!
I PULLED AN ALL-NIGHTER MAKING CLOTHES...
I'M SORRY...

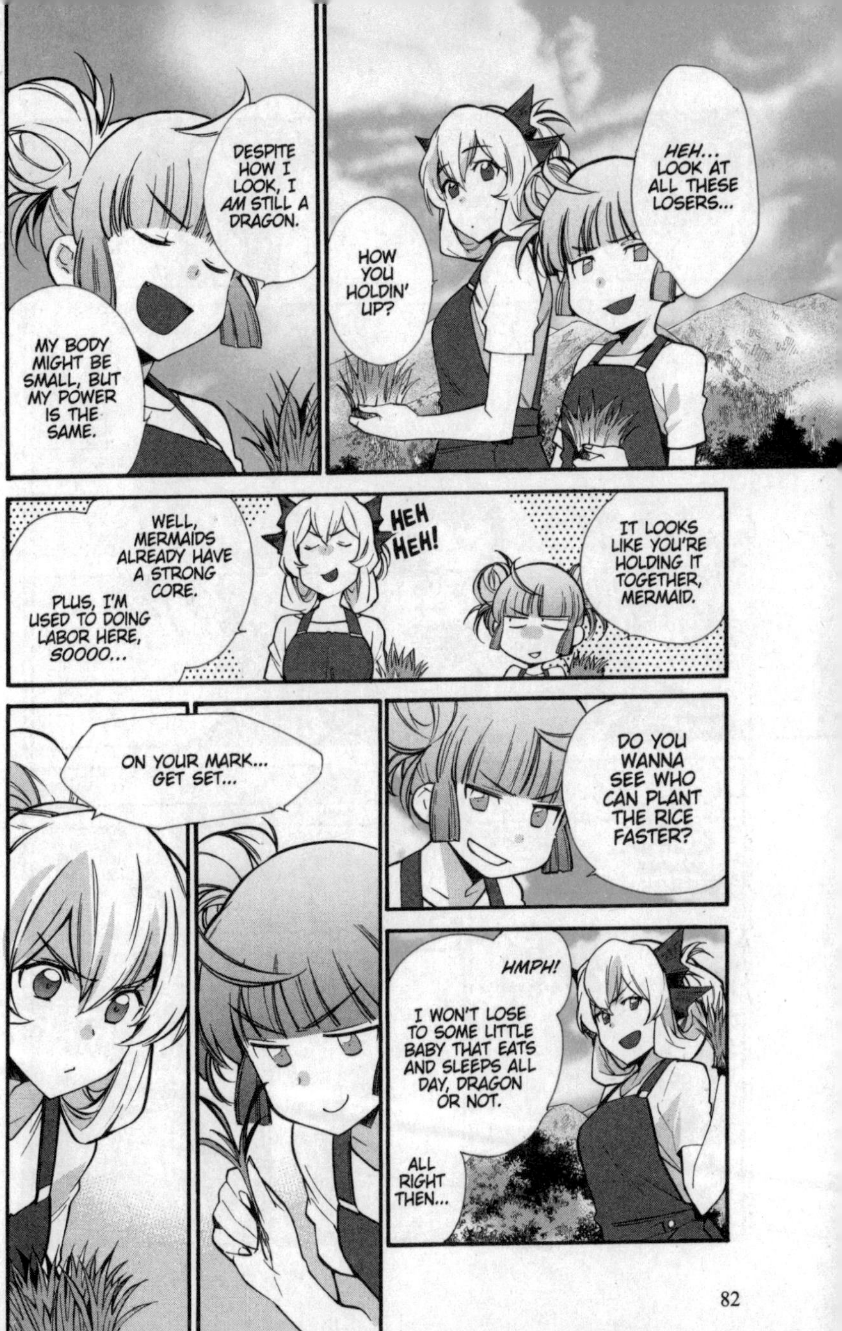
HEH... LOOK AT ALL THESE LOSERS...
HOW YOU HOLDIN' UP?
DESPITE HOW I LOOK, I AM STILL A DRAGON.
MY BODY MIGHT BE SMALL, BUT MY POWER IS THE SAME.
IT LOOKS LIKE YOU'RE HOLDING IT TOGETHER, MERMAID.
HEH HEH!
WELL, MERMAIDS ALREADY HAVE A STRONG CORE.
PLUS, I'M USED TO DOING LABOR HERE, SOOOO...
DO YOU WANNA SEE WHO CAN PLANT THE RICE FASTER?
HMPH!
I WON'T LOSE TO SOME LITTLE BABY THAT EATS AND SLEEPS ALL DAY, DRAGON OR NOT.
ALL RIGHT THEN...
ON YOUR MARK... GET SET...

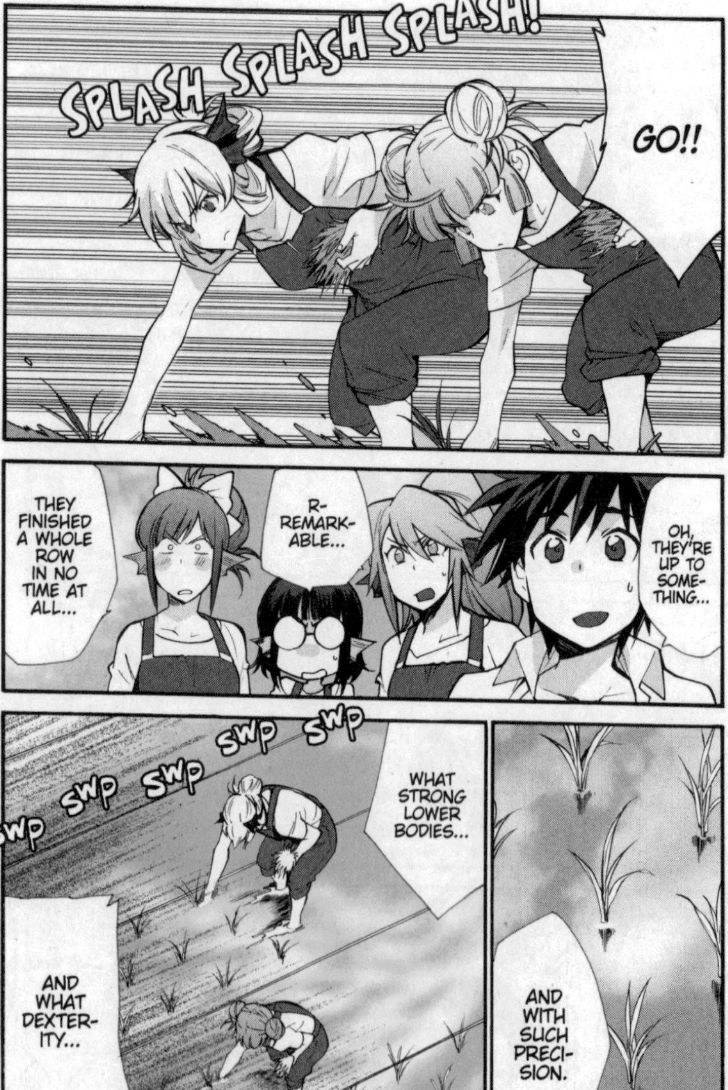

SPLASH SPLASH SPLASH!
GO!!
OH, THEY'RE UP TO SOMETHING...
R-REMARKABLE...
THEY FINISHED A WHOLE ROW IN NO TIME AT ALL...
AND WITH SUCH PRECISION.
swp swp swp swp swp
WHAT STRONG LOWER BODIES...
AND WHAT DEXTERITY...

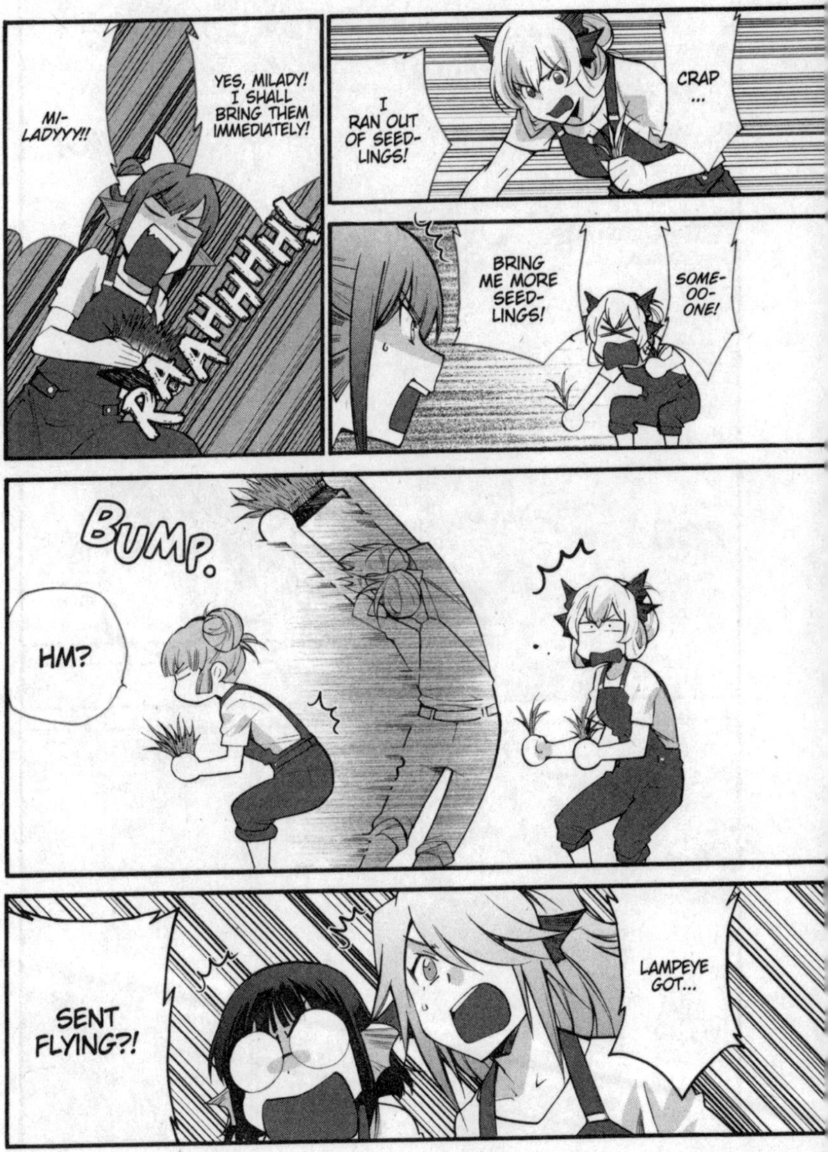
CRAP ...
I RAN OUT OF SEED-LINGS!
SOME-OO-ONE!
BRING ME MORE SEED-LINGS!
YES, MILADY! I SHALL BRING THEM IMMEDIATELY!
MI-LADYYY!!
RAAHHHH!
BUMP.
HM?
LAMPEYE GOT...
SENT FLYING?!

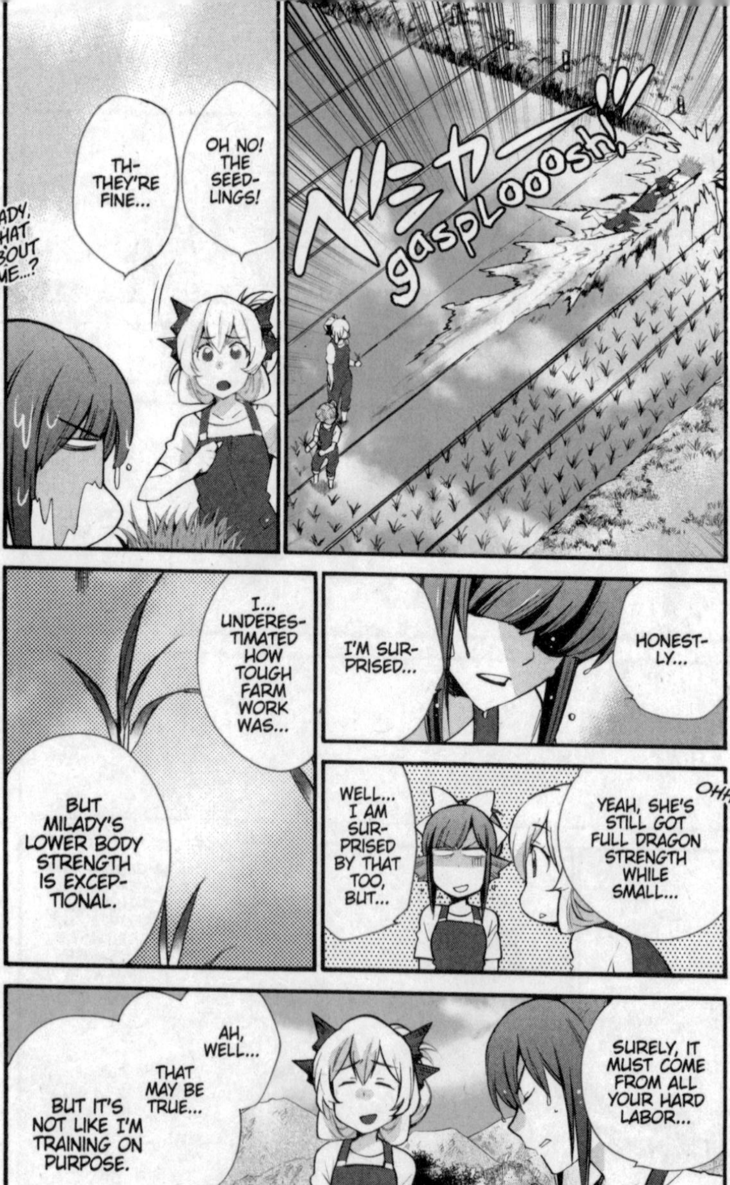
gasplooosh!!
OH NO! THE SEEDLINGS!
TH- THEY'RE FINE...
MILADY, WHAT ABOUT ME...?
HONESTLY...
I'M SURPRISED...
OHHH.
YEAH, SHE'S STILL GOT FULL DRAGON STRENGTH WHILE SMALL...
WELL... I AM SURPRISED BY THAT TOO, BUT...
I... UNDERESTIMATED HOW TOUGH FARM WORK WAS...
BUT MILADY'S LOWER BODY STRENGTH IS EXCEPTIONAL.
SURELY, IT MUST COME FROM ALL YOUR HARD LABOR...
AH, WELL...
THAT MAY BE TRUE...
BUT IT'S NOT LIKE I'M TRAINING ON PURPOSE.

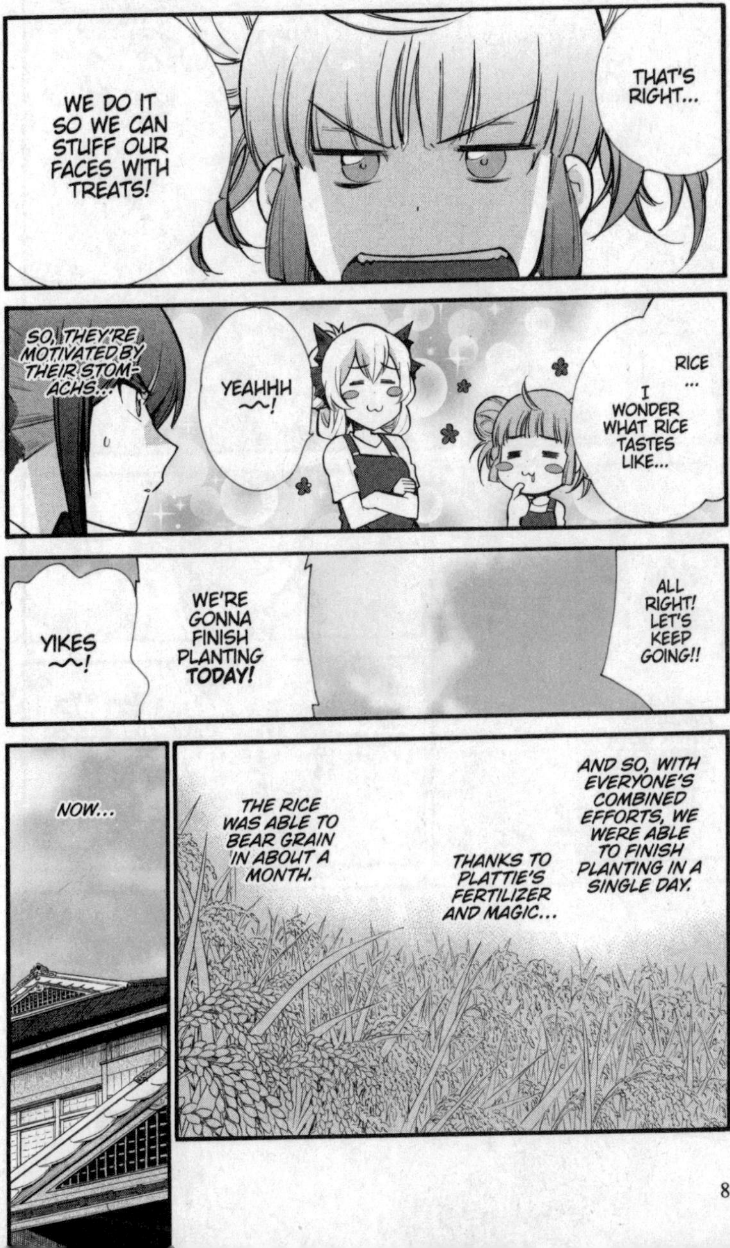
THAT'S RIGHT...
WE DO IT SO WE CAN STUFF OUR FACES WITH TREATS!
RICE ... I WONDER WHAT RICE TASTES LIKE...
YEAHHH ~!
SO, THEY'RE MOTIVATED BY THEIR STOM-ACHS...
ALL RIGHT! LET'S KEEP GOING!!
WE'RE GONNA FINISH PLANTING TODAY!
YIKES ~!
AND SO, WITH EVERYONE'S COMBINED EFFORTS, WE WERE ABLE TO FINISH PLANTING IN A SINGLE DAY.
THANKS TO PLATTIE'S FERTILIZER AND MAGIC...
THE RICE WAS ABLE TO BEAR GRAIN IN ABOUT A MONTH.
NOW...

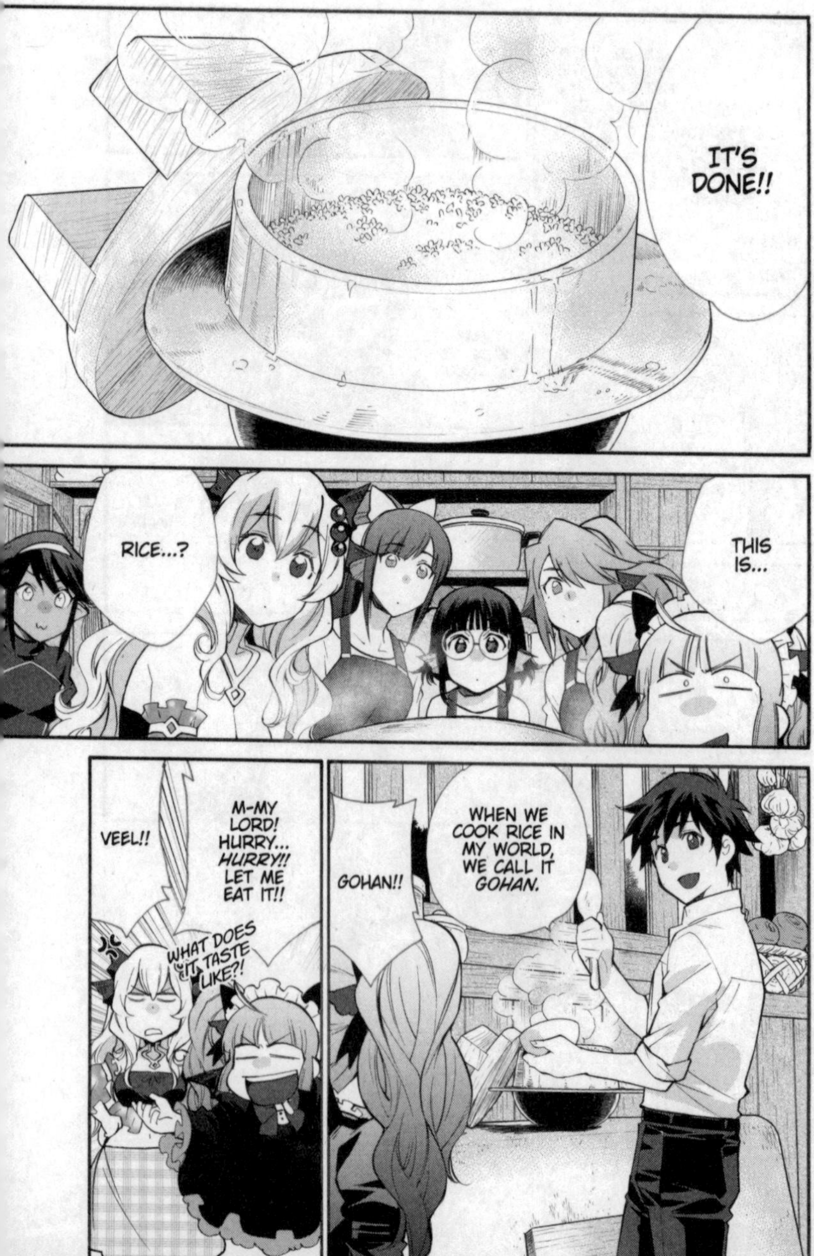
IT'S DONE!!
THIS IS...
RICE...?
WHEN WE COOK RICE IN MY WORLD, WE CALL IT GOHAN.
GOHAN!!
M-MY LORD! HURRY... HURRY!! LET ME EAT IT!!
VEEL!!
WHAT DOES IT TASTE LIKE?!

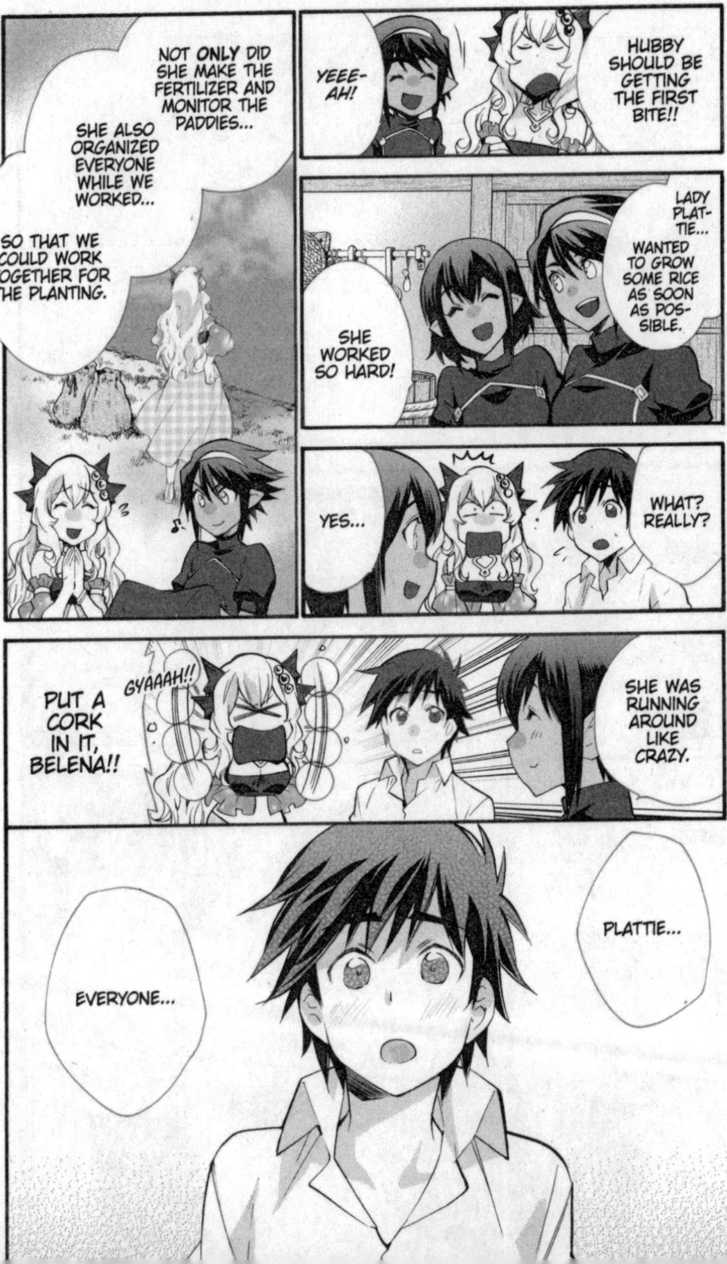
HUBBY SHOULD BE GETTING THE FIRST BITE!!
YEEE-AH!
LADY PLATTIE... WANTED TO GROW SOME RICE AS SOON AS POSSIBLE.
SHE WORKED SO HARD!
WHAT? REALLY?
YES...
NOT ONLY DID SHE MAKE THE FERTILIZER AND MONITOR THE PADDIES...
SHE ALSO ORGANIZED EVERYONE WHILE WE WORKED...
SO THAT WE COULD WORK TOGETHER FOR THE PLANTING.
SHE WAS RUNNING AROUND LIKE CRAZY.
GYAAAH!!
PUT A CORK IN IT, BELENA!!
PLATTIE...
EVERYONE...

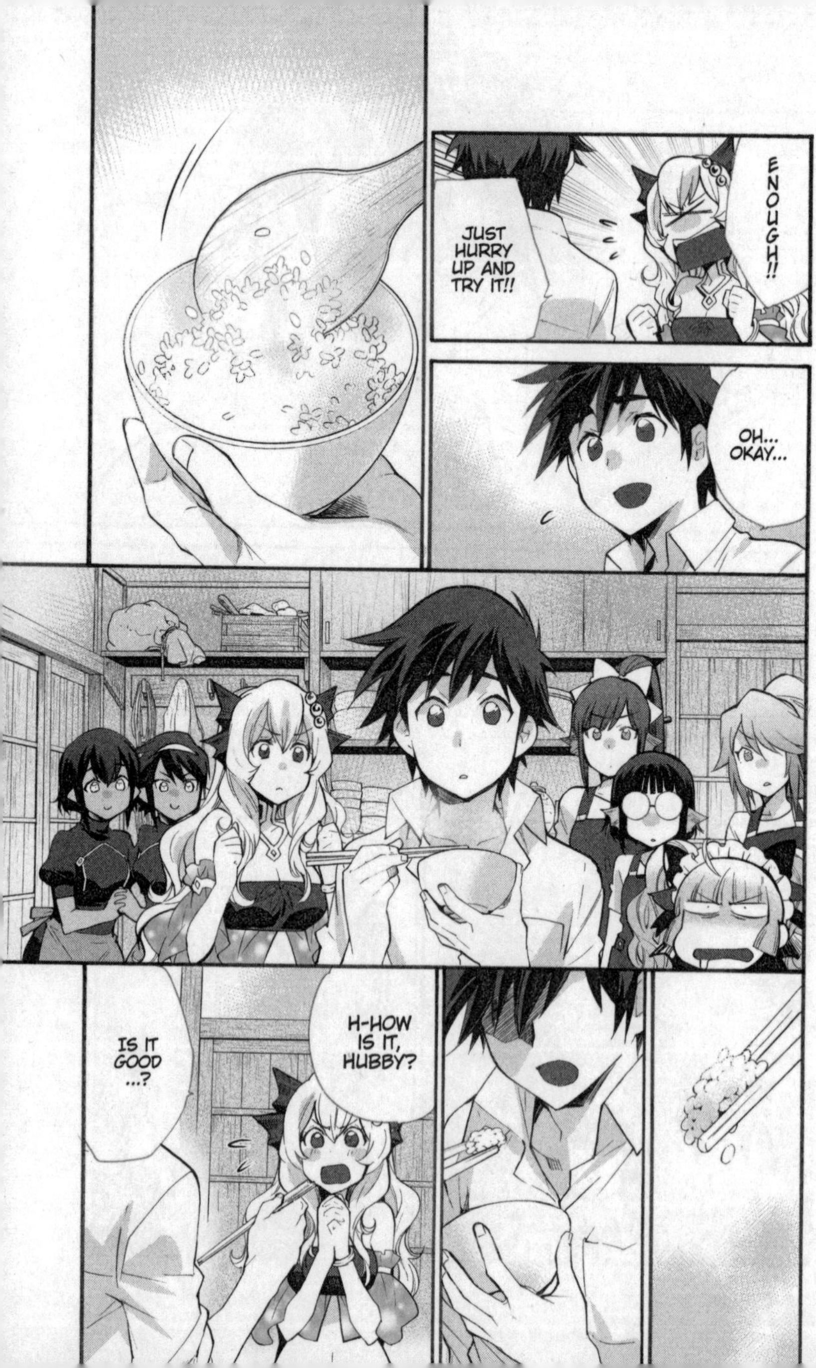
ENOUGH!!
JUST HURRY UP AND TRY IT!!
OH... OKAY...
H-HOW IS IT, HUBBY?
IS IT GOOD ...?

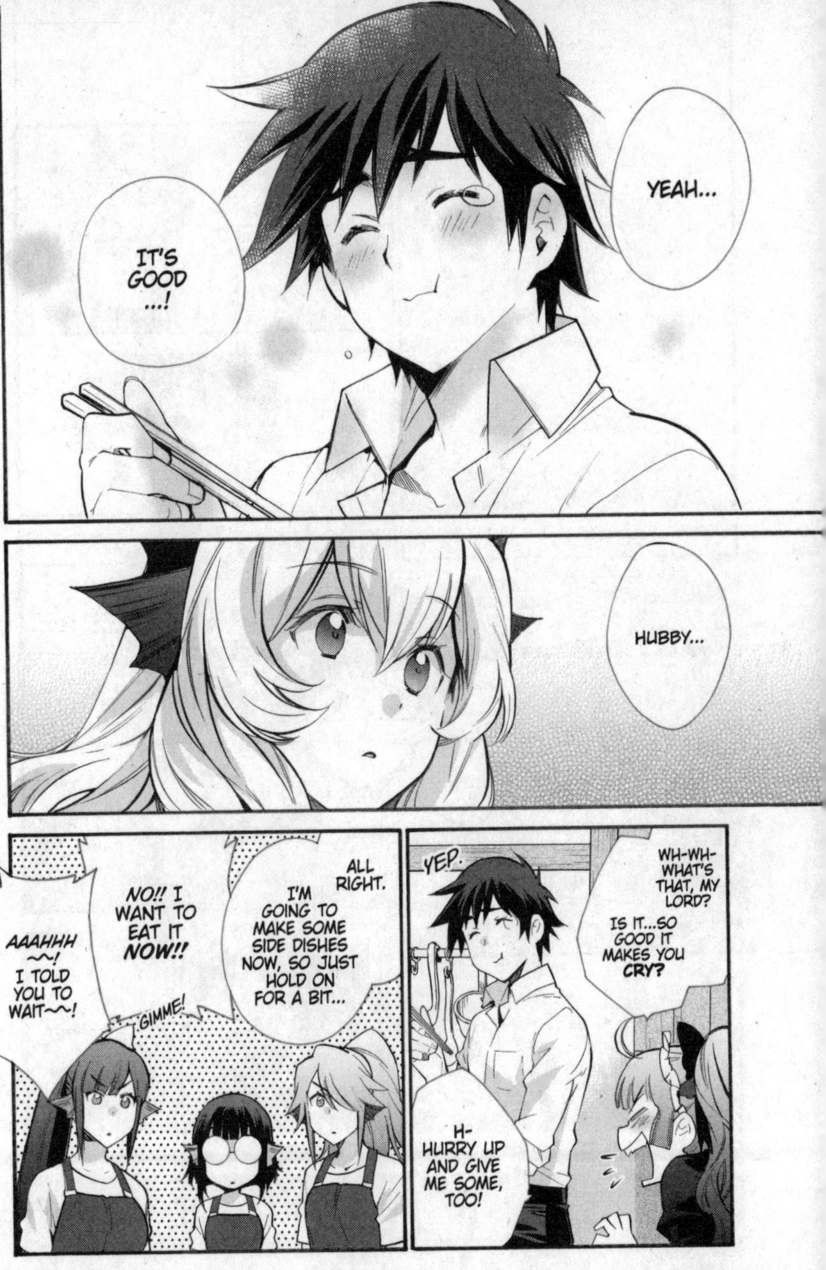
YEAH...
IT'S GOOD...!
HUBBY...
WH-WH-WHAT'S THAT, MY LORD?
IS IT...SO GOOD IT MAKES YOU CRY?
YEP.
H-HURRY UP AND GIVE ME SOME, TOO!
ALL RIGHT.
I'M GOING TO MAKE SOME SIDE DISHES NOW, SO JUST HOLD ON FOR A BIT...
NO!! I WANT TO EAT IT NOW!!
GIMME!
AAAHHH~~! I TOLD YOU TO WAIT~~!

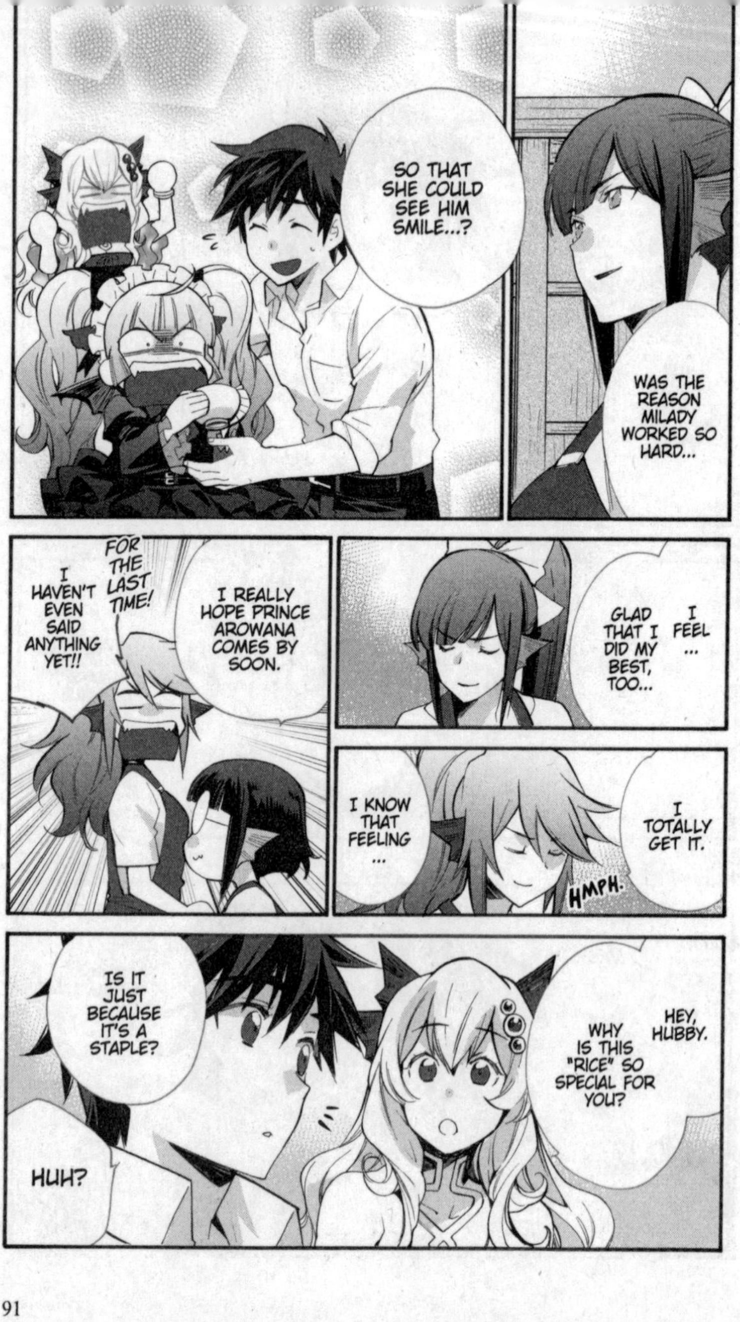
WAS THE REASON MILADY WORKED SO HARD...
SO THAT SHE COULD SEE HIM SMILE...?
I FEEL ...
GLAD THAT I DID MY BEST, TOO...
I TOTALLY GET IT.
HMPH.
I KNOW THAT FEELING ...
I REALLY HOPE PRINCE AROWANA COMES BY SOON.
FOR THE LAST TIME!
I HAVEN'T EVEN SAID ANYTHING YET!!
HEY, HUBBY.
WHY IS THIS "RICE" SO SPECIAL FOR YOU?
IS IT JUST BECAUSE IT'S A STAPLE?
HUH?

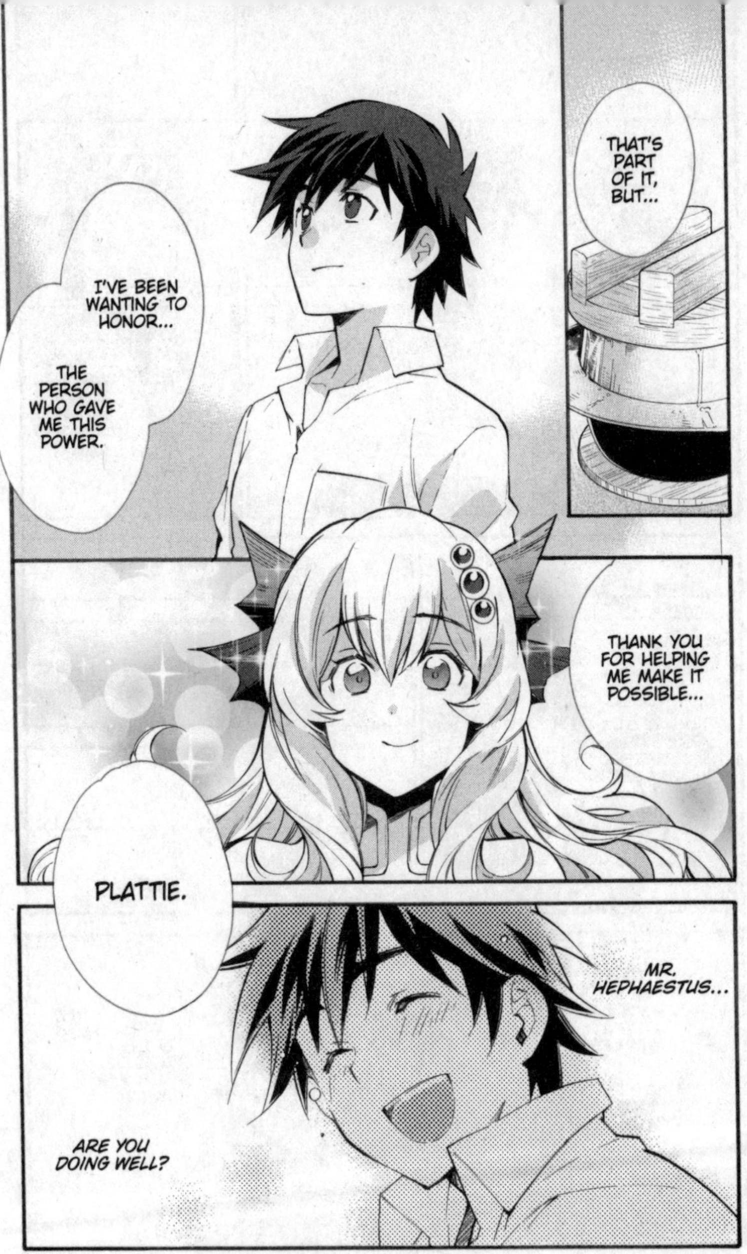
THAT'S PART OF IT, BUT...
I'VE BEEN WANTING TO HONOR...
THE PERSON WHO GAVE ME THIS POWER.
THANK YOU FOR HELPING ME MAKE IT POSSIBLE...
PLATTIE.
MR. HEPHAESTUS...
ARE YOU DOING WELL?

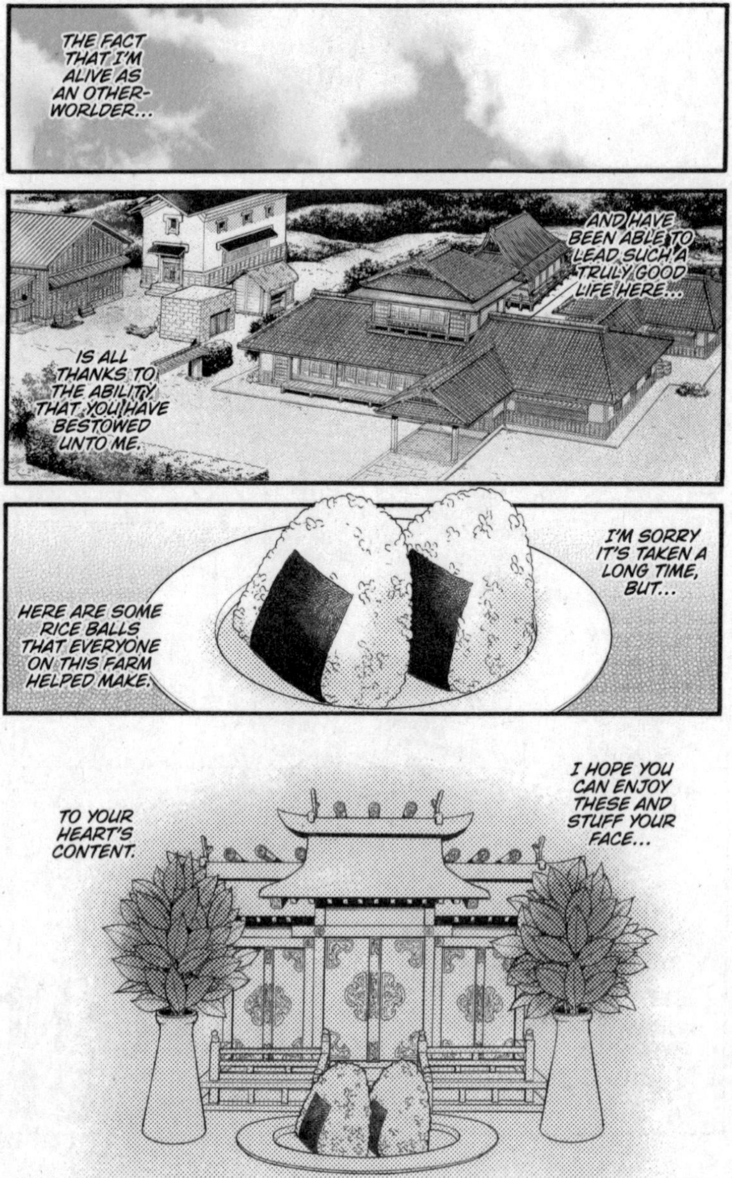
THE FACT THAT I'M ALIVE AS AN OTHER-WORLDER...
AND HAVE BEEN ABLE TO LEAD SUCH A TRULY GOOD LIFE HERE...
IS ALL THANKS TO THE ABILITY THAT YOU HAVE BESTOWED UNTO ME.
I'M SORRY IT'S TAKEN A LONG TIME, BUT...
HERE ARE SOME RICE BALLS THAT EVERYONE ON THIS FARM HELPED MAKE.
I HOPE YOU CAN ENJOY THESE AND STUFF YOUR FACE...
TO YOUR HEART'S CONTENT.

LET'S BUY THE LAND and CULTIVATE IT IN A DIFFERENT WORLD

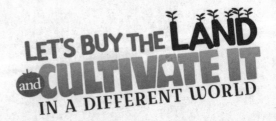

CHAPTER 23

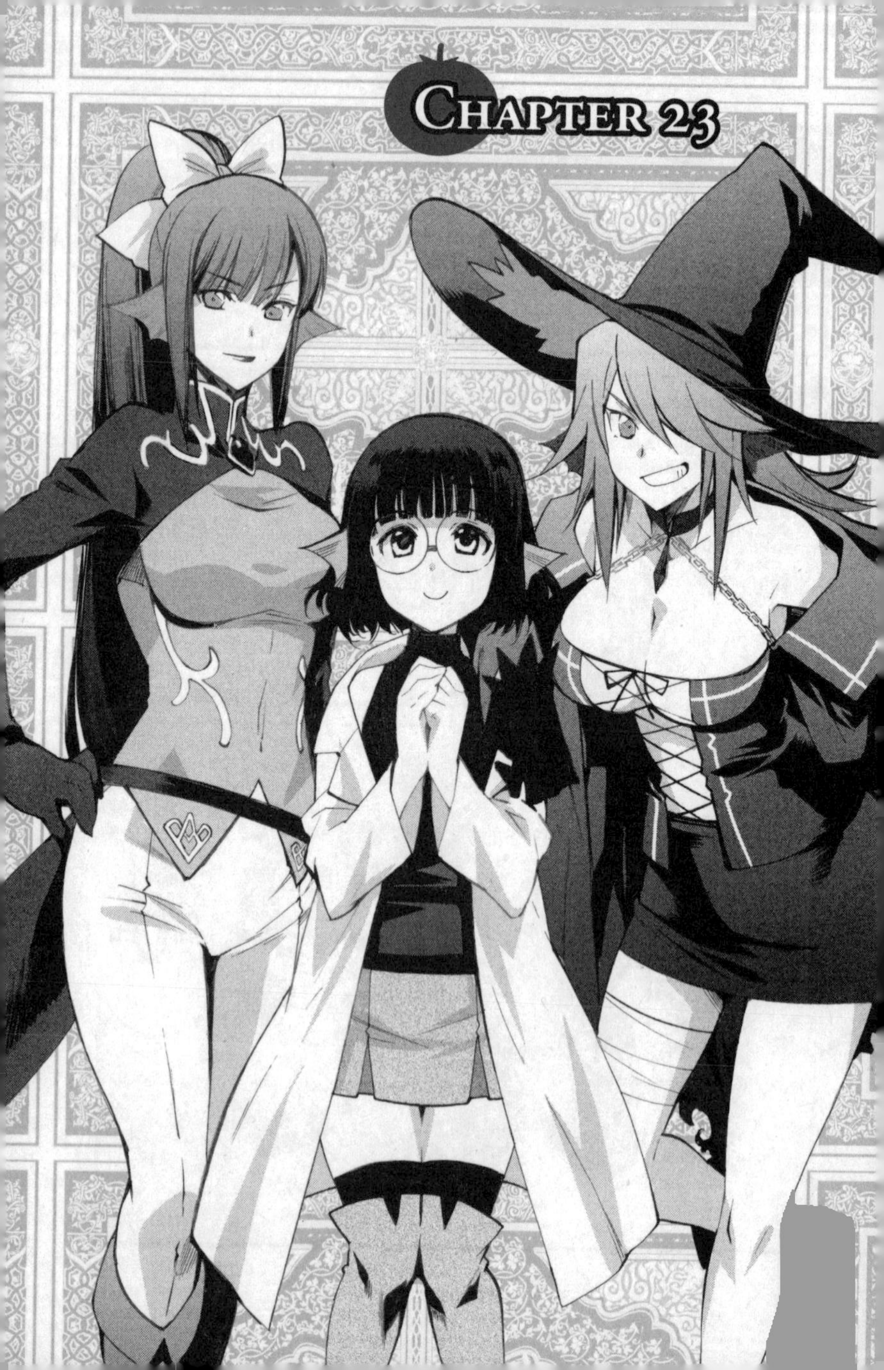

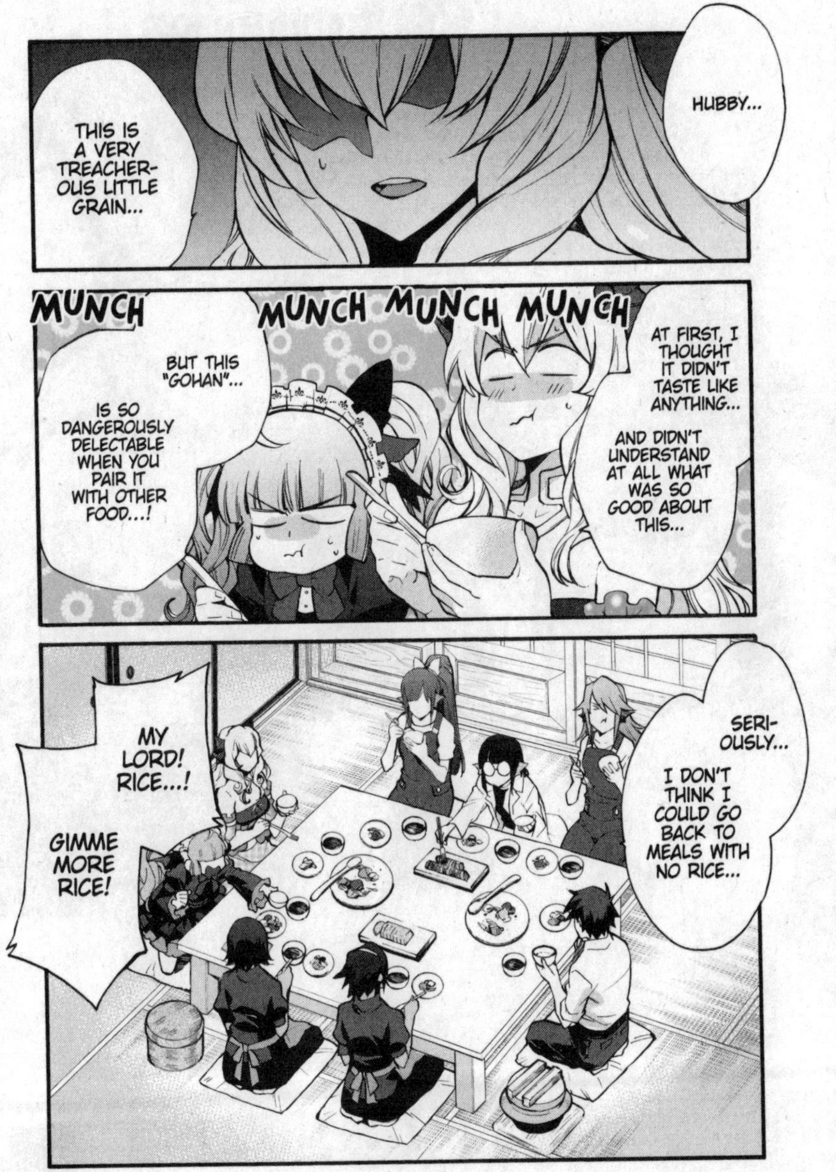
HUBBY...
THIS IS A VERY TREACHER-OUS LITTLE GRAIN...
MUNCH MUNCH MUNCH MUNCH
AT FIRST, I THOUGHT IT DIDN'T TASTE LIKE ANYTHING...
AND DIDN'T UNDERSTAND AT ALL WHAT WAS SO GOOD ABOUT THIS...
BUT THIS "GOHAN"...
IS SO DANGEROUSLY DELECTABLE WHEN YOU PAIR IT WITH OTHER FOOD...!
SERI-OUSLY...
I DON'T THINK I COULD GO BACK TO MEALS WITH NO RICE...
MY LORD! RICE...!
GIMME MORE RICE!

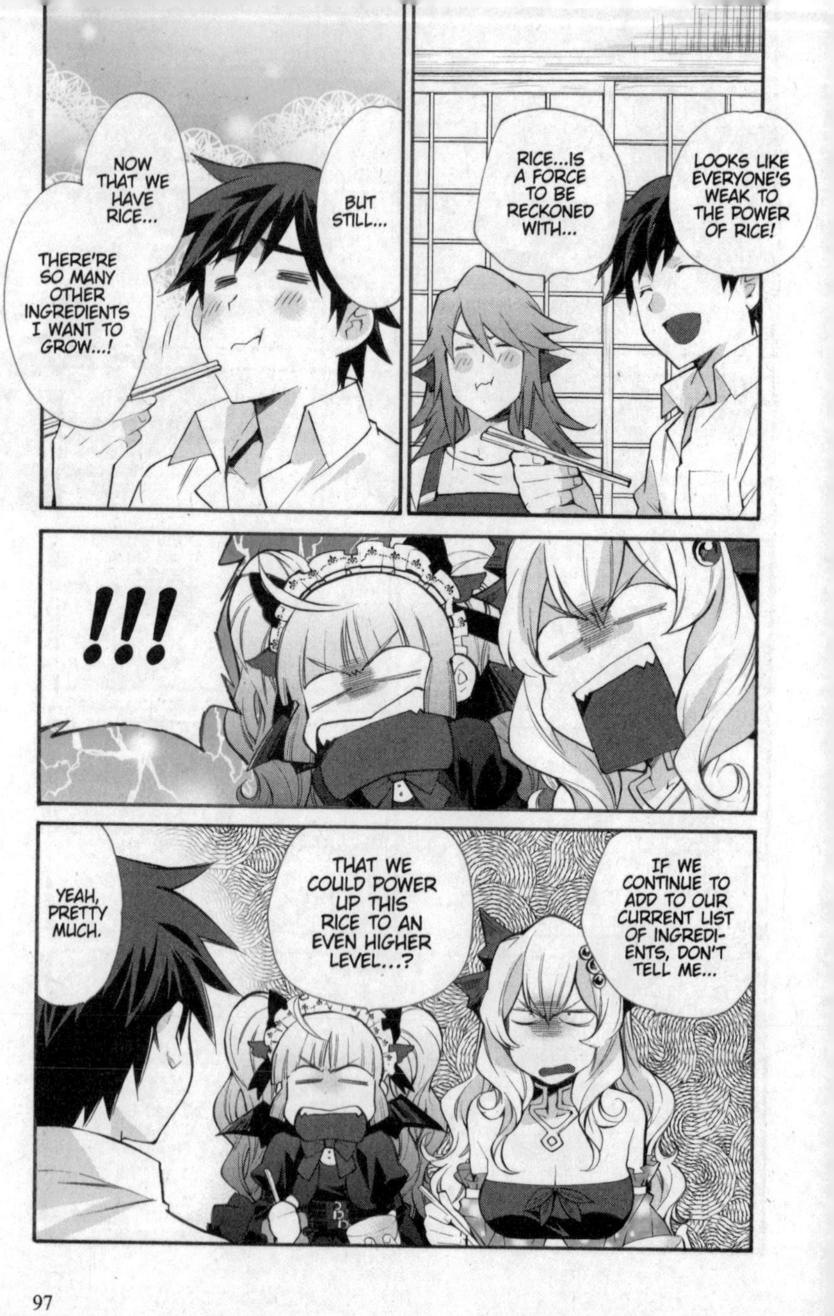
LOOKS LIKE EVERYONE'S WEAK TO THE POWER OF RICE!
RICE...IS A FORCE TO BE RECKONED WITH...
BUT STILL...
NOW THAT WE HAVE RICE...
THERE'RE SO MANY OTHER INGREDIENTS I WANT TO GROW...!
!!!
IF WE CONTINUE TO ADD TO OUR CURRENT LIST OF INGREDI-ENTS, DON'T TELL ME...
THAT WE COULD POWER UP THIS RICE TO AN EVEN HIGHER LEVEL...?
YEAH, PRETTY MUCH.

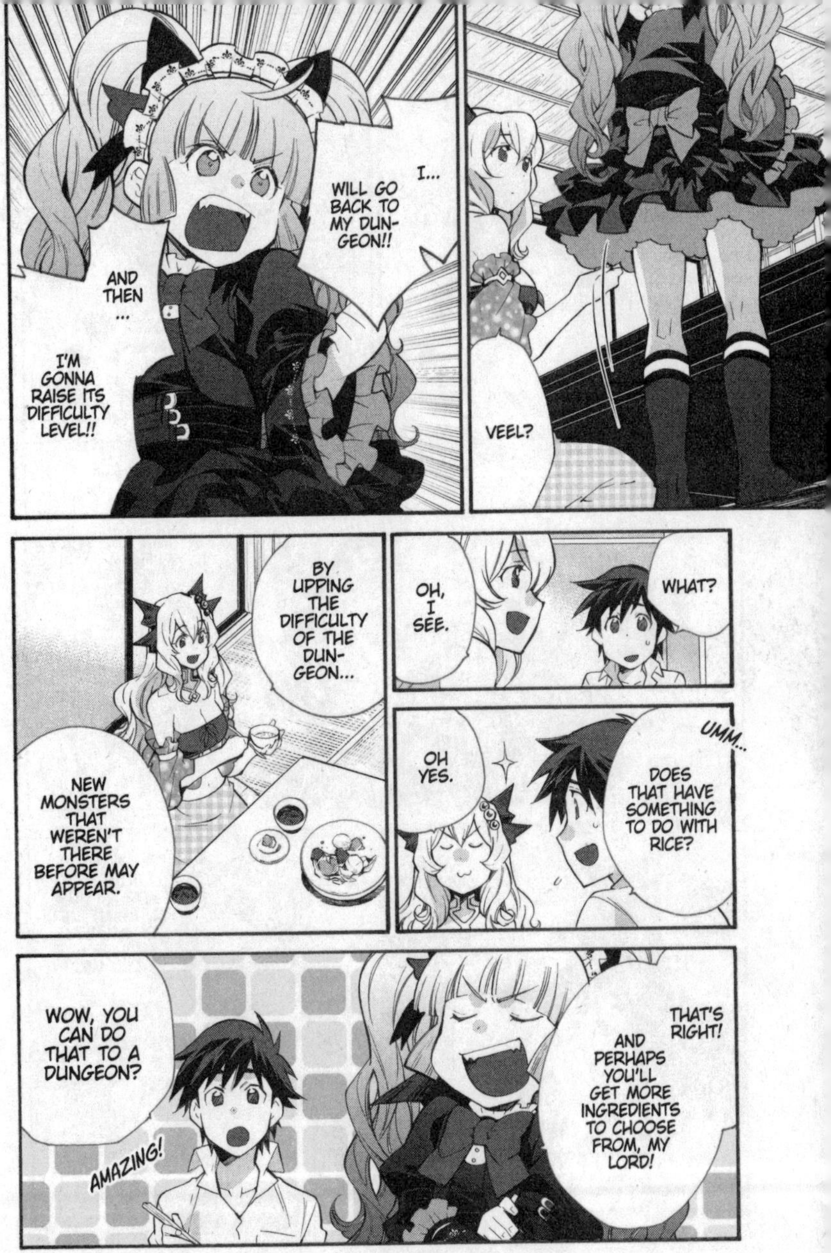
VEEL?
I...
WILL GO BACK TO MY DUNGEON!!
AND THEN ...
I'M GONNA RAISE ITS DIFFICULTY LEVEL!!
WHAT?
OH, I SEE.
UMM...
DOES THAT HAVE SOMETHING TO DO WITH RICE?
OH YES.
BY UPPING THE DIFFICULTY OF THE DUNGEON...
NEW MONSTERS THAT WEREN'T THERE BEFORE MAY APPEAR.
THAT'S RIGHT!
AND PERHAPS YOU'LL GET MORE INGREDIENTS TO CHOOSE FROM, MY LORD!
WOW, YOU CAN DO THAT TO A DUNGEON?
AMAZING!

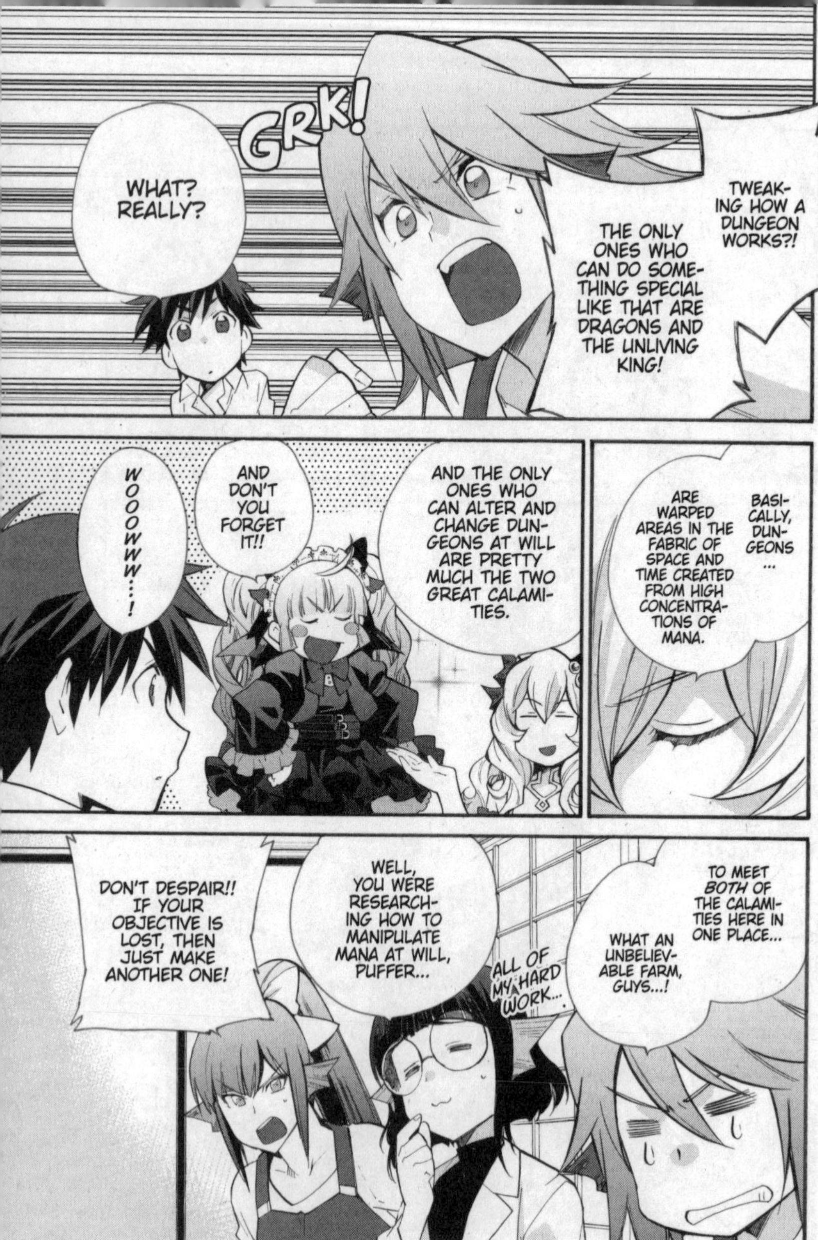
TWEAKING HOW A DUNGEON WORKS?!
THE ONLY ONES WHO CAN DO SOMETHING SPECIAL LIKE THAT ARE DRAGONS AND THE UNLIVING KING!
GRK!
WHAT? REALLY?
BASICALLY, DUNGEONS...
ARE WARPED AREAS IN THE FABRIC OF SPACE AND TIME CREATED FROM HIGH CONCENTRATIONS OF MANA.
AND THE ONLY ONES WHO CAN ALTER AND CHANGE DUNGEONS AT WILL ARE PRETTY MUCH THE TWO GREAT CALAMITIES.
AND DON'T YOU FORGET IT!!
WOOOWWW...!
TO MEET *BOTH* OF THE CALAMITIES HERE IN ONE PLACE...
WHAT AN UNBELIEVABLE FARM, GUYS...!
ALL OF MY HARD WORK...
WELL, YOU WERE RESEARCHING HOW TO MANIPULATE MANA AT WILL, PUFFER...
DON'T DESPAIR!! IF YOUR OBJECTIVE IS LOST, THEN JUST MAKE ANOTHER ONE!

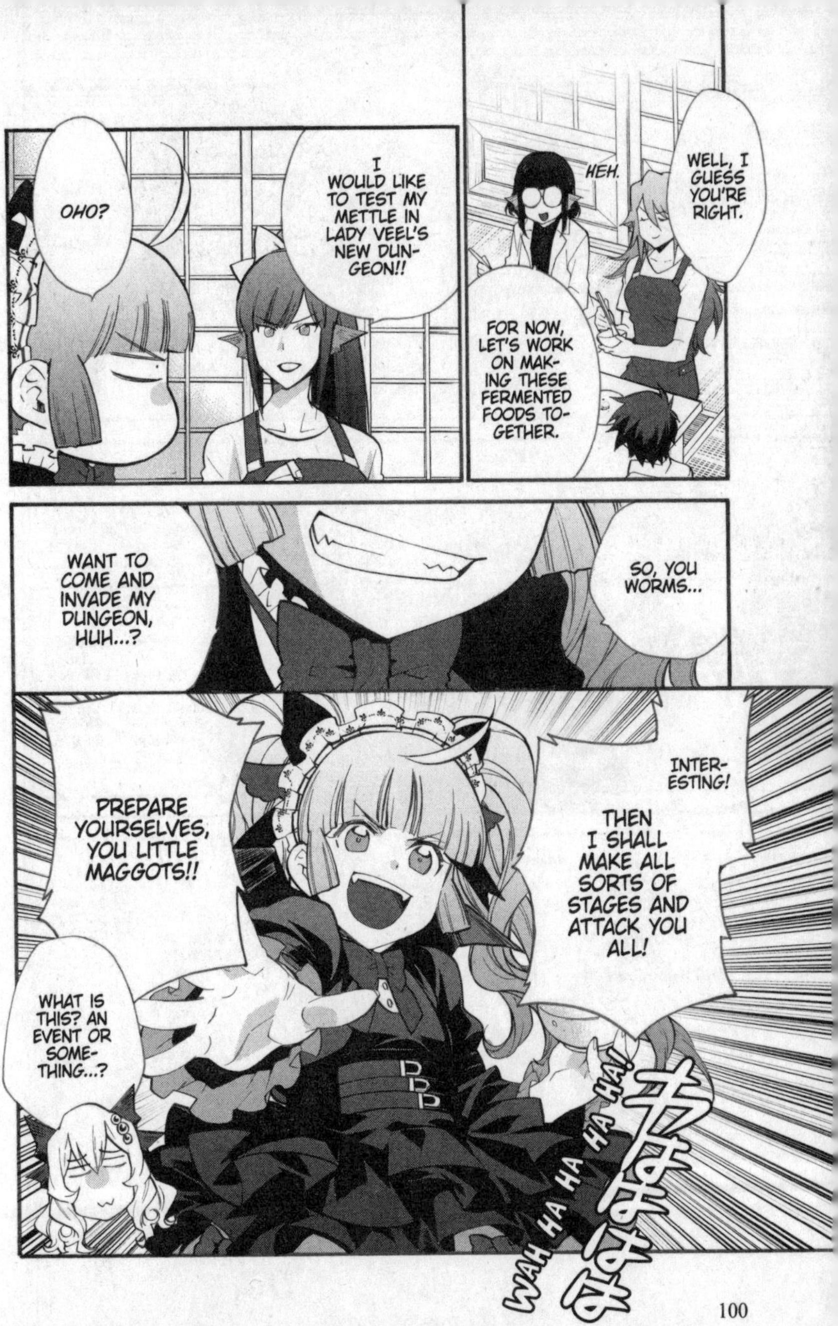
WELL, I GUESS YOU'RE RIGHT.
HEH.
FOR NOW, LET'S WORK ON MAKING THESE FERMENTED FOODS TOGETHER.
I WOULD LIKE TO TEST MY METTLE IN LADY VEEL'S NEW DUNGEON!!
OHO?
SO, YOU WORMS...
WANT TO COME AND INVADE MY DUNGEON, HUH...?
INTERESTING!
THEN I SHALL MAKE ALL SORTS OF STAGES AND ATTACK YOU ALL!
PREPARE YOURSELVES, YOU LITTLE MAGGOTS!!
WAH HA HA HA HA!
WHAT IS THIS? AN EVENT OR SOMETHING...?

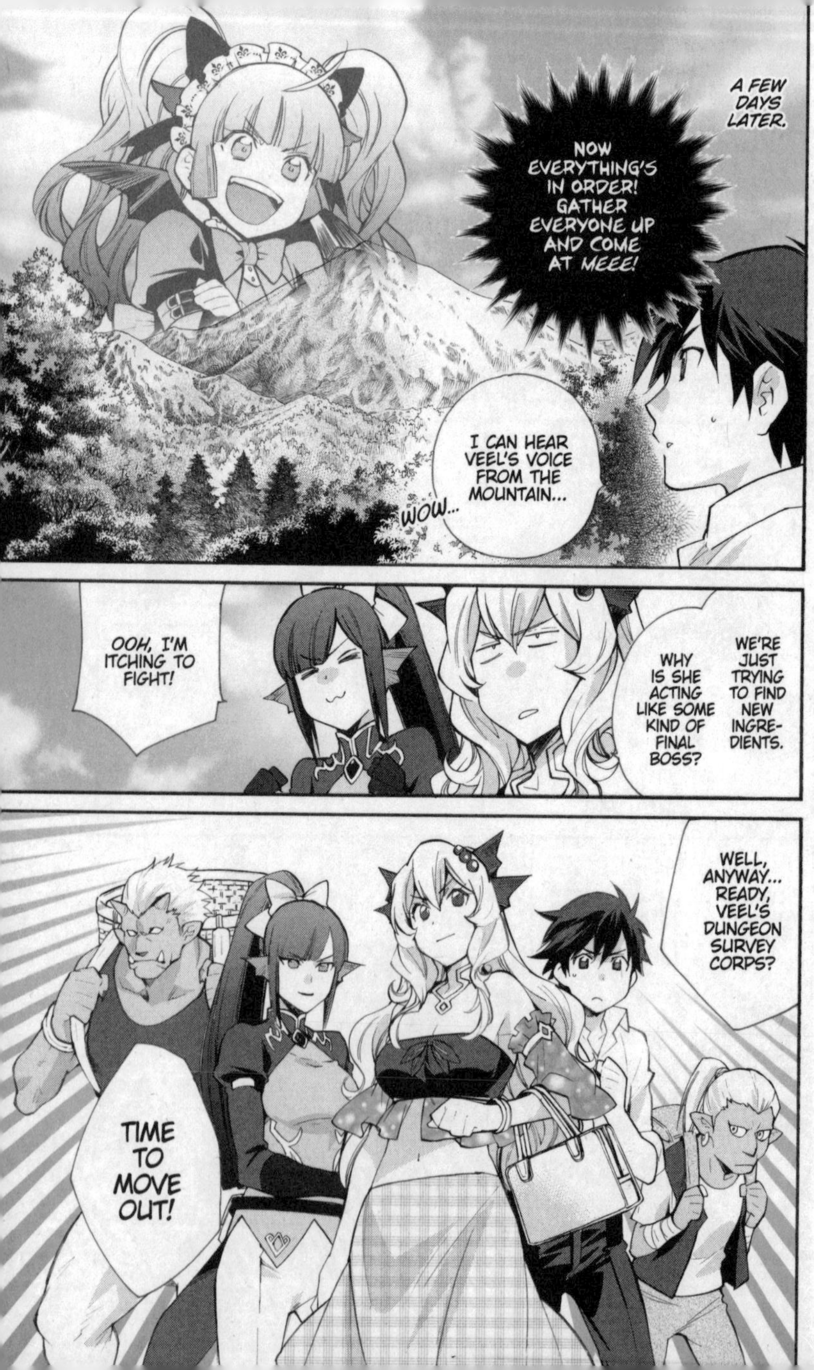
A FEW DAYS LATER.
NOW EVERYTHING'S IN ORDER! GATHER EVERYONE UP AND COME AT MEEE!
I CAN HEAR VEEL'S VOICE FROM THE MOUNTAIN...
WOW...
WE'RE JUST TRYING TO FIND NEW INGRE-DIENTS.
WHY IS SHE ACTING LIKE SOME KIND OF FINAL BOSS?
OOH, I'M ITCHING TO FIGHT!
WELL, ANYWAY... READY, VEEL'S DUNGEON SURVEY CORPS?
TIME TO MOVE OUT!

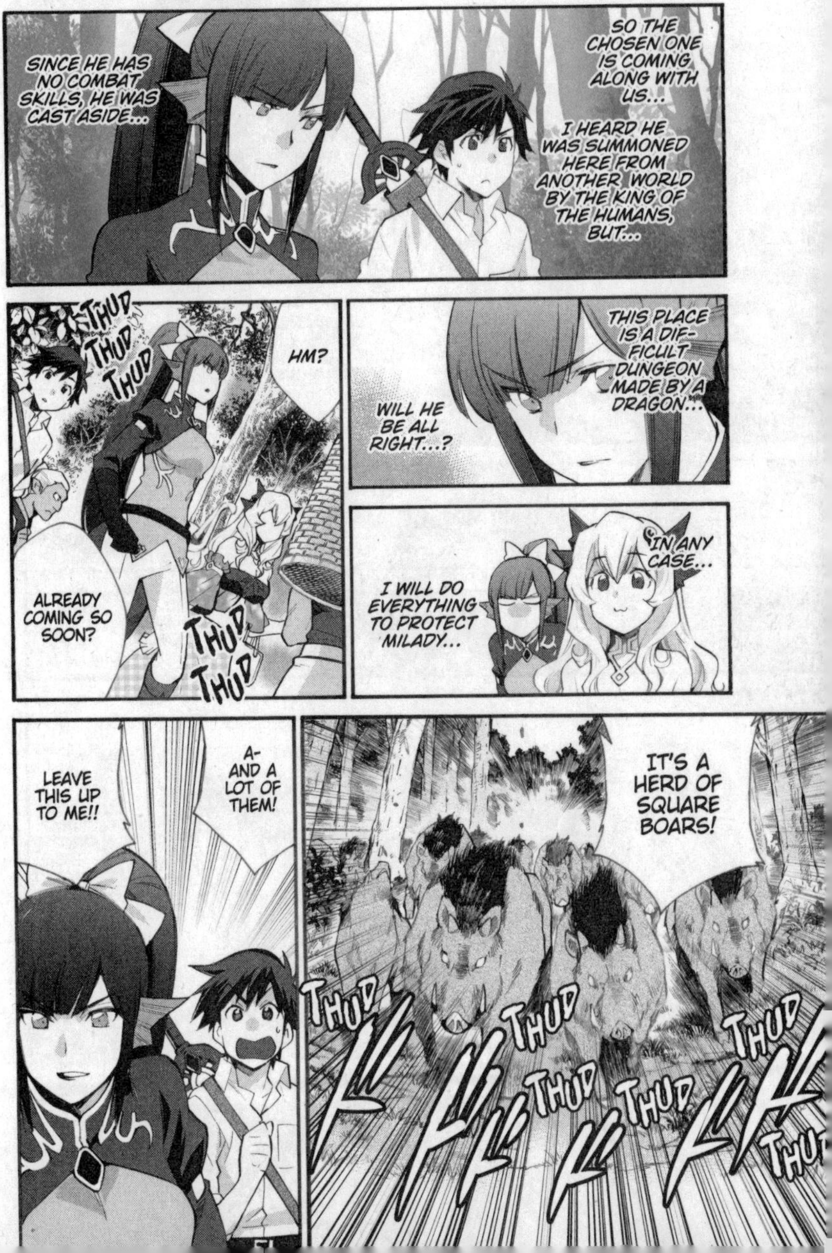
SO THE CHOSEN ONE IS COMING ALONG WITH US...
I HEARD HE WAS SUMMONED HERE FROM ANOTHER WORLD BY THE KING OF THE HUMANS, BUT...
SINCE HE HAS NO COMBAT SKILLS, HE WAS CAST ASIDE...
THIS PLACE IS A DIF- FICULT DUNGEON MADE BY A DRAGON...
WILL HE BE ALL RIGHT...?
IN ANY CASE...
I WILL DO EVERYTHING TO PROTECT MILADY...
HM?
THUD THUD THUD
ALREADY COMING SO SOON?
THUD THUD
IT'S A HERD OF SQUARE BOARS!
THUD THUD THUD THUD THUD THUD
A- AND A LOT OF THEM!
LEAVE THIS UP TO ME!!

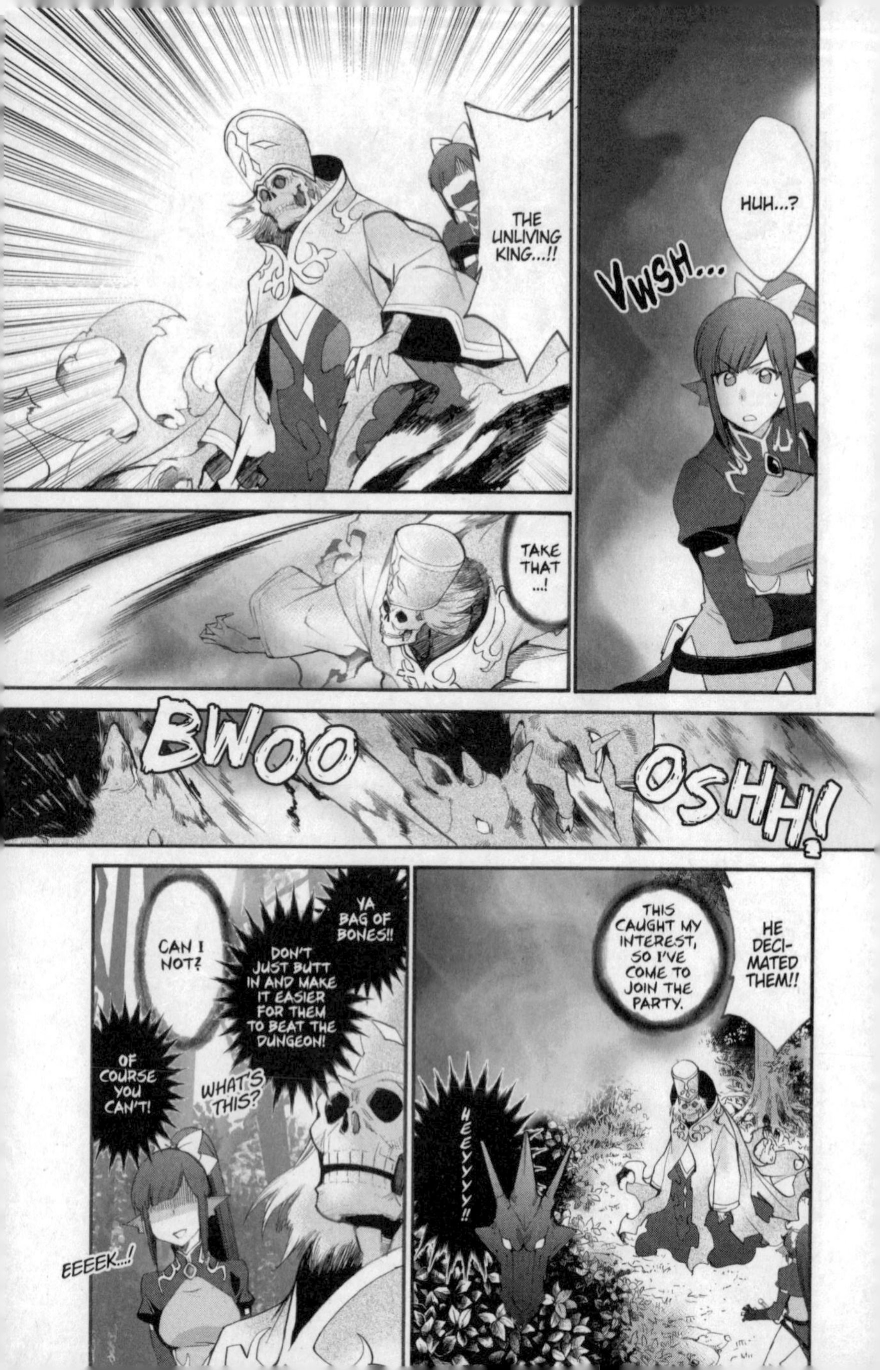
HUH...?
VWSH...
THE UNLIVING KING...!!
TAKE THAT ...!
BWOOOSHH!
HE DECIMATED THEM!!
THIS CAUGHT MY INTEREST, SO I'VE COME TO JOIN THE PARTY.
HEEYYYY!!
YA BAG OF BONES!!
DON'T JUST BUTT IN AND MAKE IT EASIER FOR THEM TO BEAT THE DUNGEON!
CAN I NOT?
WHAT'S THIS?
OF COURSE YOU CAN'T!
EEEEK...!

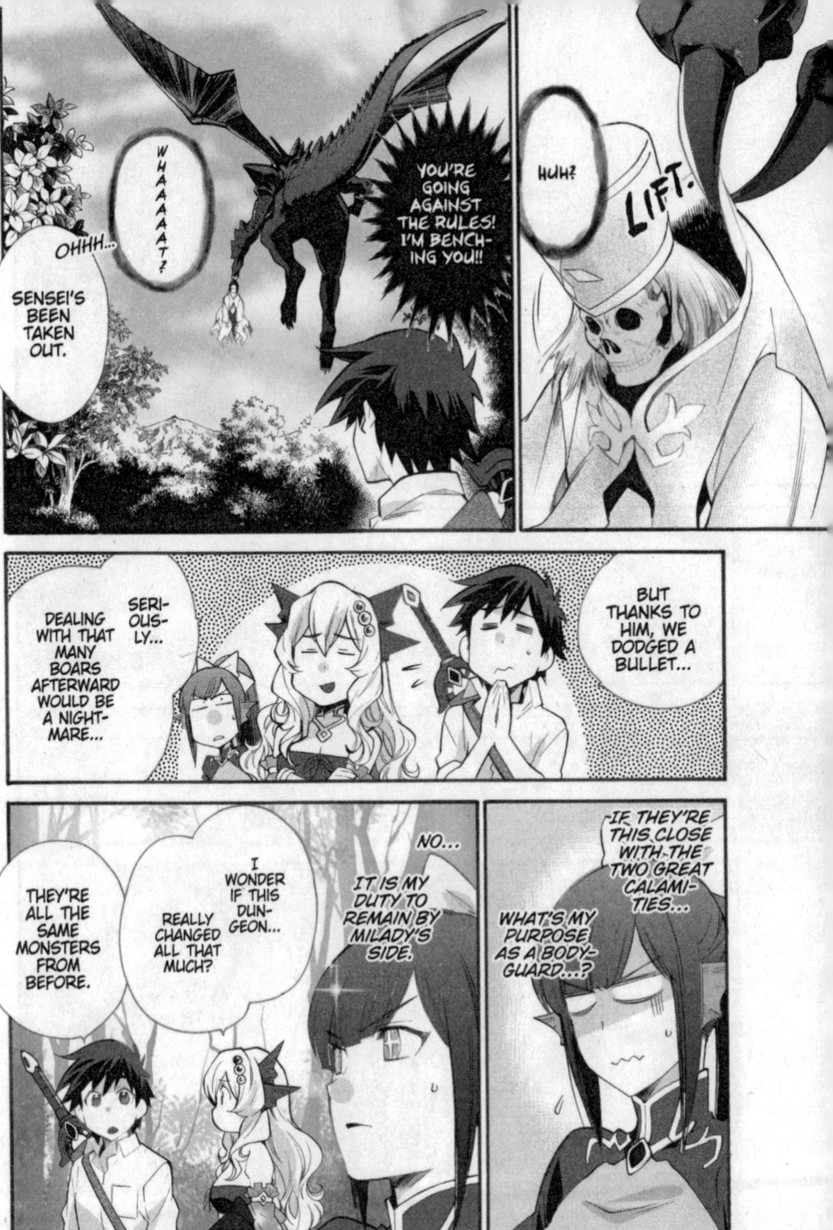
HUH?
LIFT.
YOU'RE GOING AGAINST THE RULES! I'M BENCHING YOU!!
WHAAAAAAT?
OHHH...
SENSEI'S BEEN TAKEN OUT.
BUT THANKS TO HIM, WE DODGED A BULLET...
SERIOUSLY...
DEALING WITH THAT MANY BOARS AFTERWARD WOULD BE A NIGHTMARE...
IF THEY'RE THIS CLOSE WITH THE TWO GREAT CALAMITIES...
WHAT'S MY PURPOSE AS A BODYGUARD...?
NO...
IT IS MY DUTY TO REMAIN BY MILADY'S SIDE.
I WONDER IF THIS DUNGEON...
REALLY CHANGED ALL THAT MUCH?
THEY'RE ALL THE SAME MONSTERS FROM BEFORE.

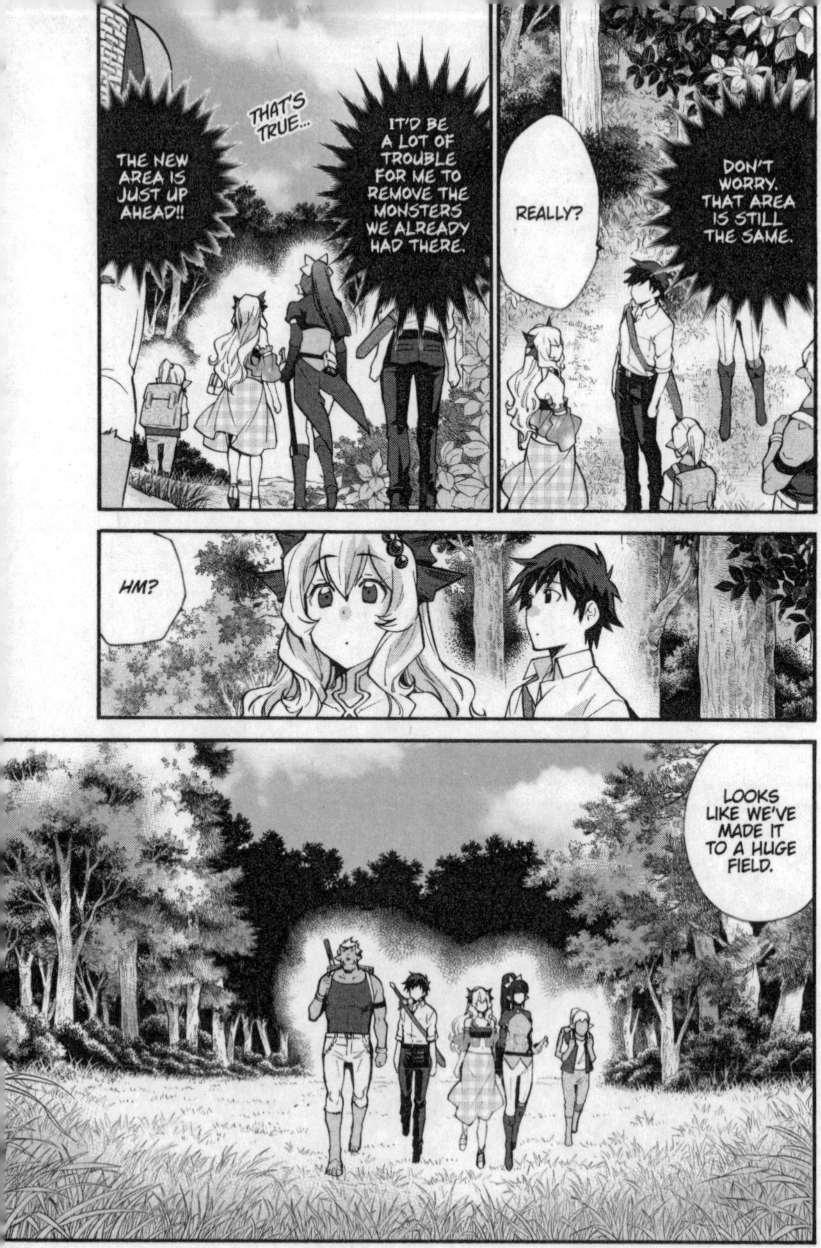
DON'T WORRY. THAT AREA IS STILL THE SAME.
REALLY?
IT'D BE A LOT OF TROUBLE FOR ME TO REMOVE THE MONSTERS WE ALREADY HAD THERE.
THAT'S TRUE...
THE NEW AREA IS JUST UP AHEAD!!
HM?
LOOKS LIKE WE'VE MADE IT TO A HUGE FIELD.

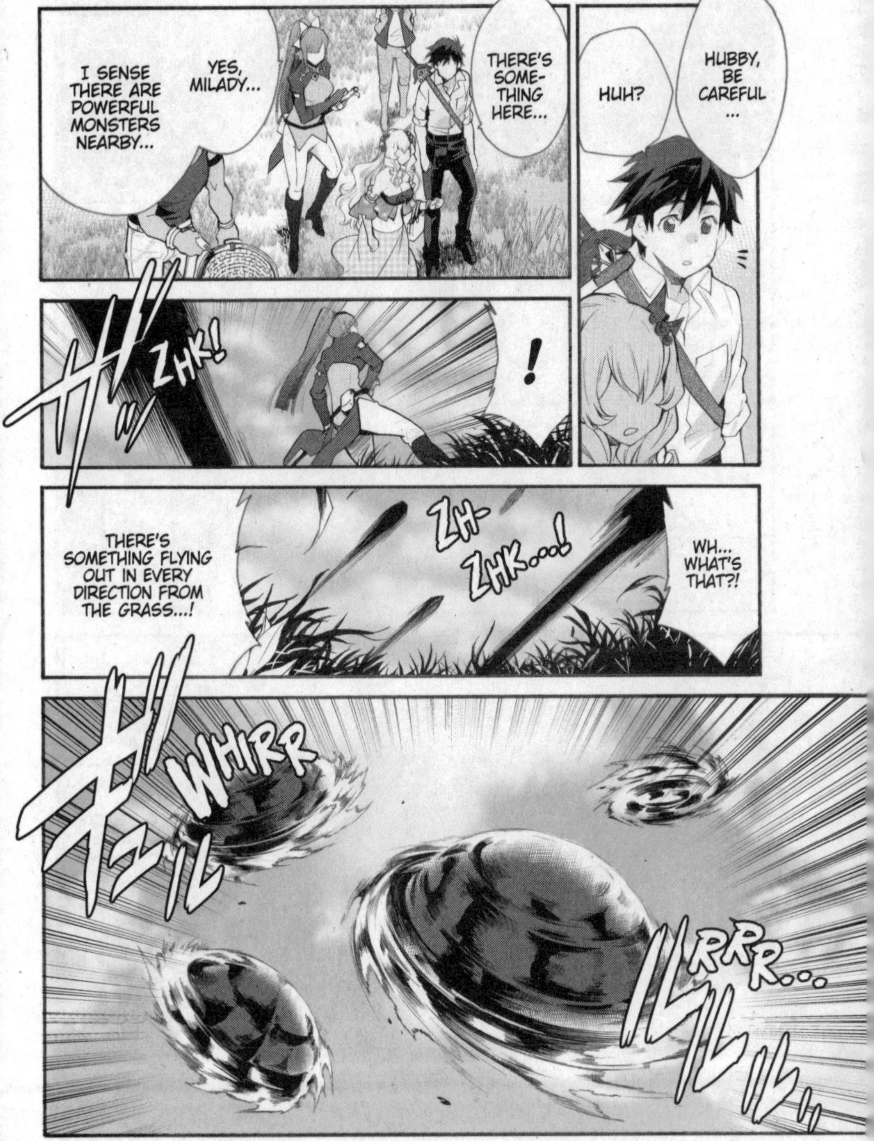
HUBBY, BE CAREFUL ...
HUH?
THERE'S SOME-THING HERE...
YES, MILADY...
I SENSE THERE ARE POWERFUL MONSTERS NEARBY...
!
ZHK!
WH... WHAT'S THAT?!
ZH-ZHK...!
THERE'S SOMETHING FLYING OUT IN EVERY DIRECTION FROM THE GRASS...!
RRR...
WHIRR

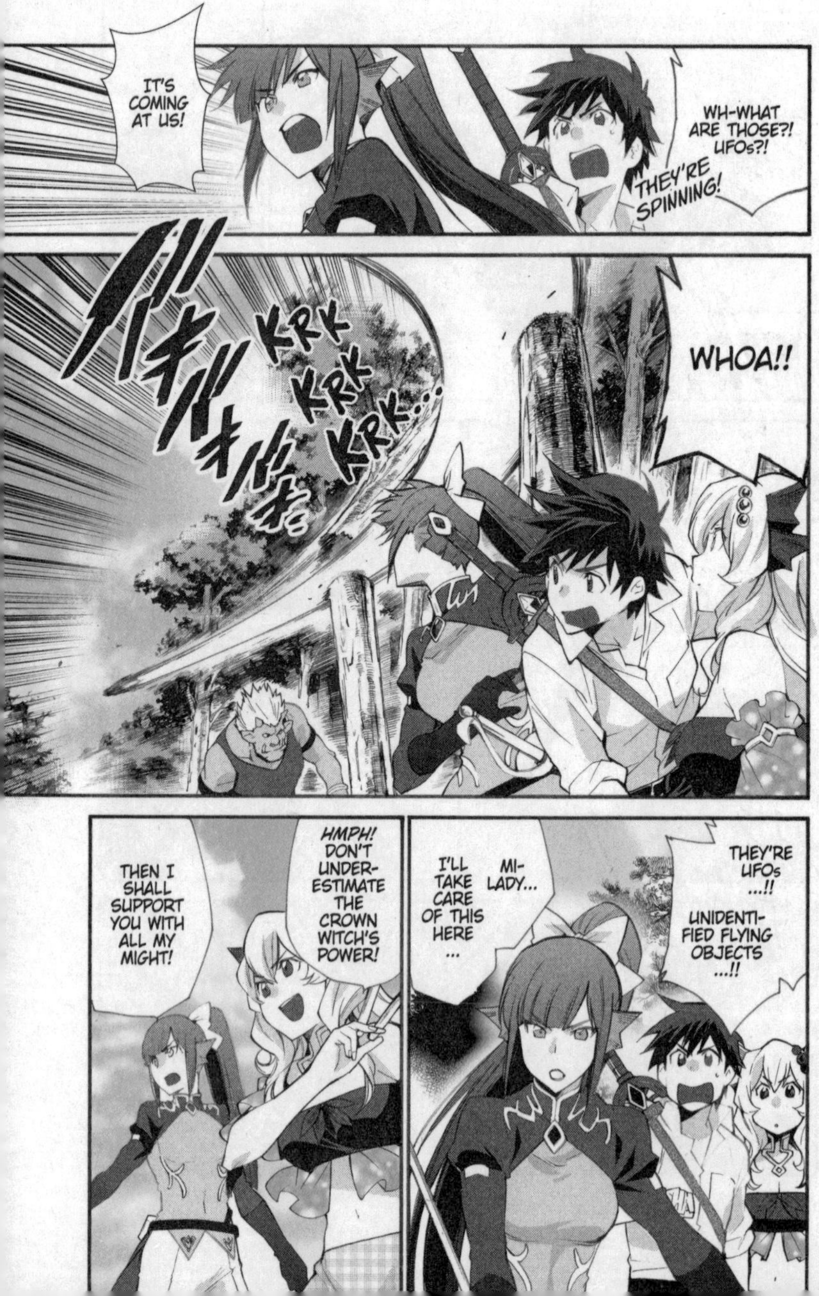
WH-WHAT ARE THOSE?! UFOs?!
THEY'RE SPINNING!
IT'S COMING AT US!
WHOA!!
KRK KRK KRK...
THEY'RE UFOs ...!!
UNIDENTI-FIED FLYING OBJECTS ...!!
MI-LADY...
I'LL TAKE CARE OF THIS HERE ...
HMPH! DON'T UNDER-ESTIMATE THE CROWN WITCH'S POWER!
THEN I SHALL SUPPORT YOU WITH ALL MY MIGHT!

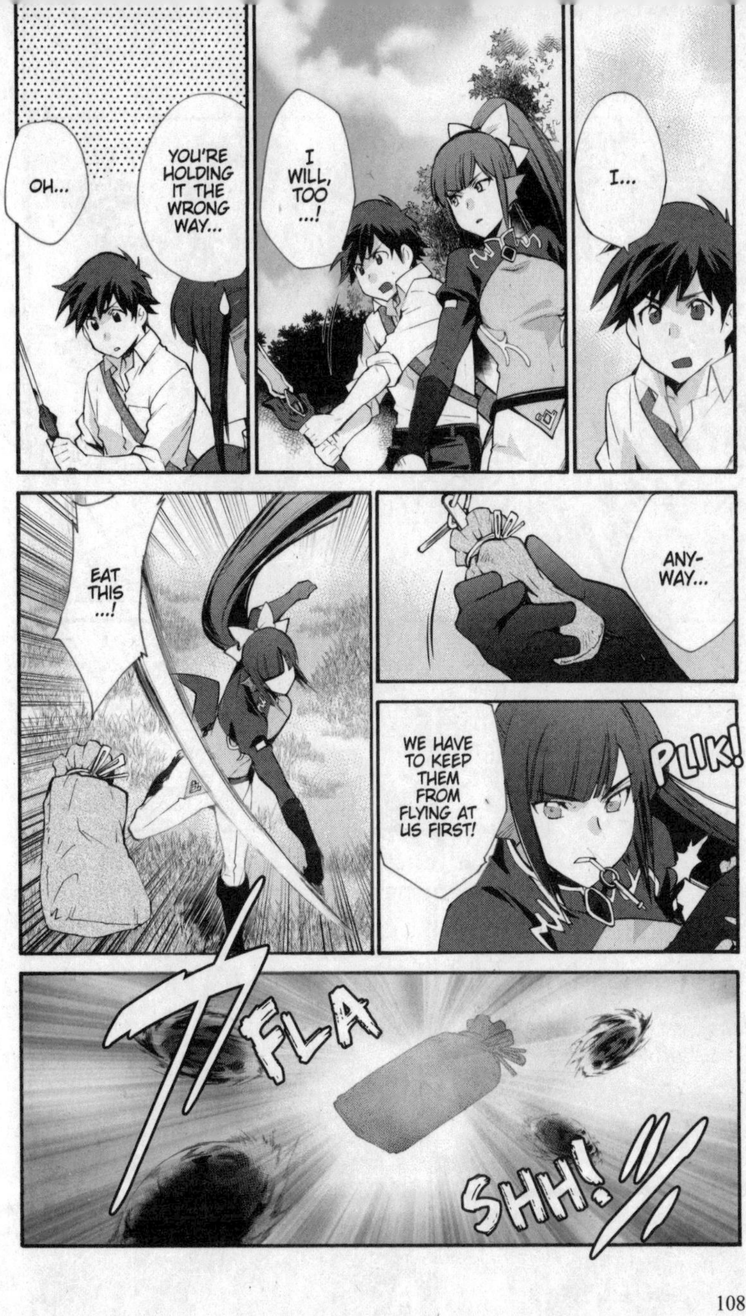
I...
I WILL, TOO ...!
YOU'RE HOLDING IT THE WRONG WAY...
OH...
ANY-WAY...
WE HAVE TO KEEP THEM FROM FLYING AT US FIRST!
PLIK!
EAT THIS ...!
FLA
SHH!

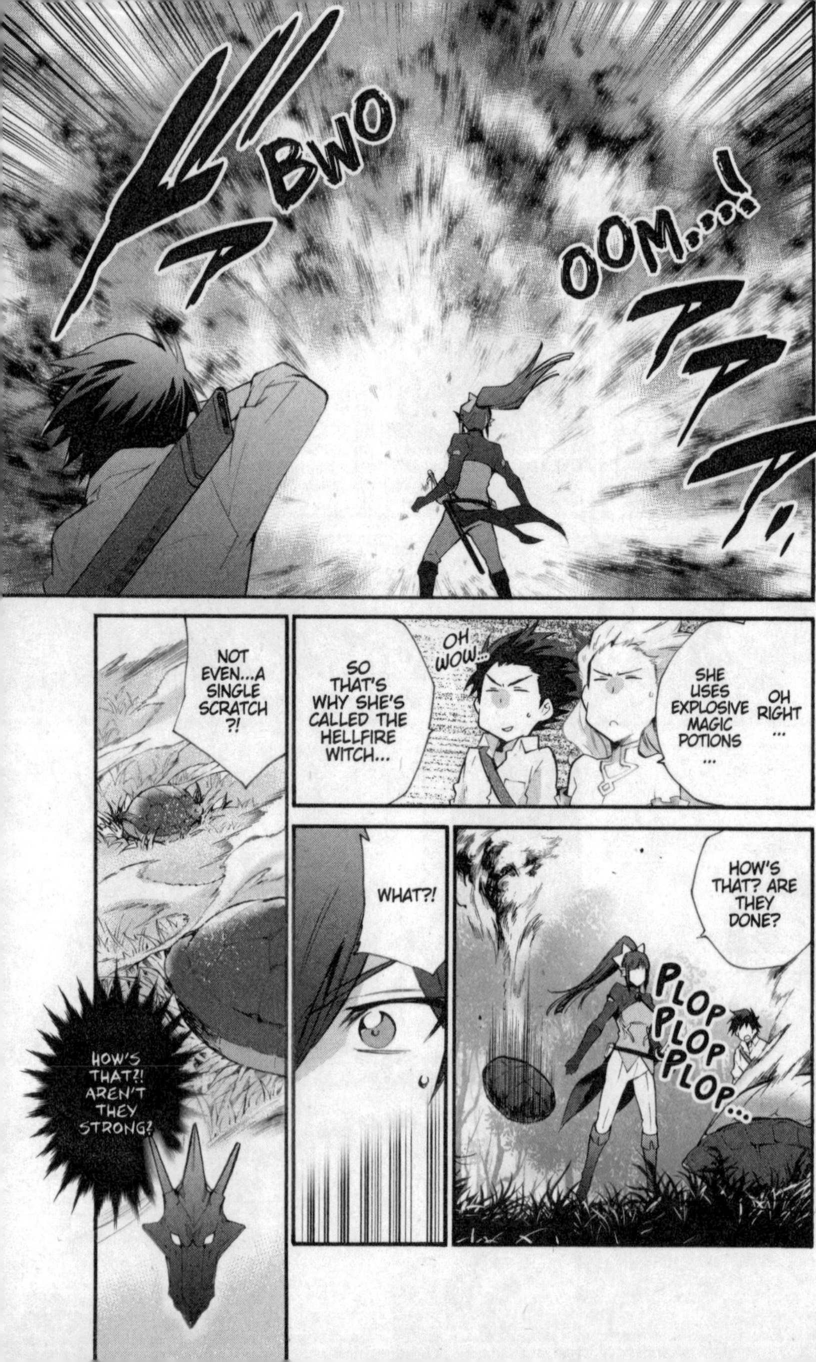
BWO
OOM...!
OH RIGHT ...
SHE USES EXPLOSIVE MAGIC POTIONS ...
OH WOW...
SO THAT'S WHY SHE'S CALLED THE HELLFIRE WITCH...
HOW'S THAT? ARE THEY DONE?
PLOP PLOP PLOP...
WHAT?!
NOT EVEN...A SINGLE SCRATCH?!
HOW'S THAT?! AREN'T THEY STRONG?

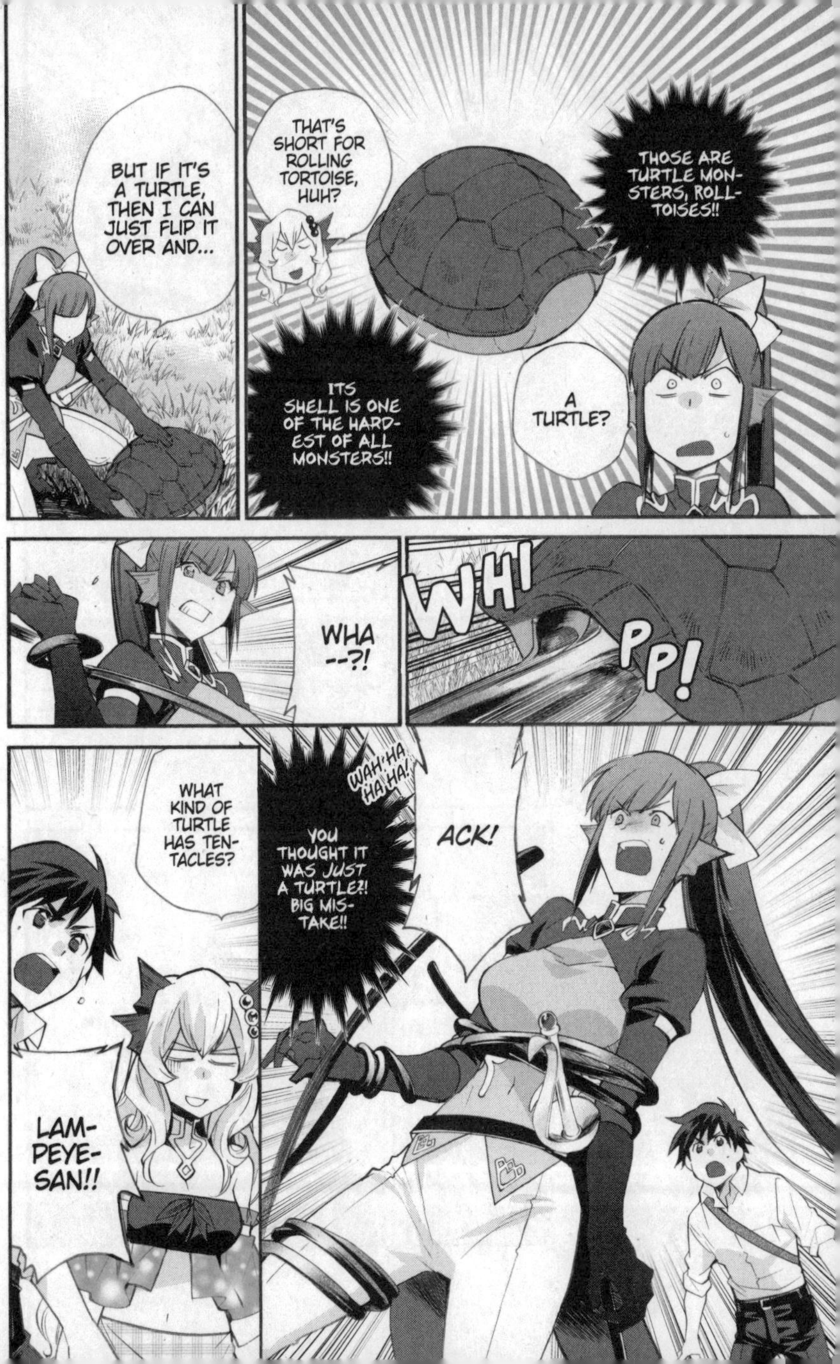
THOSE ARE TURTLE MONSTERS, ROLL-TOISES!!
THAT'S SHORT FOR ROLLING TORTOISE, HUH?
A TURTLE?
ITS SHELL IS ONE OF THE HARD-EST OF ALL MONSTERS!!
BUT IF IT'S A TURTLE, THEN I CAN JUST FLIP IT OVER AND...
WHIPP!
WHA--?!
ACK!
WAH HA HA HA!
YOU THOUGHT IT WAS JUST A TURTLE?! BIG MIS-TAKE!!
WHAT KIND OF TURTLE HAS TEN-TACLES?
LAM-PEYE-SAN!!

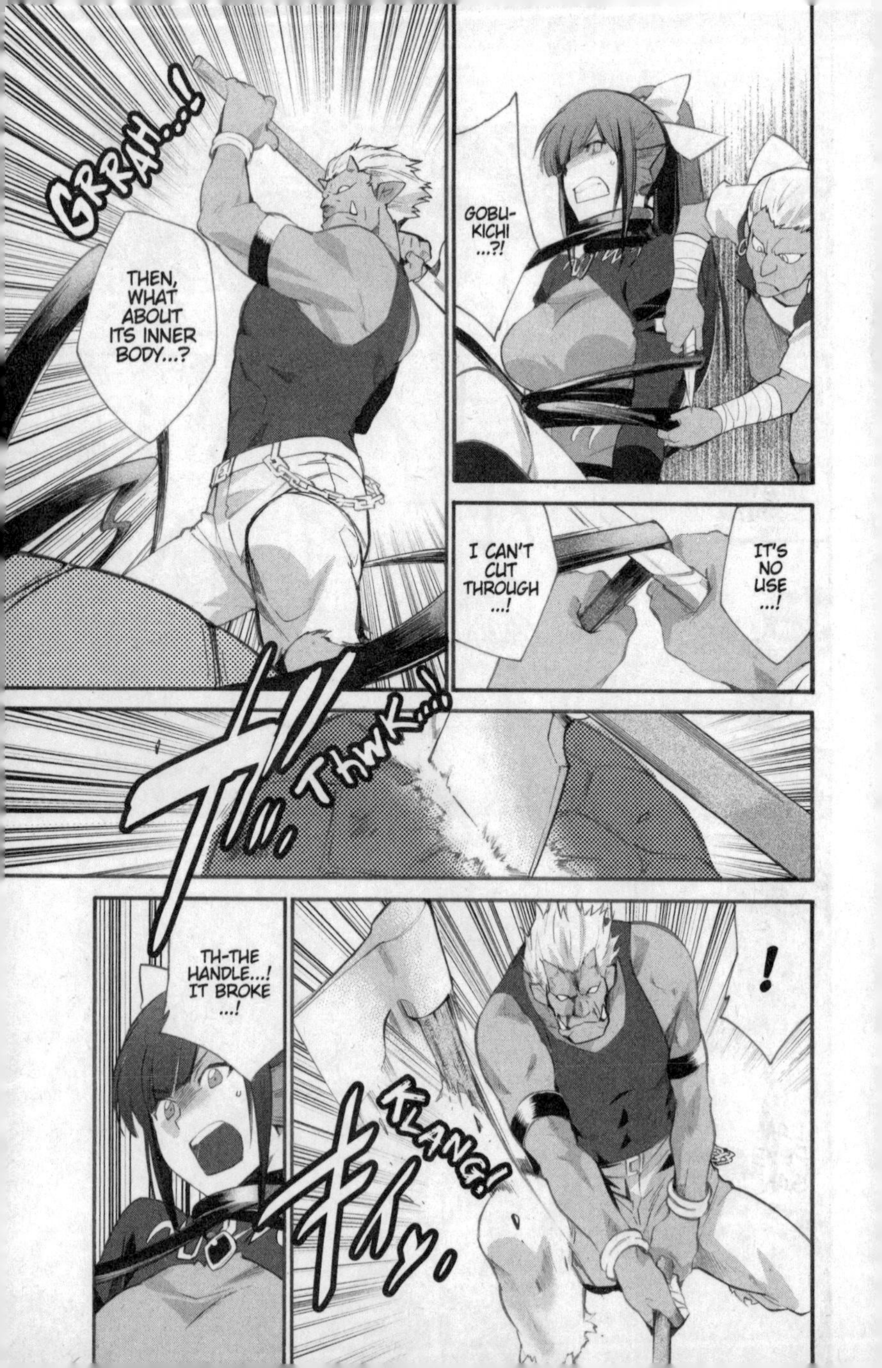
GOBU-
KICHI
...?!
IT'S
NO
USE
...!
I CAN'T
CUT
THROUGH
...!
GRRAH...!
THEN,
WHAT
ABOUT
ITS INNER
BODY...?
THWK...!
!
KLANG!
TH-THE
HANDLE...!
IT BROKE
...!

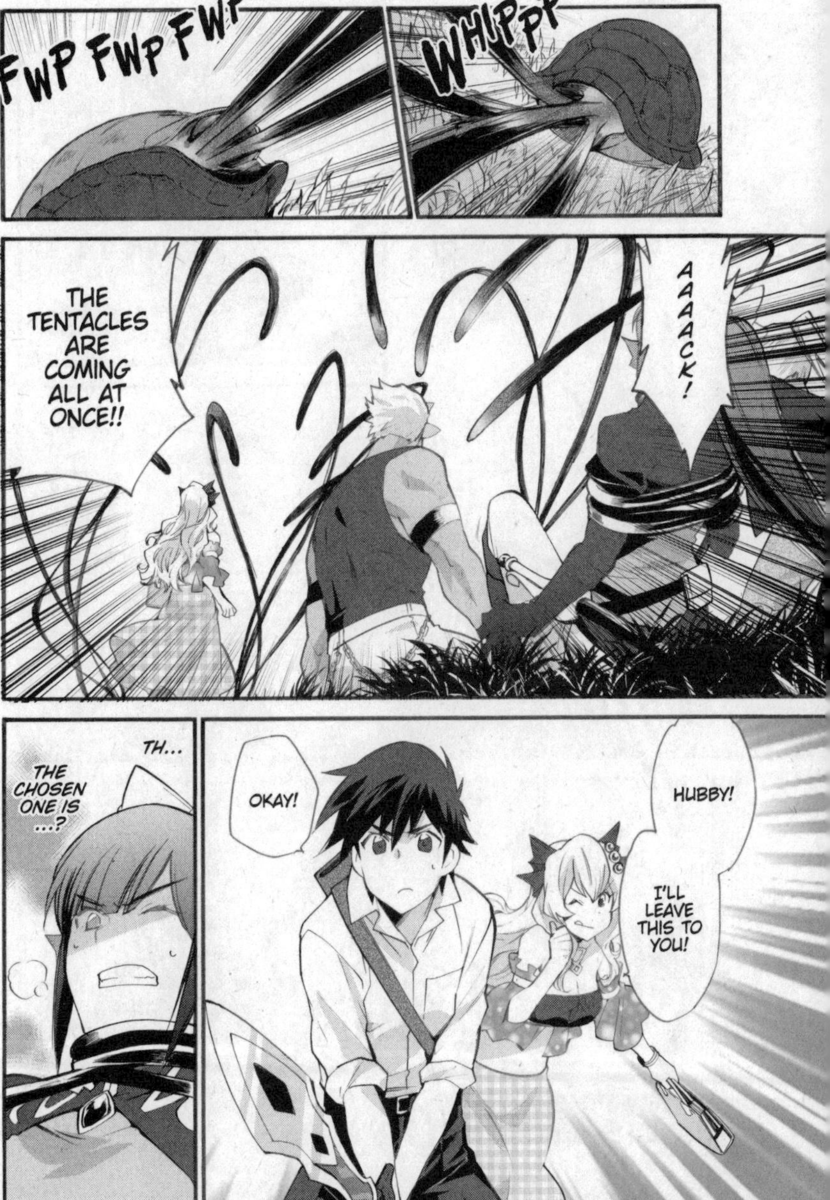
WHIPPP
FWP FWP FWP
AAAACK!
THE TENTACLES ARE COMING ALL AT ONCE!!
HUBBY!
I'LL LEAVE THIS TO YOU!
OKAY!
TH...
THE CHOSEN ONE IS ...?

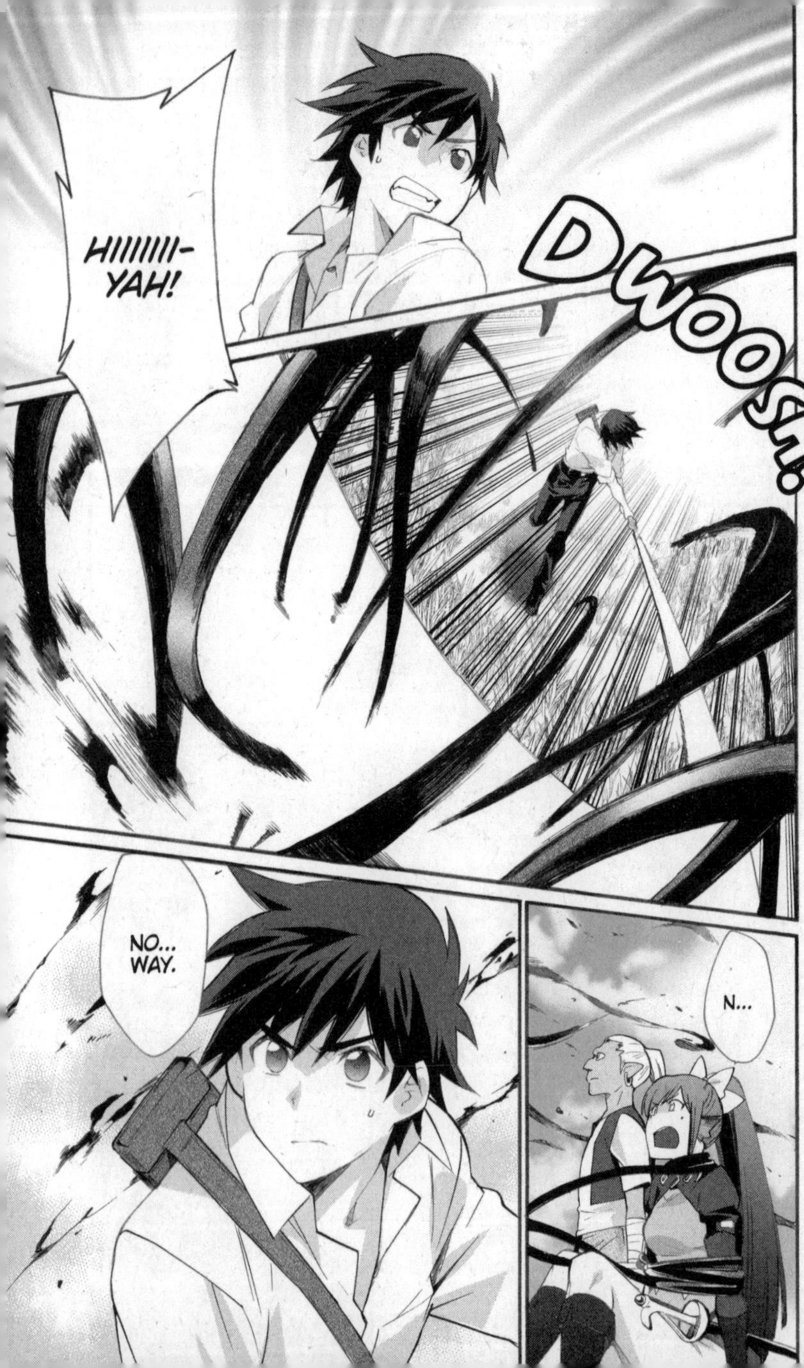
DWOOSH!!
HIIIIIII-YAH!
N...
NO... WAY.

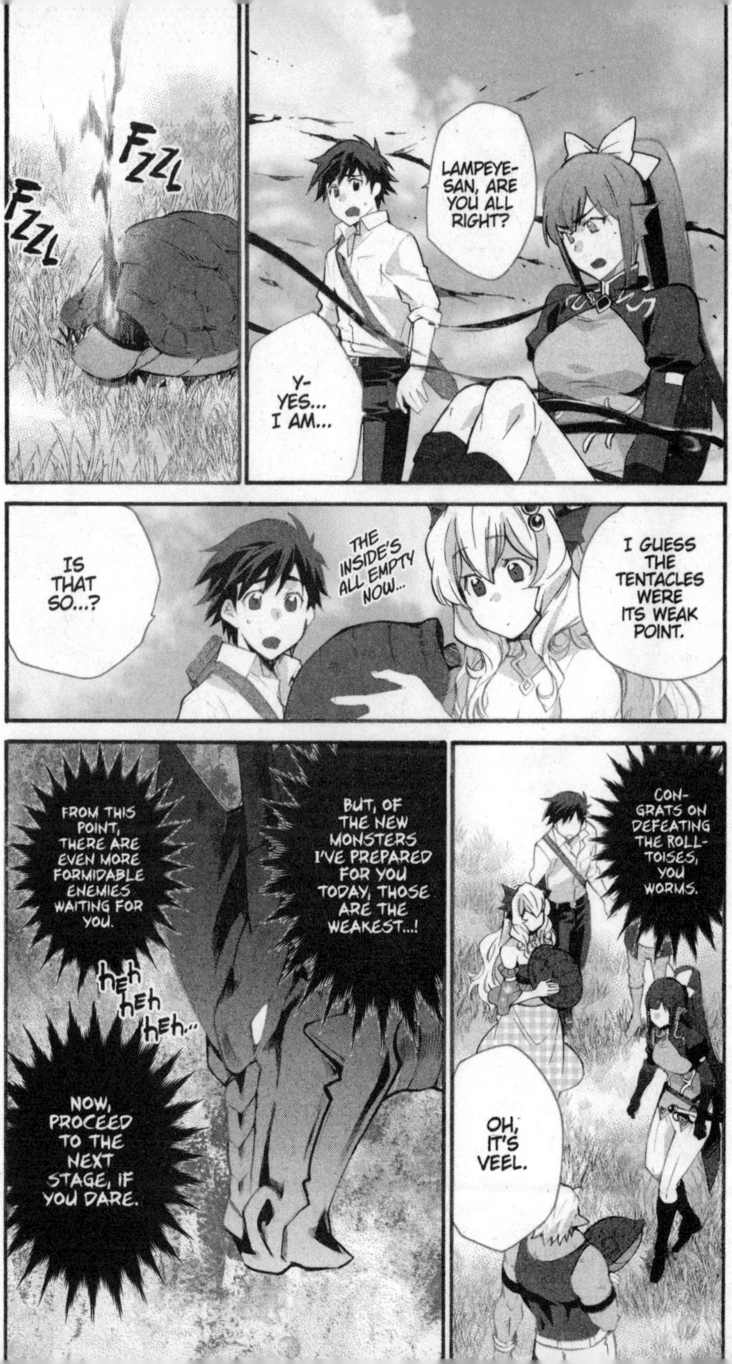
LAMPEYE-SAN, ARE YOU ALL RIGHT?
Y-YES... I AM...
FZZL
FZZL
I GUESS THE TENTACLES WERE ITS WEAK POINT.
THE INSIDE'S ALL EMPTY NOW...
IS THAT SO...?
CON-GRATS ON DEFEATING THE ROLL-TOISES, YOU WORMS.
OH, IT'S VEEL.
BUT, OF THE NEW MONSTERS I'VE PREPARED FOR YOU TODAY, THOSE ARE THE WEAKEST...!
FROM THIS POINT, THERE ARE EVEN MORE FORMIDABLE ENEMIES WAITING FOR YOU.
heh heh heh...
NOW, PROCEED TO THE NEXT STAGE, IF YOU DARE.

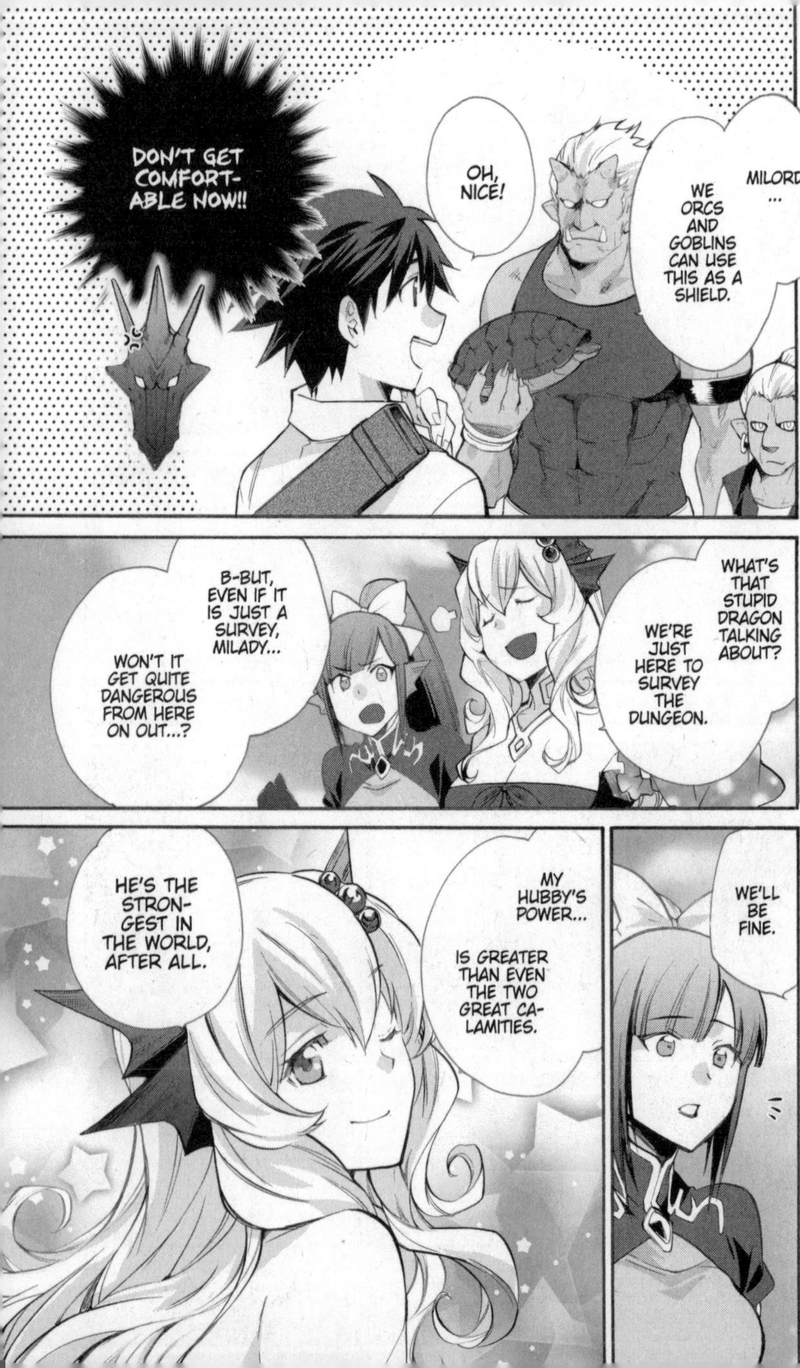
MILORD ... WE ORCS AND GOBLINS CAN USE THIS AS A SHIELD.
OH, NICE!
DON'T GET COMFORT-ABLE NOW!!
WHAT'S THAT STUPID DRAGON TALKING ABOUT? WE'RE JUST HERE TO SURVEY THE DUNGEON.
B-BUT, EVEN IF IT IS JUST A SURVEY, MILADY... WON'T IT GET QUITE DANGEROUS FROM HERE ON OUT...?
WE'LL BE FINE.
MY HUBBY'S POWER... IS GREATER THAN EVEN THE TWO GREAT CA-LAMITIES.
HE'S THE STRON-GEST IN THE WORLD, AFTER ALL.

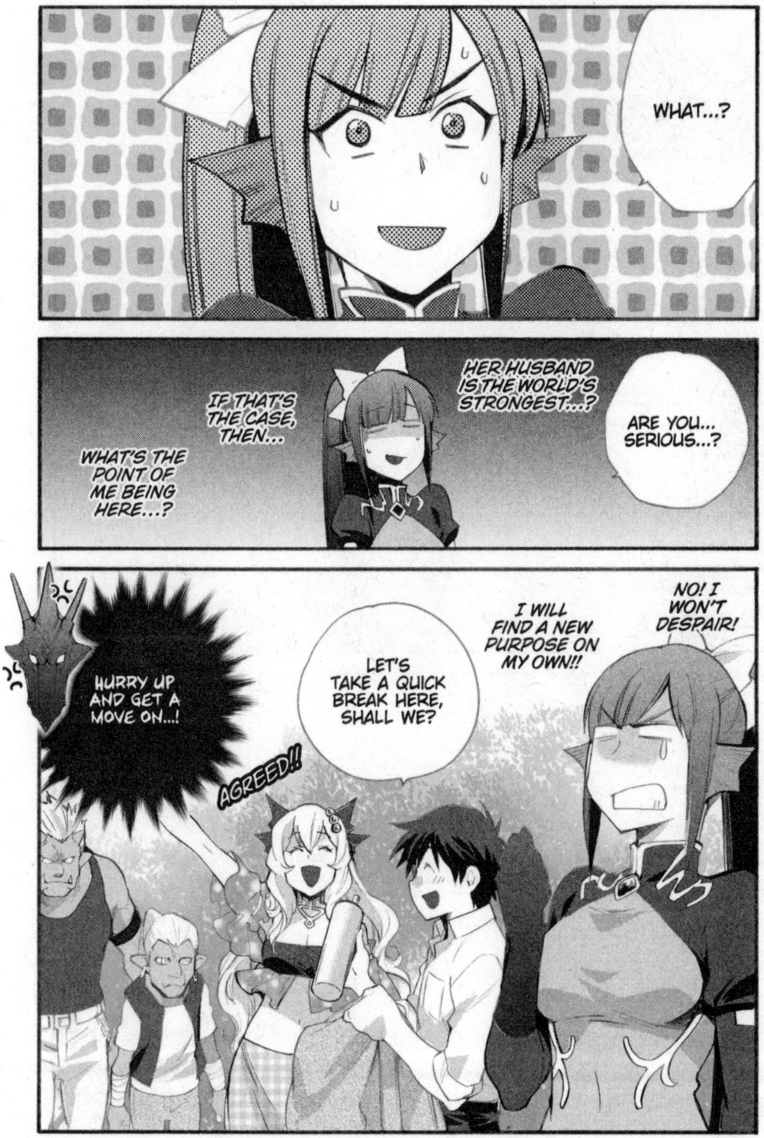
WHAT...?
ARE YOU... SERIOUS...?
HER HUSBAND IS THE WORLD'S STRONGEST...?
IF THAT'S THE CASE, THEN...
WHAT'S THE POINT OF ME BEING HERE...?
NO! I WON'T DESPAIR!
I WILL FIND A NEW PURPOSE ON MY OWN!!
LET'S TAKE A QUICK BREAK HERE, SHALL WE?
AGREED!!
HURRY UP AND GET A MOVE ON...!

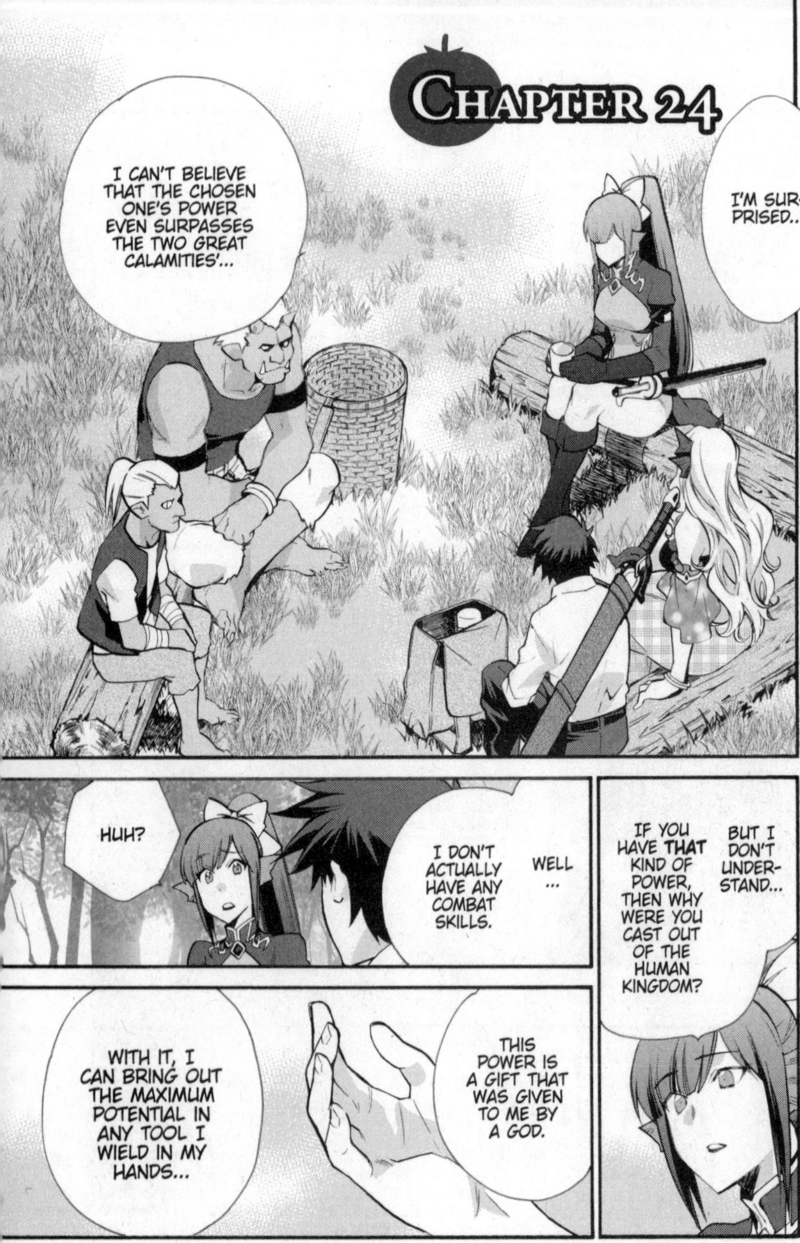
CHAPTER 24
I'M SURPRISED...
I CAN'T BELIEVE THAT THE CHOSEN ONE'S POWER EVEN SURPASSES THE TWO GREAT CALAMITIES'...
BUT I DON'T UNDERSTAND...
IF YOU HAVE **THAT** KIND OF POWER, THEN WHY WERE YOU CAST OUT OF THE HUMAN KINGDOM?
WELL ...
I DON'T ACTUALLY HAVE ANY COMBAT SKILLS.
HUH?
THIS POWER IS A GIFT THAT WAS GIVEN TO ME BY A GOD.
WITH IT, I CAN BRING OUT THE MAXIMUM POTENTIAL IN ANY TOOL I WIELD IN MY HANDS...

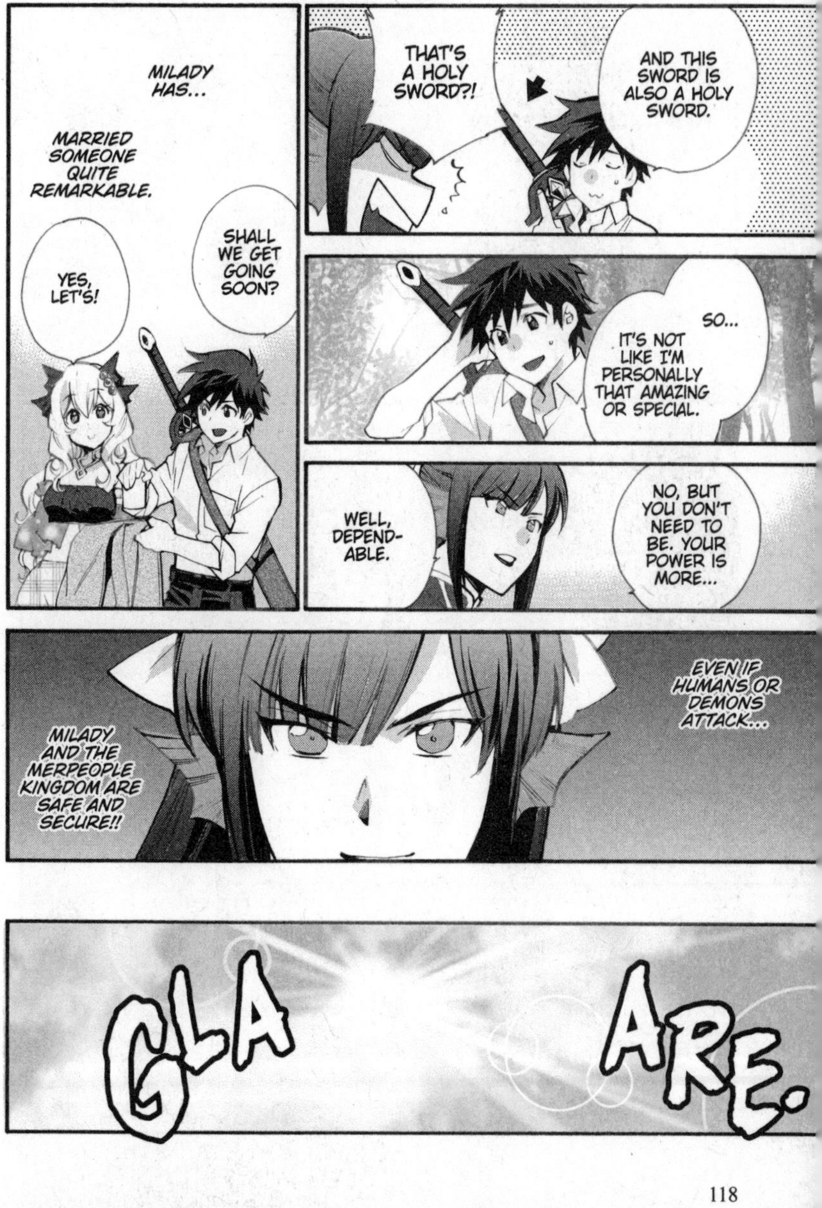
AND THIS SWORD IS ALSO A HOLY SWORD.
THAT'S A HOLY SWORD?!
SO...
IT'S NOT LIKE I'M PERSONALLY THAT AMAZING OR SPECIAL.
NO, BUT YOU DON'T NEED TO BE. YOUR POWER IS MORE...
WELL, DEPENDABLE.
MILADY HAS...
MARRIED SOMEONE QUITE REMARKABLE.
SHALL WE GET GOING SOON?
YES, LET'S!
EVEN IF HUMANS OR DEMONS ATTACK...
MILADY AND THE MERPEOPLE KINGDOM ARE SAFE AND SECURE!!
GLA
ARE.

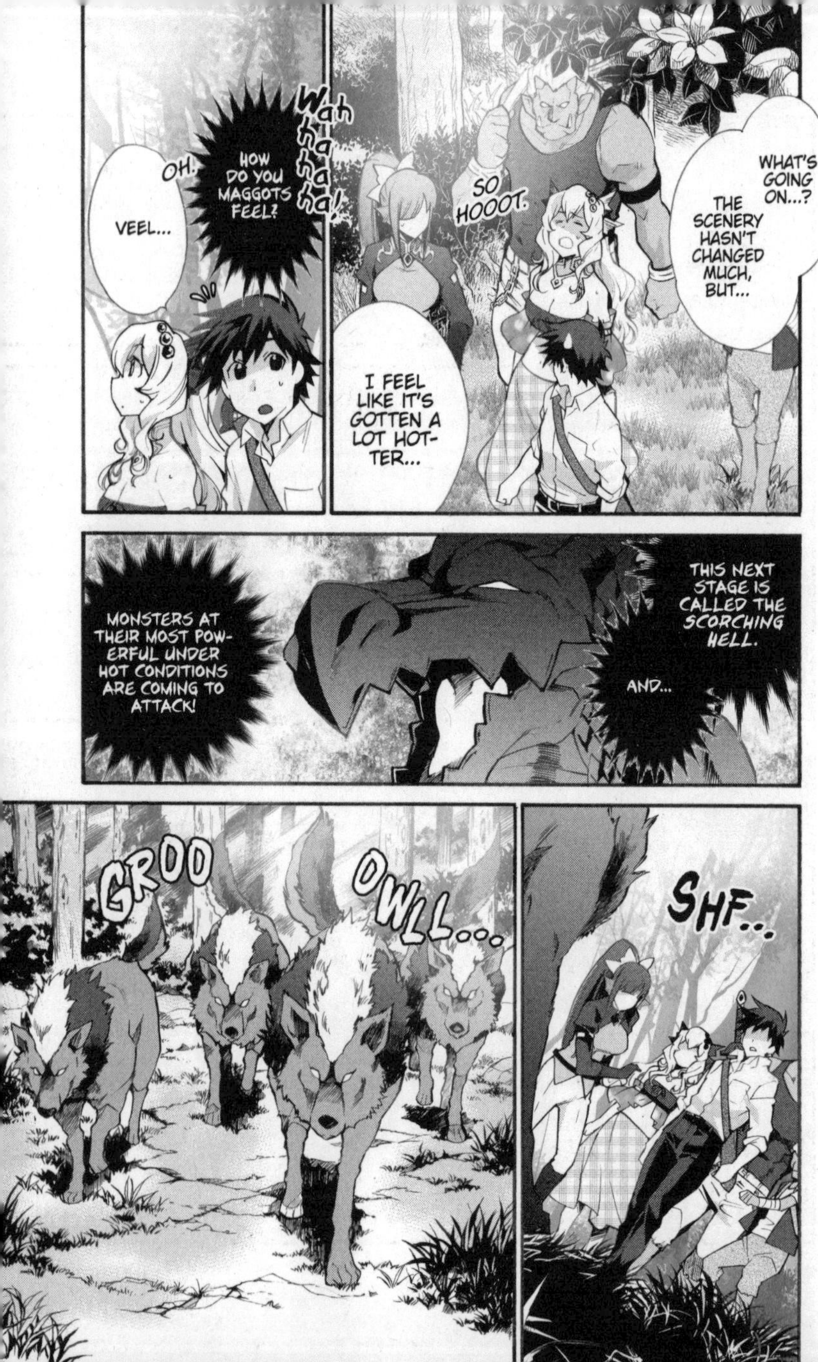
WHAT'S GOING ON...?
THE SCENERY HASN'T CHANGED MUCH, BUT...
SO HOOOT.
I FEEL LIKE IT'S GOTTEN A LOT HOT-TER...
Wah ha ha ha ha!
HOW DO YOU MAGGOTS FEEL?
OH.
VEEL...
THIS NEXT STAGE IS CALLED THE SCORCHING HELL.
AND...
MONSTERS AT THEIR MOST POW-ERFUL UNDER HOT CONDITIONS ARE COMING TO ATTACK!
SHF...
GROO OWLL...

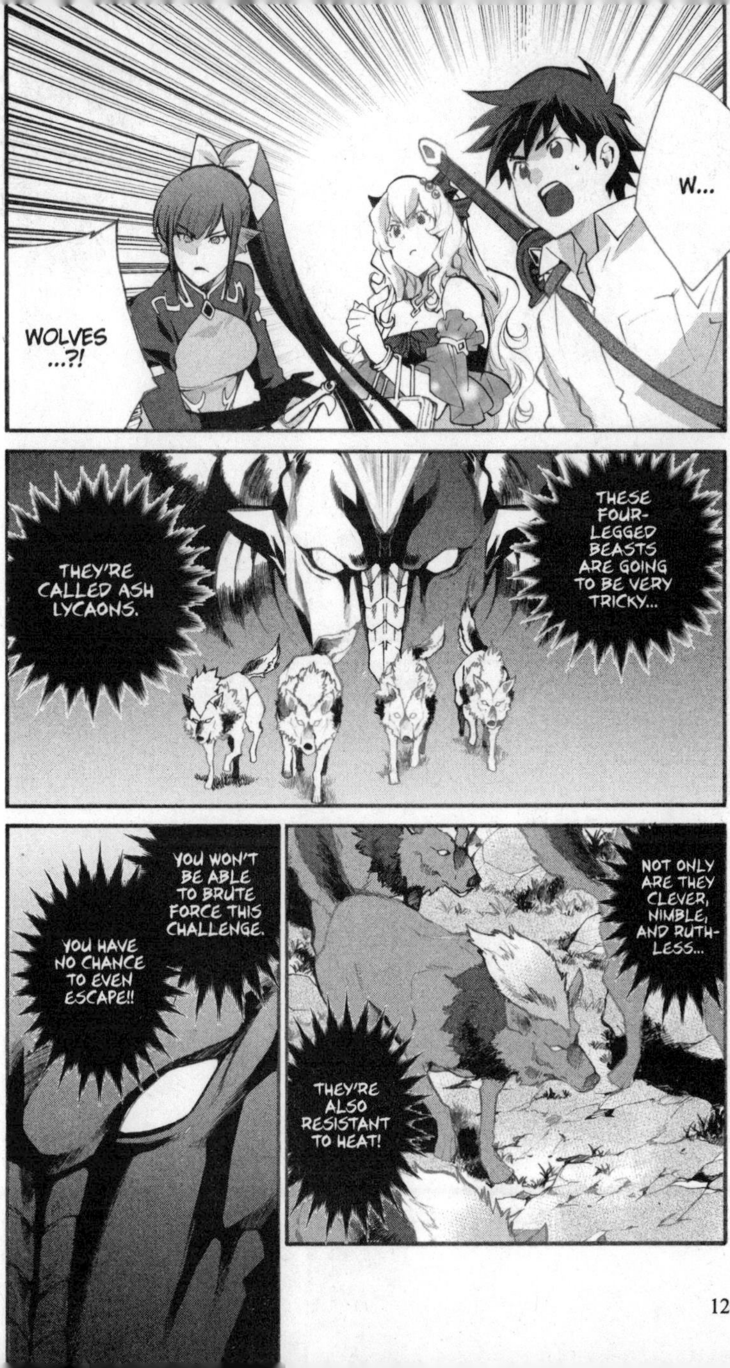
W...
WOLVES ...?!
THESE FOUR-LEGGED BEASTS ARE GOING TO BE VERY TRICKY...
THEY'RE CALLED ASH LYCAONS.
NOT ONLY ARE THEY CLEVER, NIMBLE, AND RUTH-LESS...
THEY'RE ALSO RESISTANT TO HEAT!
YOU WON'T BE ABLE TO BRUTE FORCE THIS CHALLENGE.
YOU HAVE NO CHANCE TO EVEN ESCAPE!!

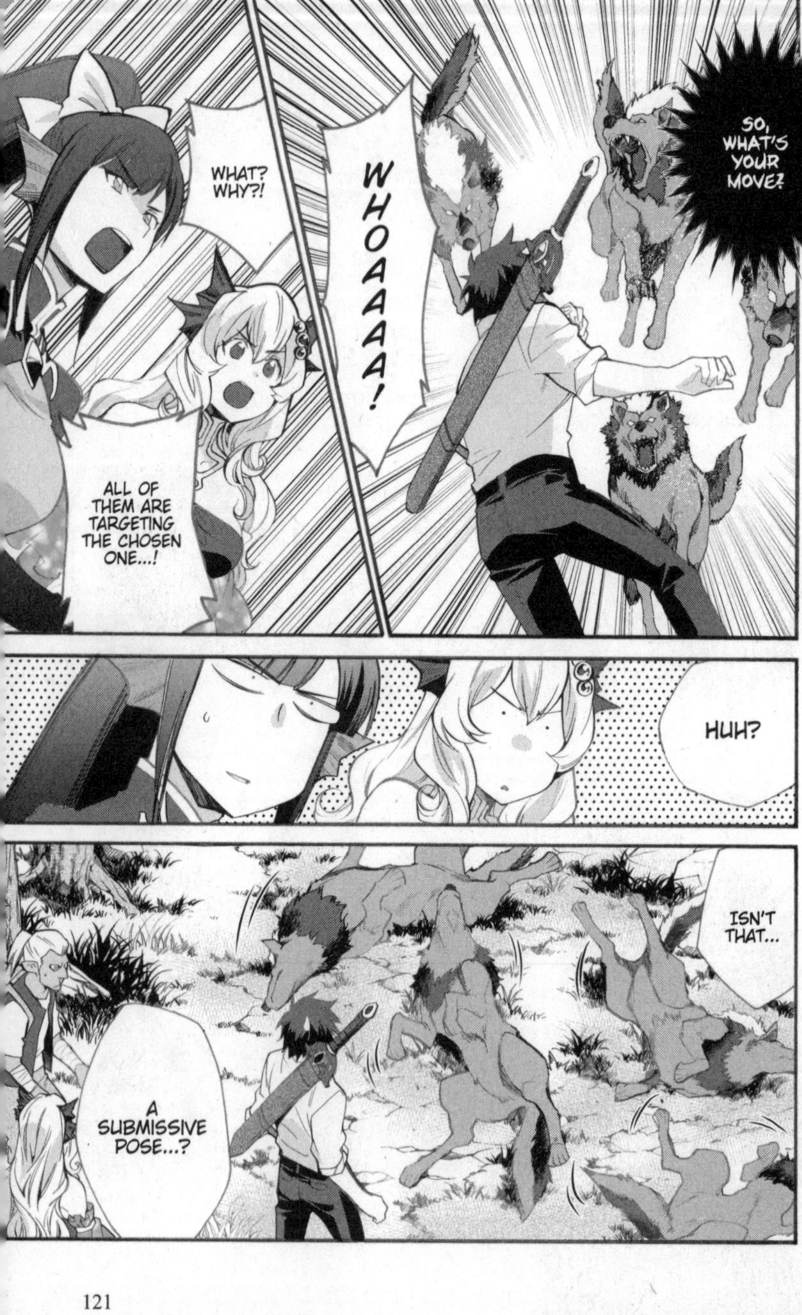
SO, WHAT'S YOUR MOVE?
WHOAAAAA!
WHAT? WHY?!
ALL OF THEM ARE TARGETING THE CHOSEN ONE...!
HUH?
ISN'T THAT...
A SUBMISSIVE POSE...?

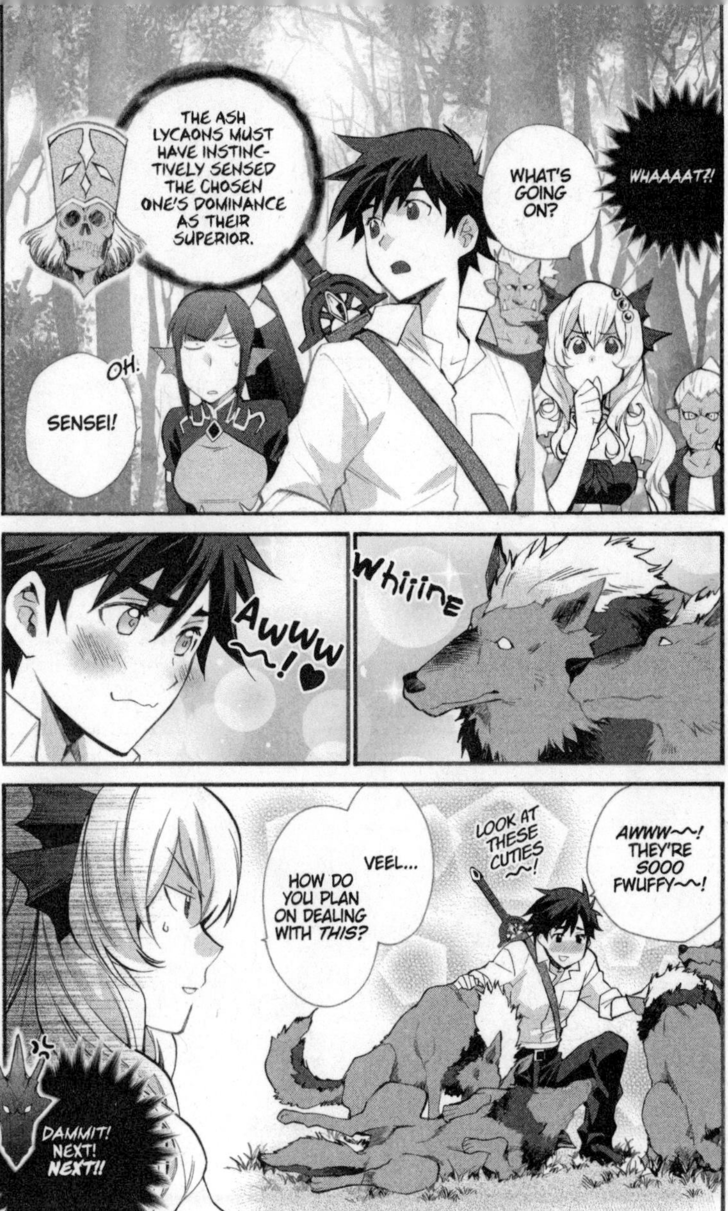
WHAAAAT?!
WHAT'S GOING ON?
THE ASH LYCAONS MUST HAVE INSTINCTIVELY SENSED THE CHOSEN ONE'S DOMINANCE AS THEIR SUPERIOR.
OH.
SENSEI!
Whiiine
Awww~! ♥
AWWW~~! THEY'RE SOOO FWUFFY~~!
LOOK AT THESE CUTIES ~~!
VEEL...
HOW DO YOU PLAN ON DEALING WITH *THIS*?
DAMMIT! NEXT! NEXT!!

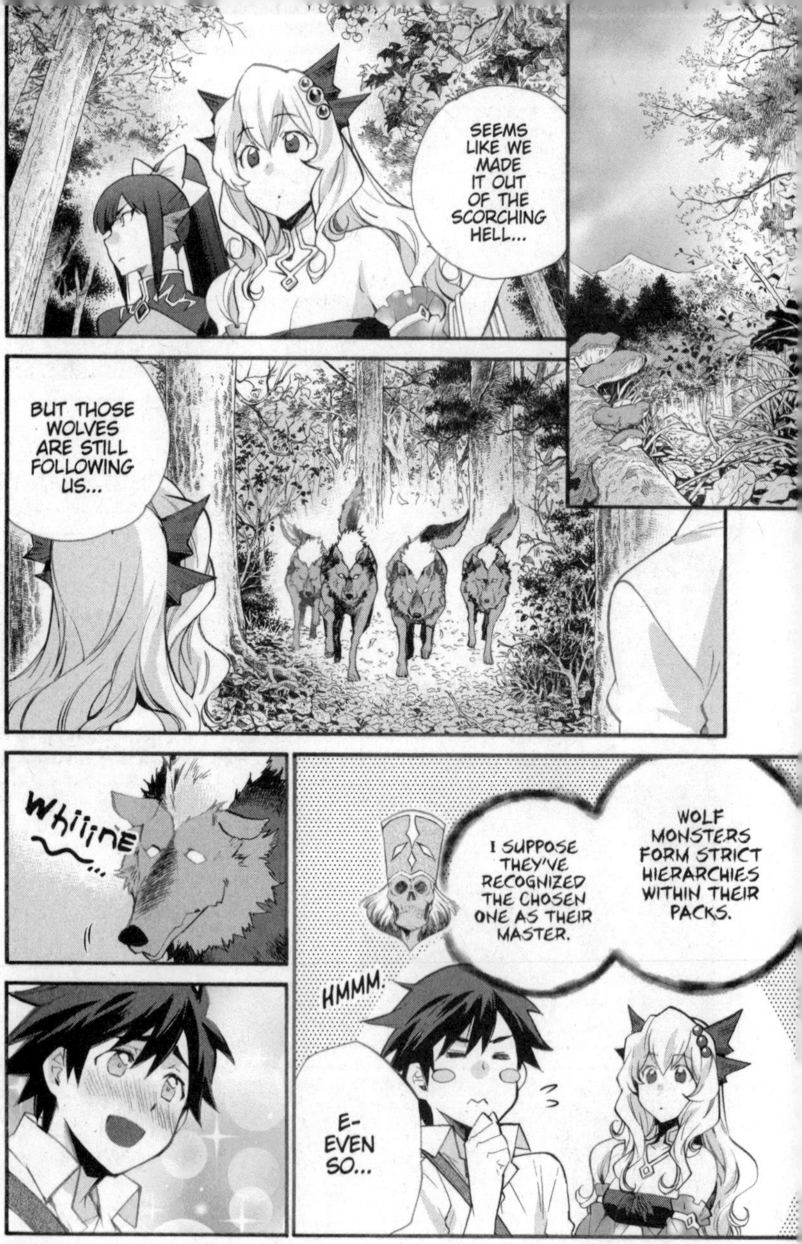
SEEMS LIKE WE MADE IT OUT OF THE SCORCHING HELL...
BUT THOSE WOLVES ARE STILL FOLLOWING US...
WOLF MONSTERS FORM STRICT HIERARCHIES WITHIN THEIR PACKS.
I SUPPOSE THEY'VE RECOGNIZED THE CHOSEN ONE AS THEIR MASTER.
HMMM.
E-EVEN SO...
Whiiine~...

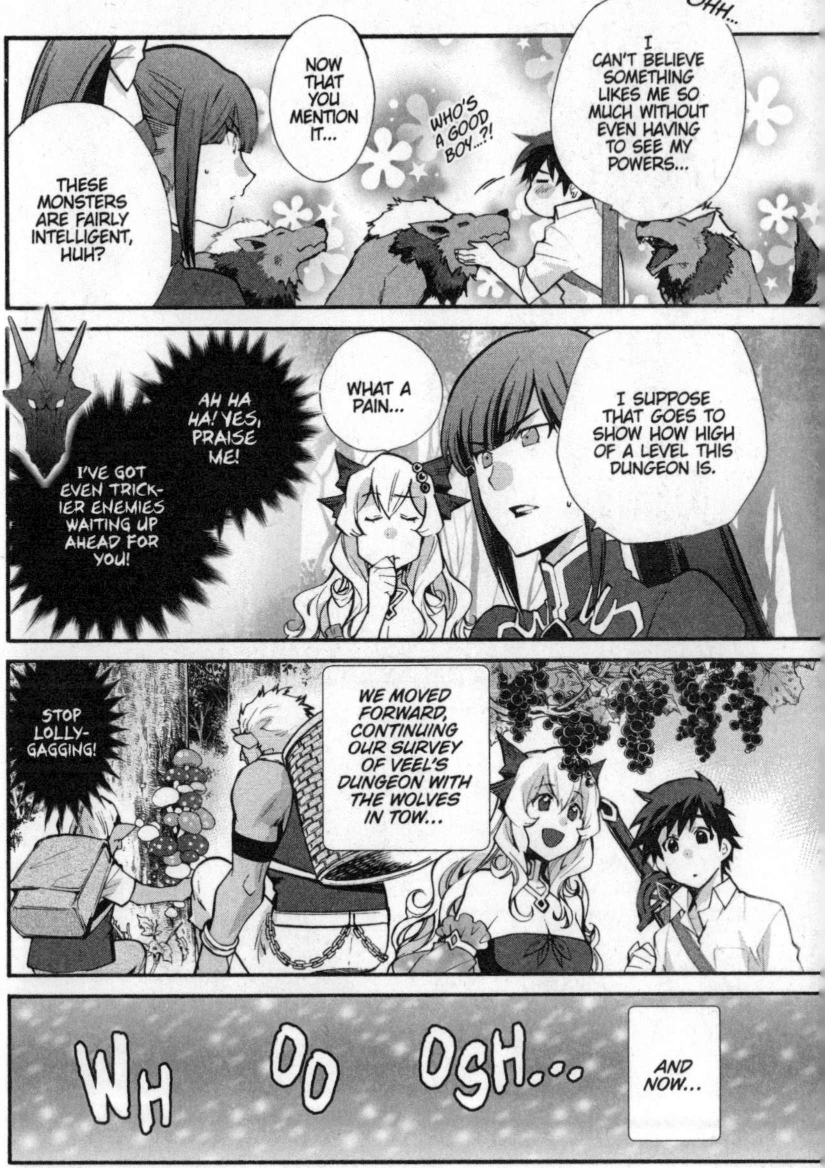
OHH...
I CAN'T BELIEVE SOMETHING LIKES ME SO MUCH WITHOUT EVEN HAVING TO SEE MY POWERS...
WHO'S A GOOD BOY...?!
NOW THAT YOU MENTION IT...
THESE MONSTERS ARE FAIRLY INTELLIGENT, HUH?
I SUPPOSE THAT GOES TO SHOW HOW HIGH OF A LEVEL THIS DUNGEON IS.
WHAT A PAIN...
AH HA HA! YES, PRAISE ME!
I'VE GOT EVEN TRICK-IER ENEMIES WAITING UP AHEAD FOR YOU!
WE MOVED FORWARD, CONTINUING OUR SURVEY OF VEEL'S DUNGEON WITH THE WOLVES IN TOW...
STOP LOLLY-GAGGING!
AND NOW...
WH OO OSH...

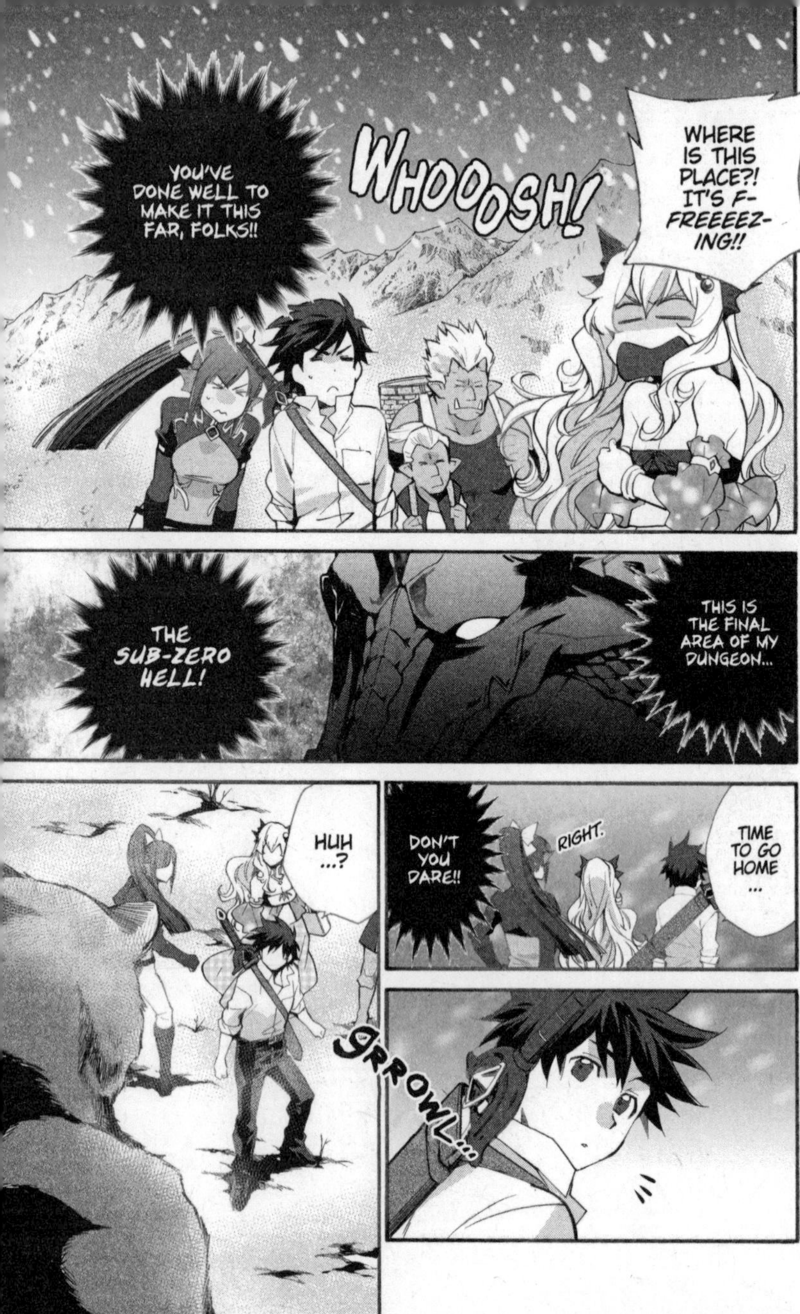
WHERE IS THIS PLACE?! IT'S F-FREEEEZ-ING!!
WHOOOSH!
YOU'VE DONE WELL TO MAKE IT THIS FAR, FOLKS!!
THIS IS THE FINAL AREA OF MY DUNGEON...
THE SUB-ZERO HELL!
TIME TO GO HOME ...
RIGHT.
DON'T YOU DARE!!
GRROWL...
HUH ...?

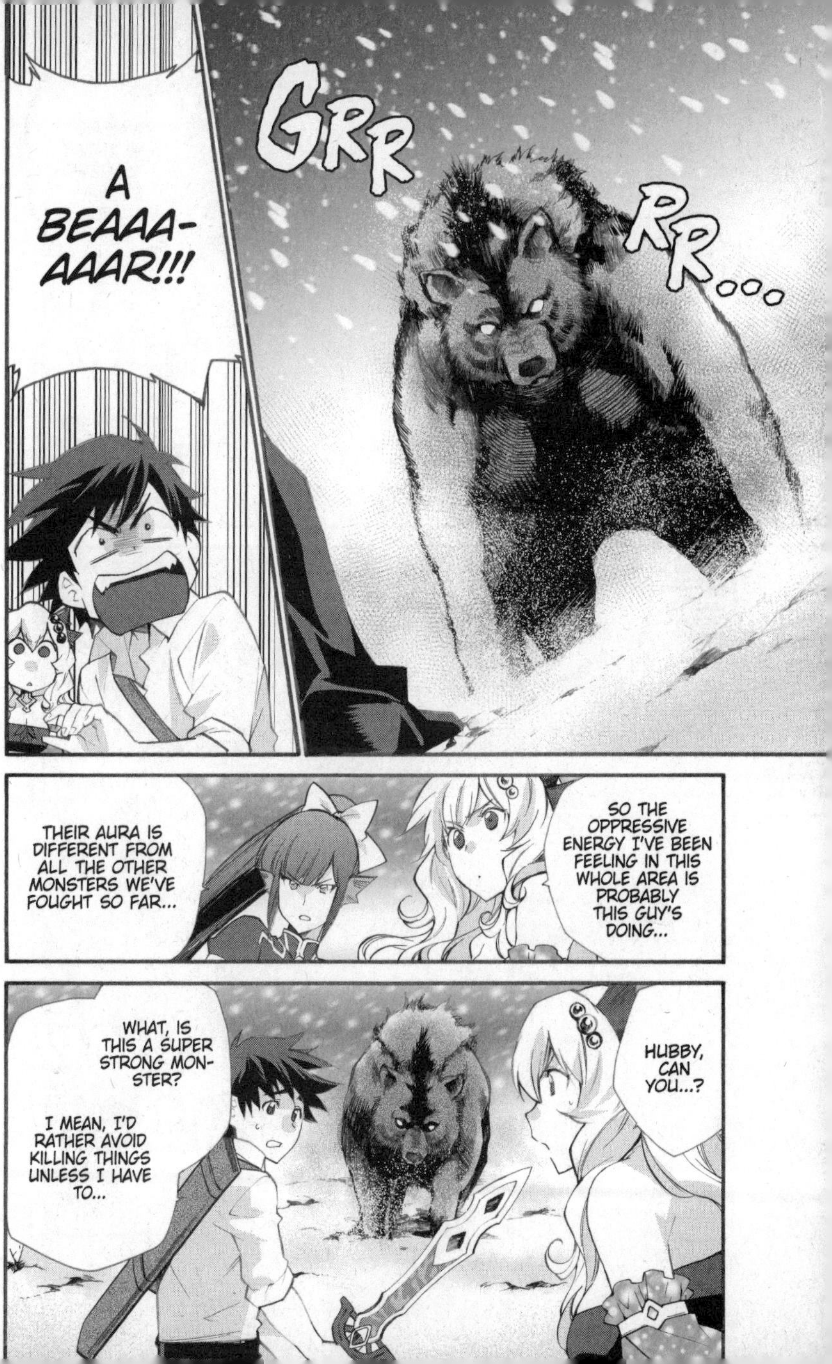
GRR
RR...
A BEAAAA-AAAR!!!
SO THE OPPRESSIVE ENERGY I'VE BEEN FEELING IN THIS WHOLE AREA IS PROBABLY THIS GUY'S DOING...
THEIR AURA IS DIFFERENT FROM ALL THE OTHER MONSTERS WE'VE FOUGHT SO FAR...
HUBBY, CAN YOU...?
WHAT, IS THIS A SUPER STRONG MON-STER?
I MEAN, I'D RATHER AVOID KILLING THINGS UNLESS I HAVE TO...

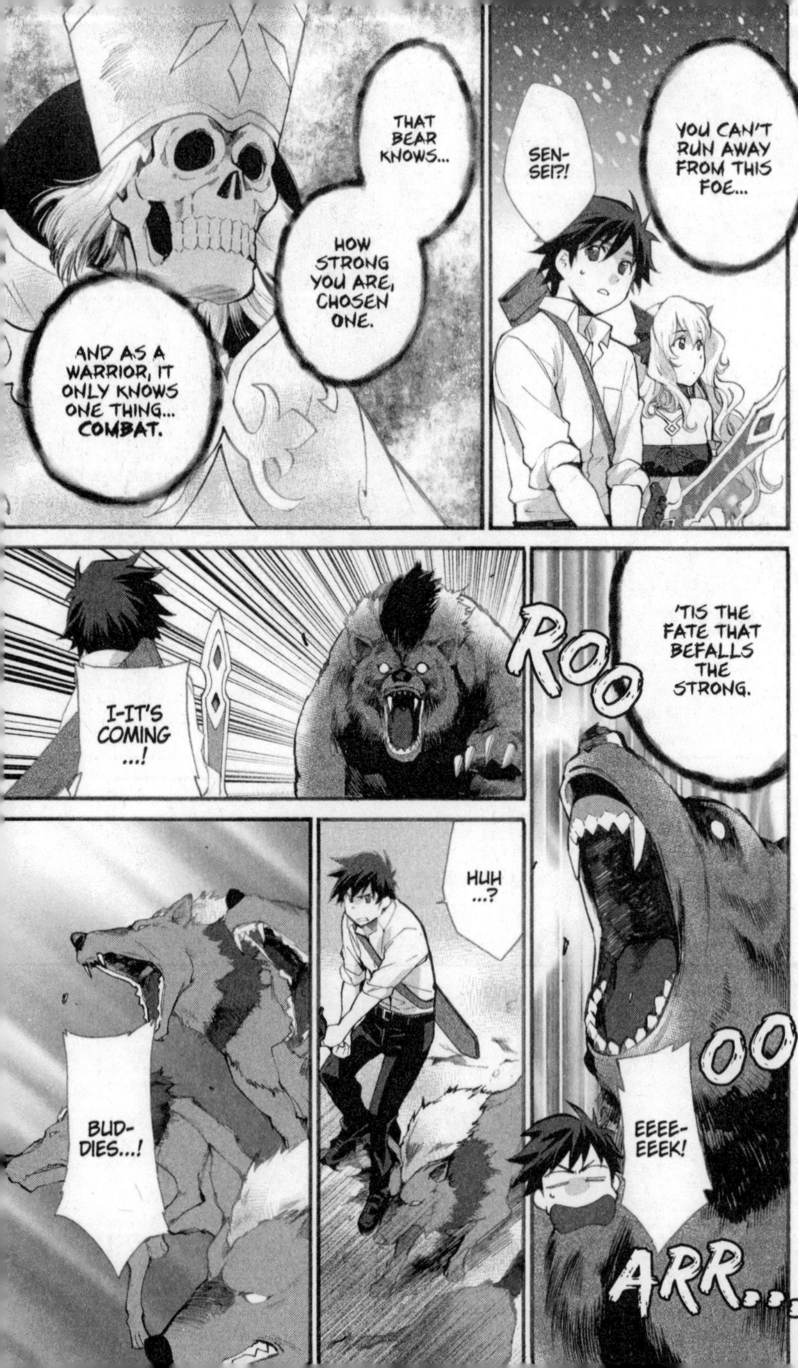
YOU CAN'T RUN AWAY FROM THIS FOE...
SEN-SEI?!
THAT BEAR KNOWS...
HOW STRONG YOU ARE, CHOSEN ONE.
AND AS A WARRIOR, IT ONLY KNOWS ONE THING... COMBAT.
'TIS THE FATE THAT BEFALLS THE STRONG.
ROO
OO
EEEE-EEEK!
ARR...!
I-IT'S COMING ...!
HUH ...?
BUD-DIES...!

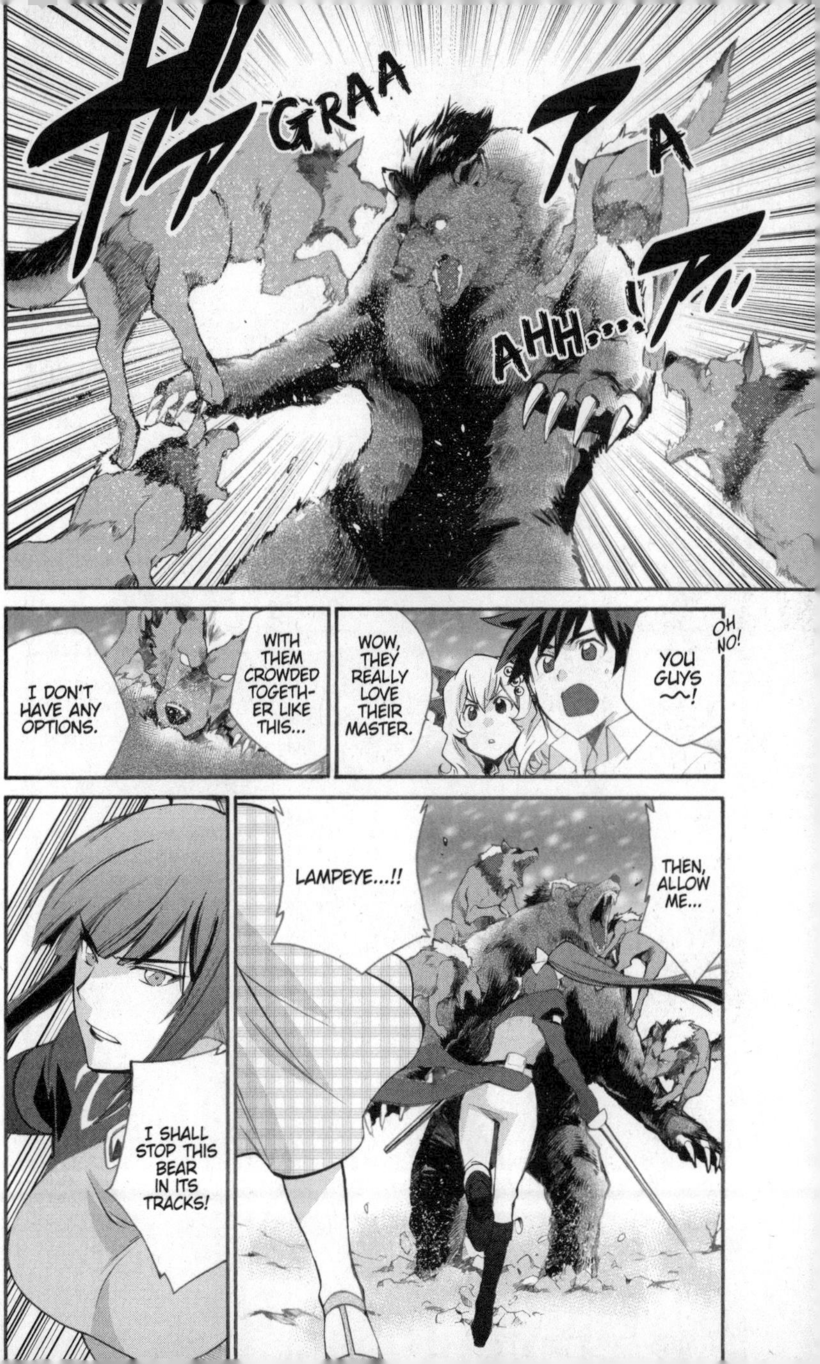
GRAA
A
AHH...!
OH NO!
YOU GUYS~!
WOW, THEY REALLY LOVE THEIR MASTER.
WITH THEM CROWDED TOGETH-ER LIKE THIS...
I DON'T HAVE ANY OPTIONS.
THEN, ALLOW ME...
LAMPEYE...!!
I SHALL STOP THIS BEAR IN ITS TRACKS!

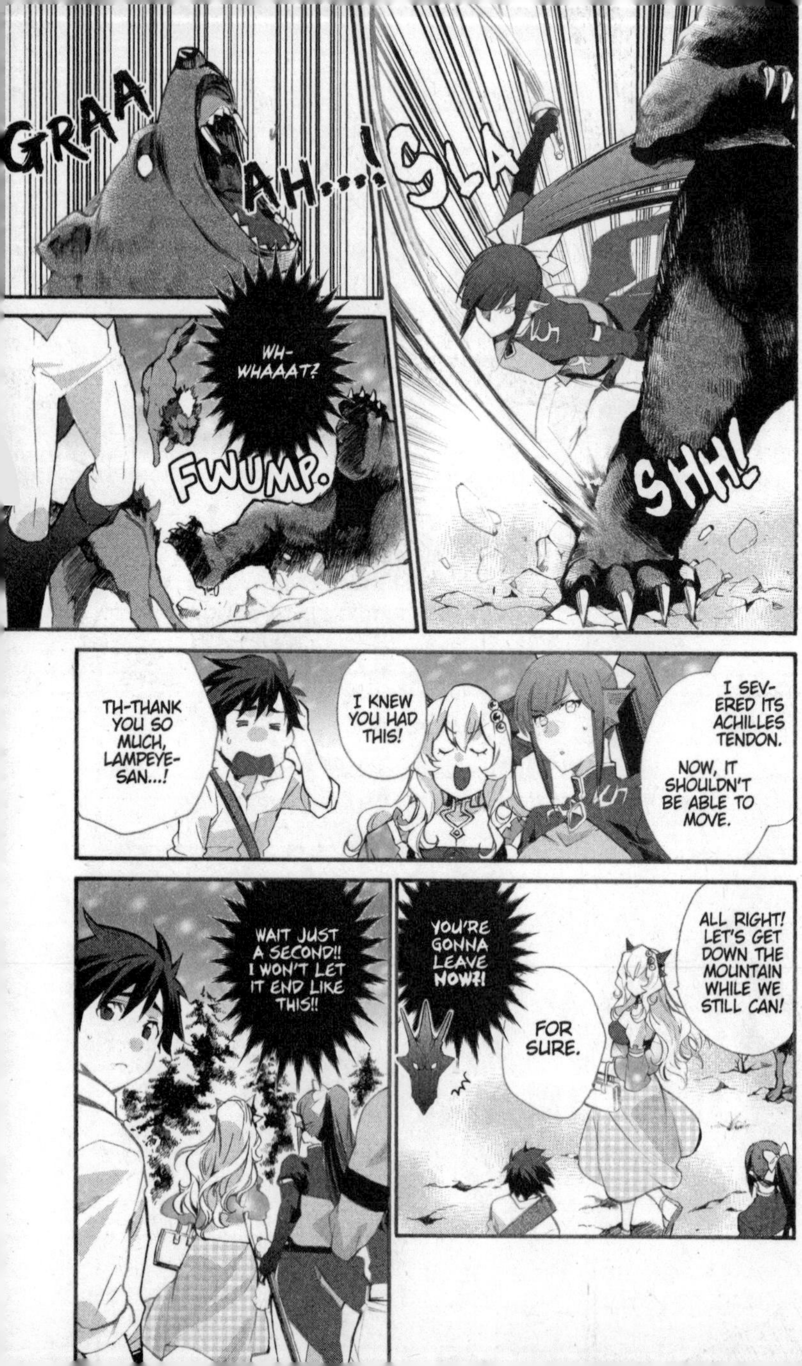
SLA
SHH!
GRAA
AH...!
WH-WHAAAT?
FWUMP.
I SEVERED ITS ACHILLES TENDON.
NOW, IT SHOULDN'T BE ABLE TO MOVE.
I KNEW YOU HAD THIS!
TH-THANK YOU SO MUCH, LAMPEYE-SAN...!
ALL RIGHT! LET'S GET DOWN THE MOUNTAIN WHILE WE STILL CAN!
FOR SURE.
YOU'RE GONNA LEAVE NOW?!
WAIT JUST A SECOND!! I WON'T LET IT END LIKE THIS!!

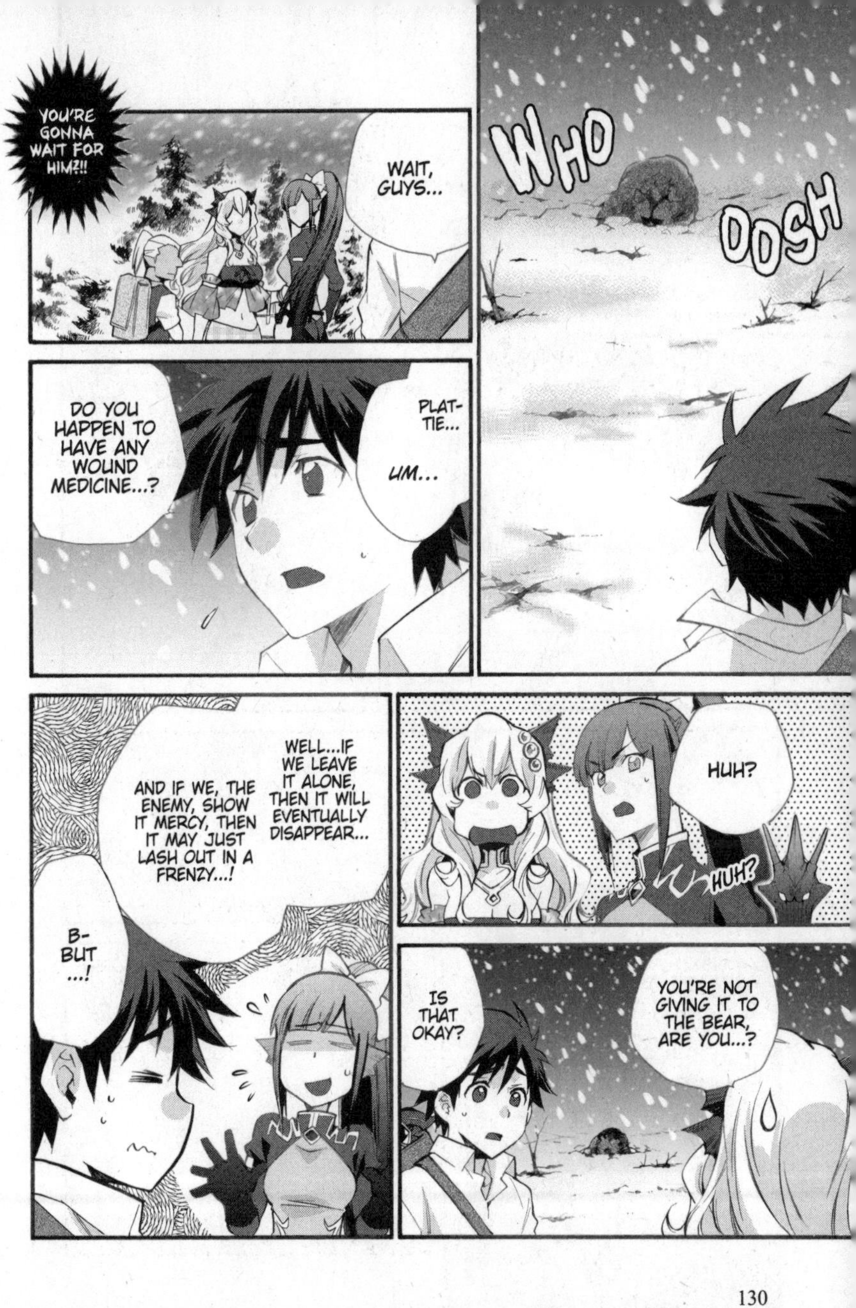
WHOOOSH
WAIT, GUYS...
YOU'RE GONNA WAIT FOR HIM?!!
PLAT-TIE...
UM...
DO YOU HAPPEN TO HAVE ANY WOUND MEDICINE...?
HUH?
HUH?
YOU'RE NOT GIVING IT TO THE BEAR, ARE YOU...?
IS THAT OKAY?
WELL...IF WE LEAVE IT ALONE, THEN IT WILL EVENTUALLY DISAPPEAR...
AND IF WE, THE ENEMY, SHOW IT MERCY, THEN IT MAY JUST LASH OUT IN A FRENZY...!
B-BUT...!

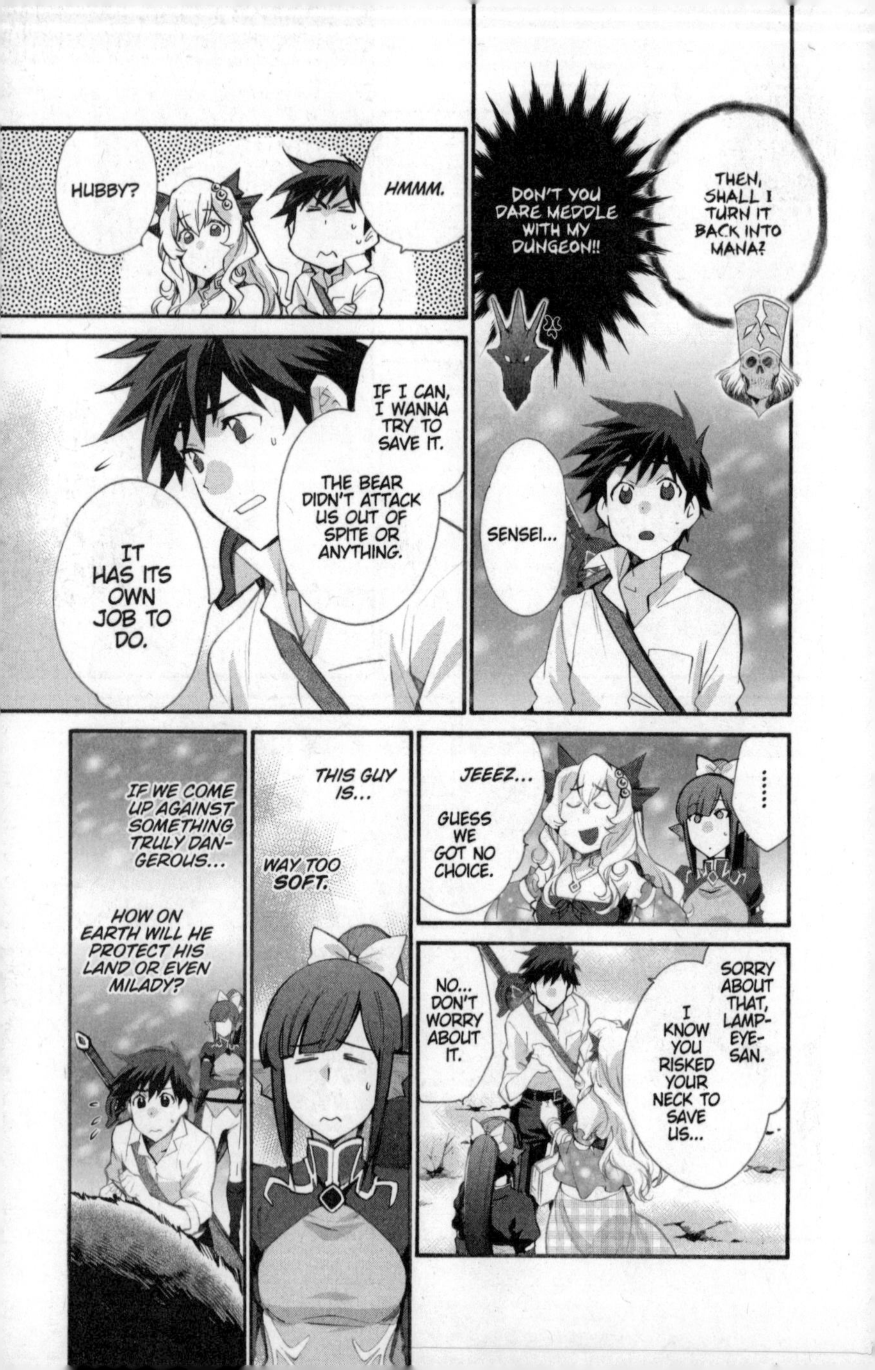
THEN, SHALL I TURN IT BACK INTO MANA?
DON'T YOU DARE MEDDLE WITH MY DUNGEON!!
SENSEI...
HMMM.
HUBBY?
IF I CAN, I WANNA TRY TO SAVE IT.
THE BEAR DIDN'T ATTACK US OUT OF SPITE OR ANYTHING.
IT HAS ITS OWN JOB TO DO.
......
JEEEZ...
GUESS WE GOT NO CHOICE.
SORRY ABOUT THAT, LAMP-EYE-SAN.
I KNOW YOU RISKED YOUR NECK TO SAVE US...
NO... DON'T WORRY ABOUT IT.
THIS GUY IS...
WAY TOO SOFT.
IF WE COME UP AGAINST SOMETHING TRULY DAN-GEROUS...
HOW ON EARTH WILL HE PROTECT HIS LAND OR EVEN MILADY?

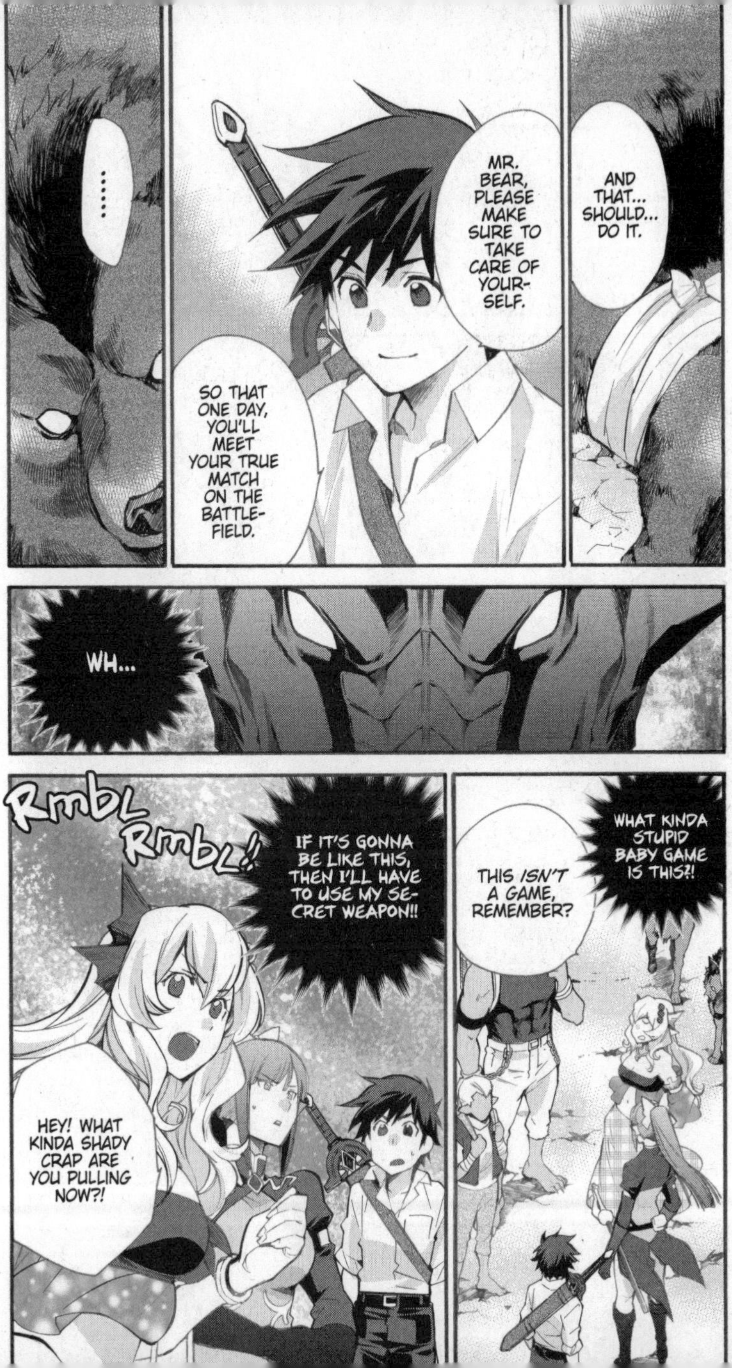
AND THAT... SHOULD... DO IT.
MR. BEAR, PLEASE MAKE SURE TO TAKE CARE OF YOUR-SELF.
SO THAT ONE DAY, YOU'LL MEET YOUR TRUE MATCH ON THE BATTLE-FIELD.
......
WH...
WHAT KINDA STUPID BABY GAME IS THIS?!
THIS *ISN'T* A GAME, REMEMBER?
IF IT'S GONNA BE LIKE THIS, THEN I'LL HAVE TO USE MY SE-CRET WEAPON!!
RmbL RmbL!!
HEY! WHAT KINDA SHADY CRAP ARE YOU PULLING NOW?!

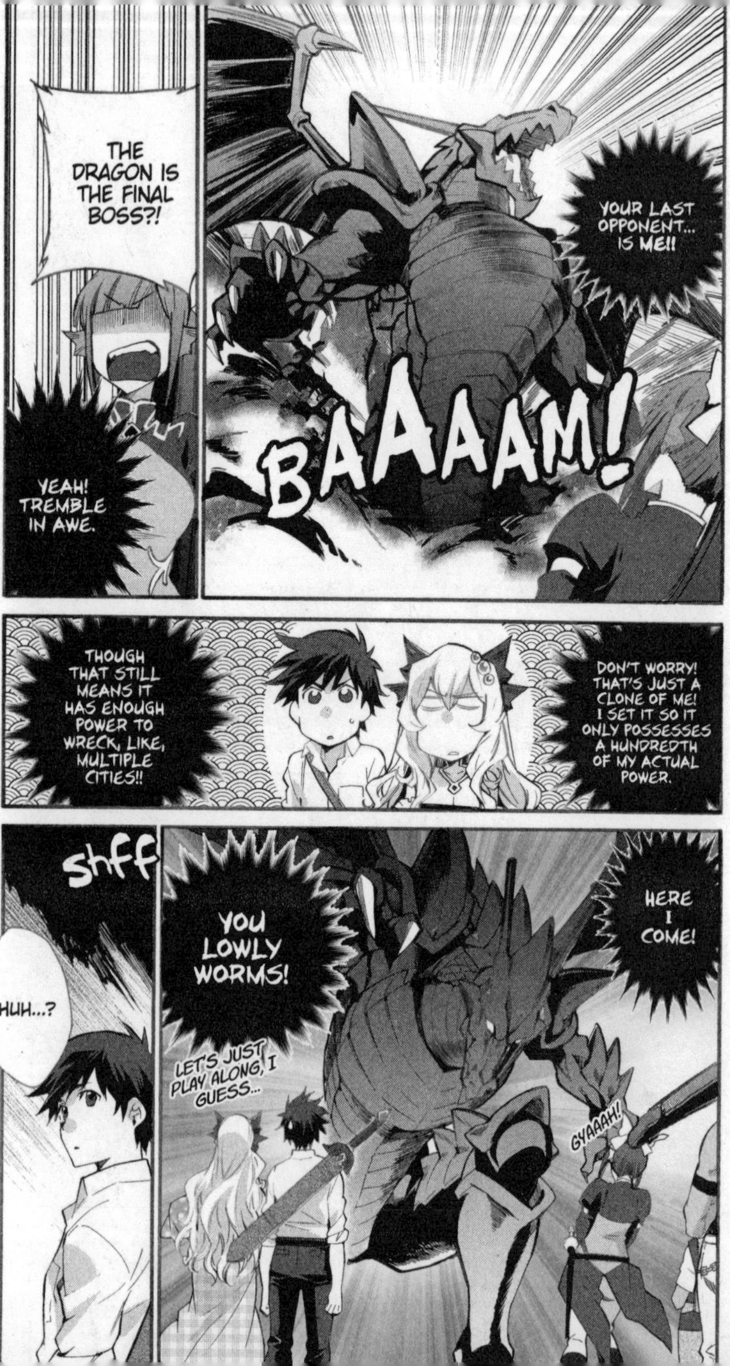
YOUR LAST OPPONENT... IS ME!!
BAAAAM!
THE DRAGON IS THE FINAL BOSS?!
YEAH! TREMBLE IN AWE.
DON'T WORRY! THAT'S JUST A CLONE OF ME! I SET IT SO IT ONLY POSSESSES A HUNDREDTH OF MY ACTUAL POWER.
THOUGH THAT STILL MEANS IT HAS ENOUGH POWER TO WRECK, LIKE, MULTIPLE CITIES!!
HERE I COME!
YOU LOWLY WORMS!
GYAAAH!
LET'S JUST PLAY ALONG, I GUESS...
shff
HUH...?

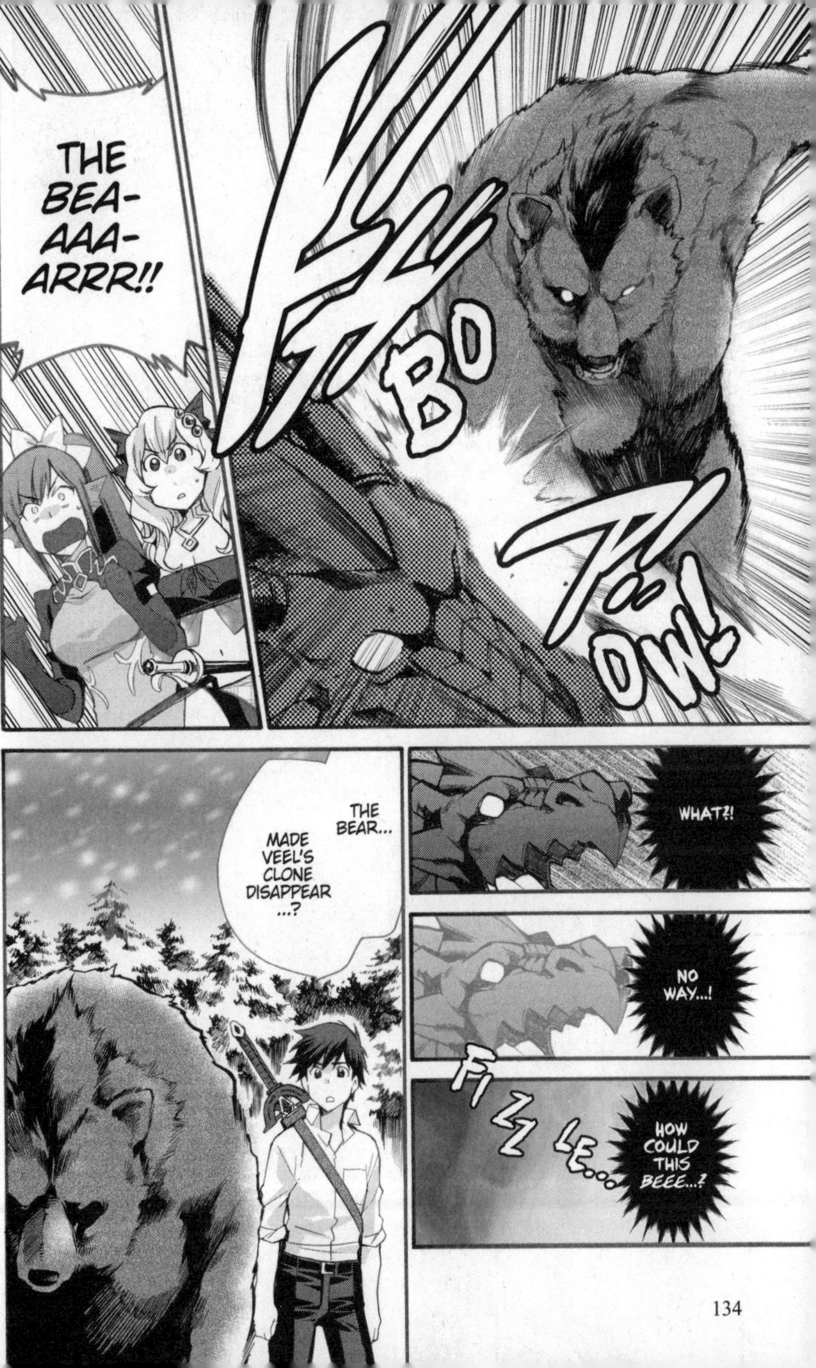
BO
OW!
THE BEA-AAA-ARRR!!
WHAT?!
NO WAY...!
FIZZLE...
HOW COULD THIS BEEE...?
THE BEAR...
MADE VEEL'S CLONE DISAPPEAR ...?

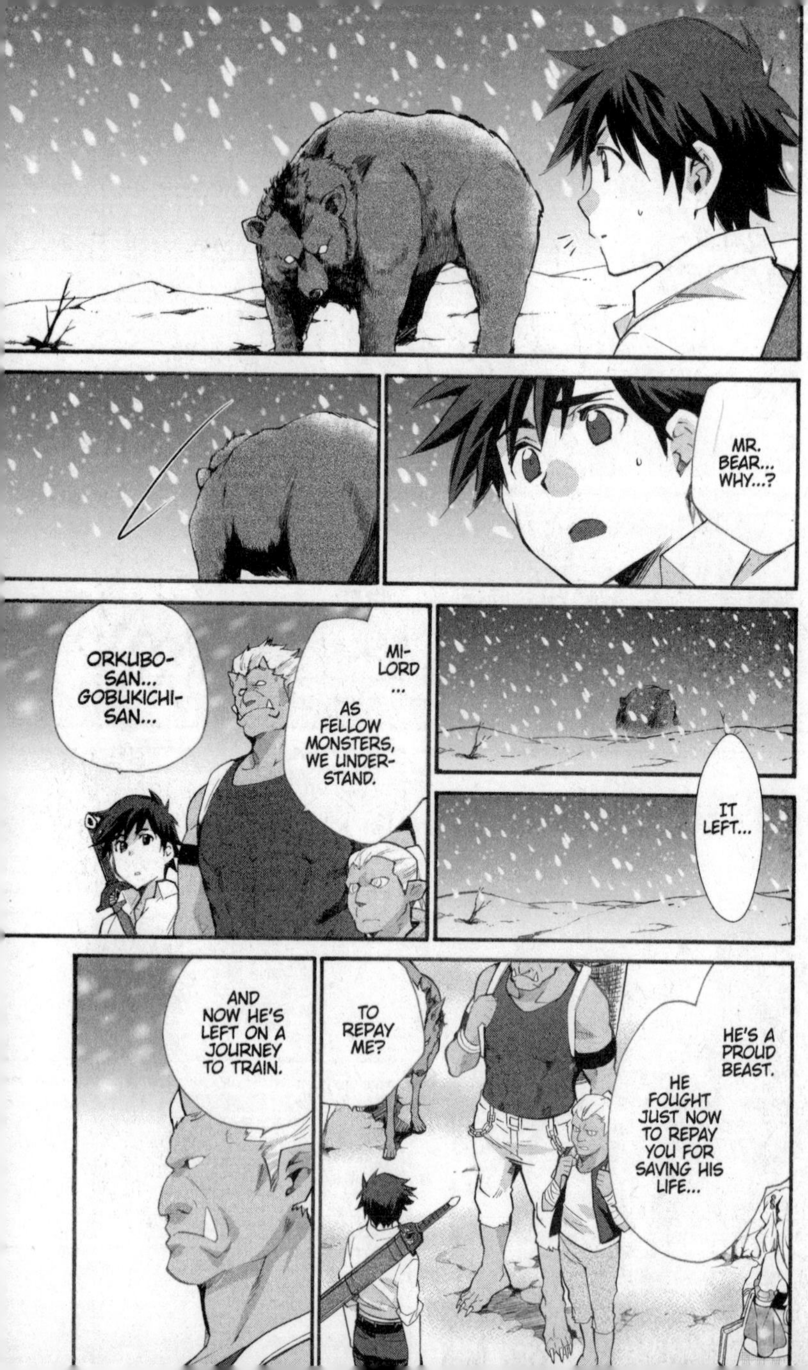
MR. BEAR... WHY...?
IT LEFT...
MI-LORD ...
AS FELLOW MONSTERS, WE UNDERSTAND.
ORKUBO-SAN... GOBUKICHI-SAN...
HE'S A PROUD BEAST.
HE FOUGHT JUST NOW TO REPAY YOU FOR SAVING HIS LIFE...
TO REPAY ME?
AND NOW HE'S LEFT ON A JOURNEY TO TRAIN.

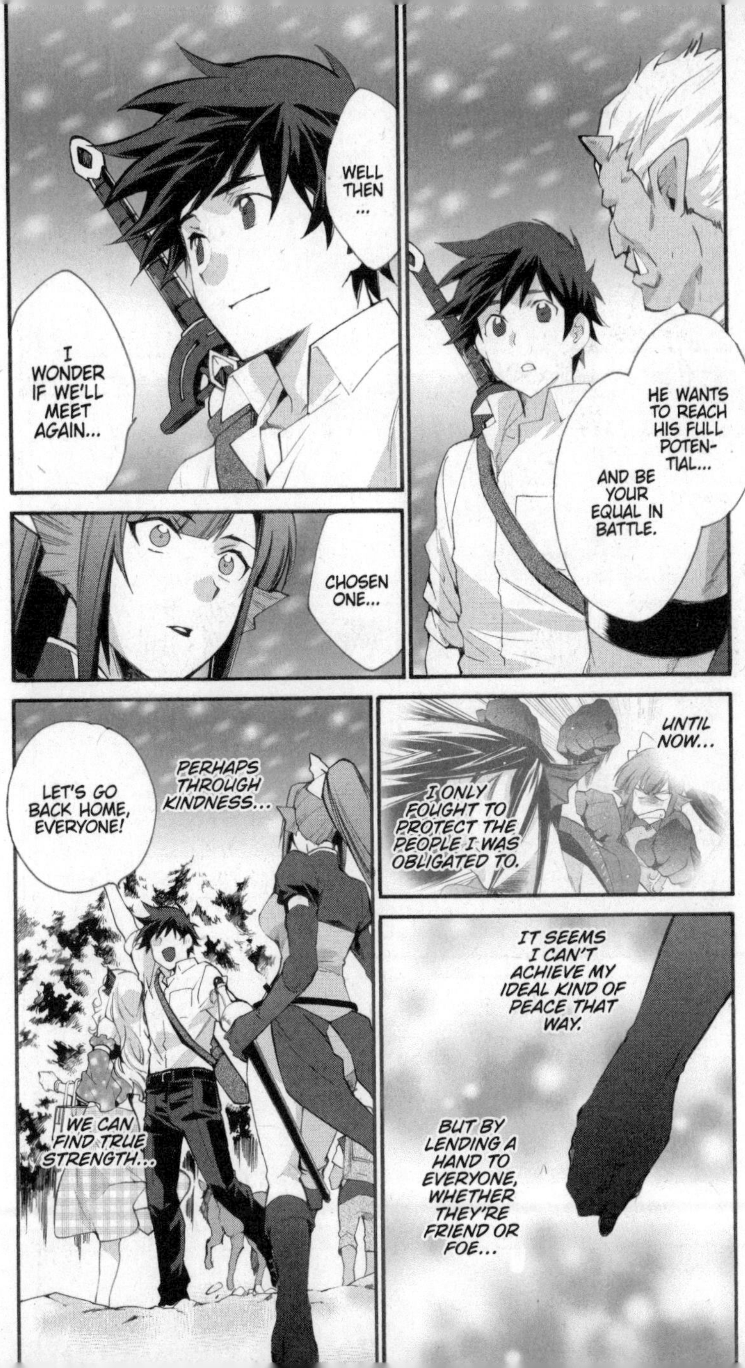
HE WANTS TO REACH HIS FULL POTEN-TIAL...
AND BE YOUR EQUAL IN BATTLE.
WELL THEN...
I WONDER IF WE'LL MEET AGAIN...
CHOSEN ONE...
UNTIL NOW...
I ONLY FOUGHT TO PROTECT THE PEOPLE I WAS OBLIGATED TO.
IT SEEMS I CAN'T ACHIEVE MY IDEAL KIND OF PEACE THAT WAY.
BUT BY LENDING A HAND TO EVERYONE, WHETHER THEY'RE FRIEND OR FOE...
LET'S GO BACK HOME, EVERYONE!
PERHAPS THROUGH KINDNESS...
WE CAN FIND TRUE STRENGTH...

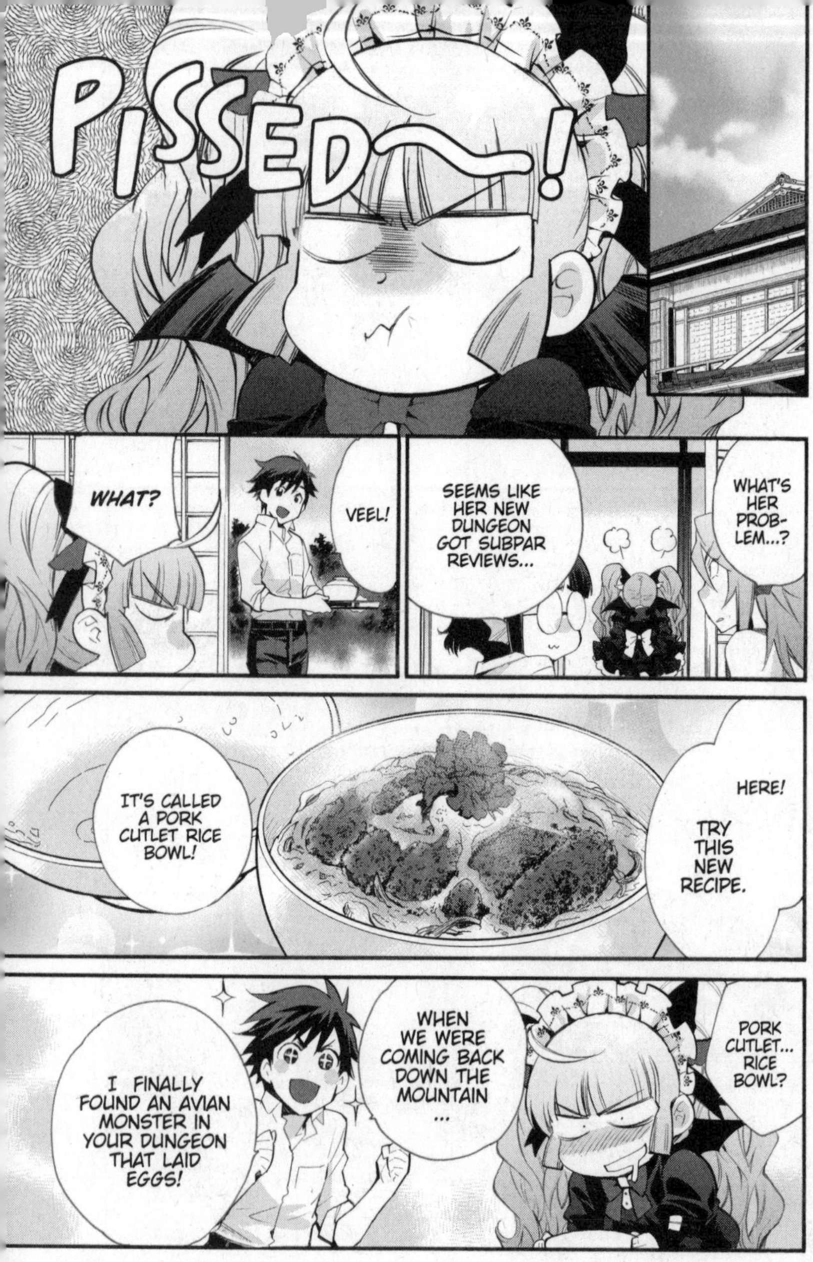
PISSED~!
WHAT'S HER PROB-LEM...?
SEEMS LIKE HER NEW DUNGEON GOT SUBPAR REVIEWS...
VEEL!
WHAT?
HERE!
TRY THIS NEW RECIPE.
IT'S CALLED A PORK CUTLET RICE BOWL!
PORK CUTLET... RICE BOWL?
WHEN WE WERE COMING BACK DOWN THE MOUNTAIN ...
I FINALLY FOUND AN AVIAN MONSTER IN YOUR DUNGEON THAT LAID EGGS!

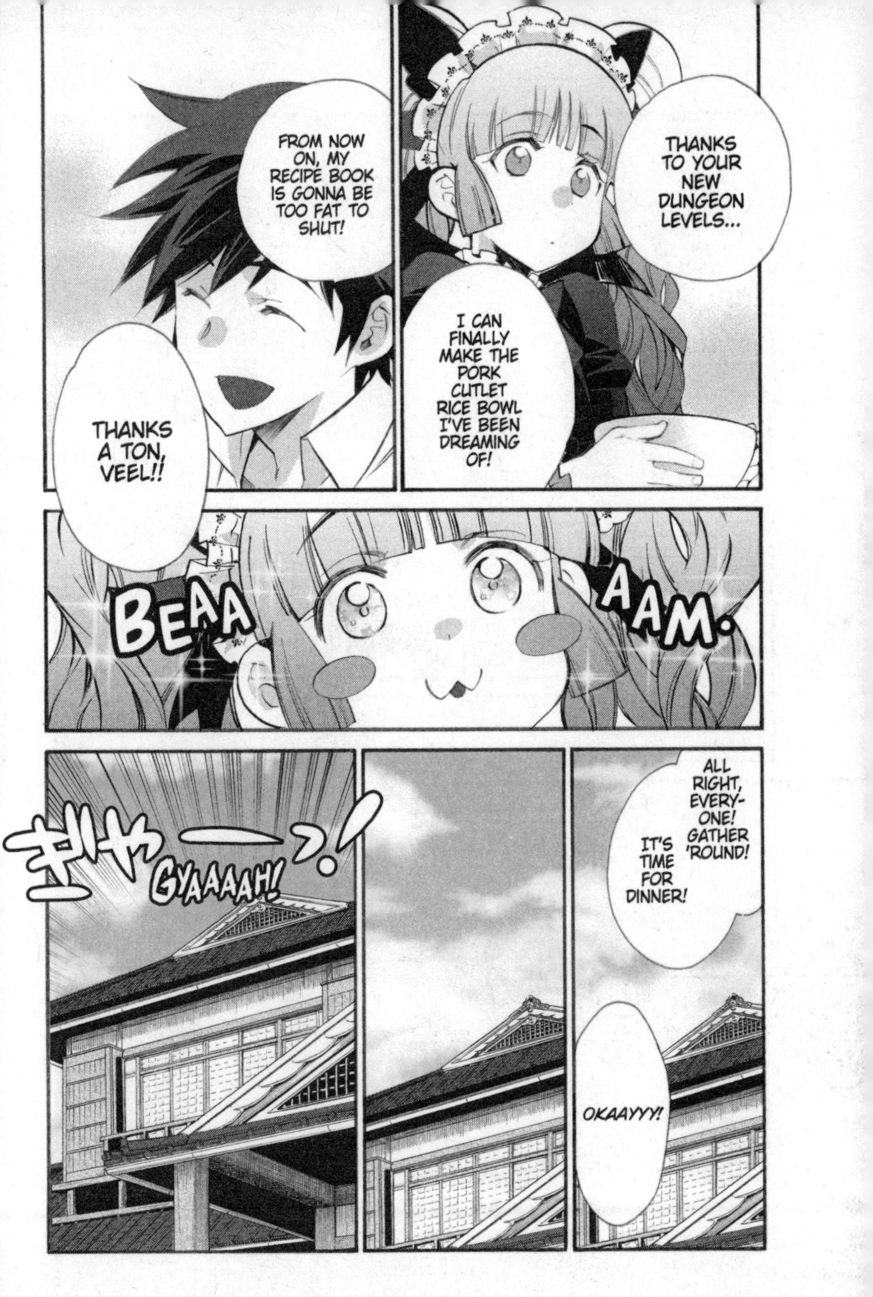
THANKS TO YOUR NEW DUNGEON LEVELS...
I CAN FINALLY MAKE THE PORK CUTLET RICE BOWL I'VE BEEN DREAMING OF!
FROM NOW ON, MY RECIPE BOOK IS GONNA BE TOO FAT TO SHUT!
THANKS A TON, VEEL!!
BEAAAAM.
ALL RIGHT, EVERYONE! GATHER 'ROUND!
IT'S TIME FOR DINNER!
OKAAYYY!
GYAAAAH!

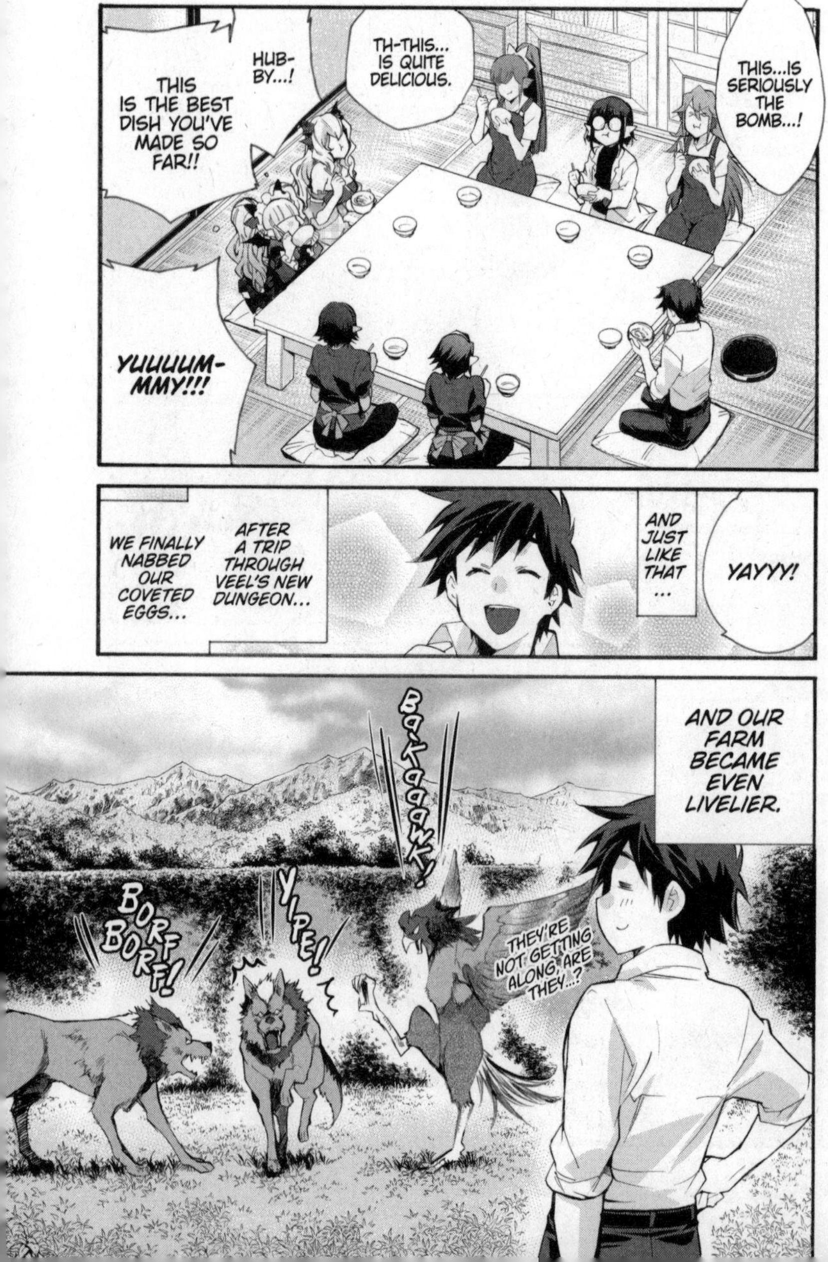
THIS...IS SERIOUSLY THE BOMB...!
TH-THIS... IS QUITE DELICIOUS.
HUB-BY...!
THIS IS THE BEST DISH YOU'VE MADE SO FAR!!
YUUUUM-MMY!!!
YAYYY!
AND JUST LIKE THAT...
AFTER A TRIP THROUGH VEEL'S NEW DUNGEON...
WE FINALLY NABBED OUR COVETED EGGS...
AND OUR FARM BECAME EVEN LIVELIER.
BAKAAAWK!
THEY'RE NOT GETTING ALONG, ARE THEY...?
YIPE!
BORF BORF!

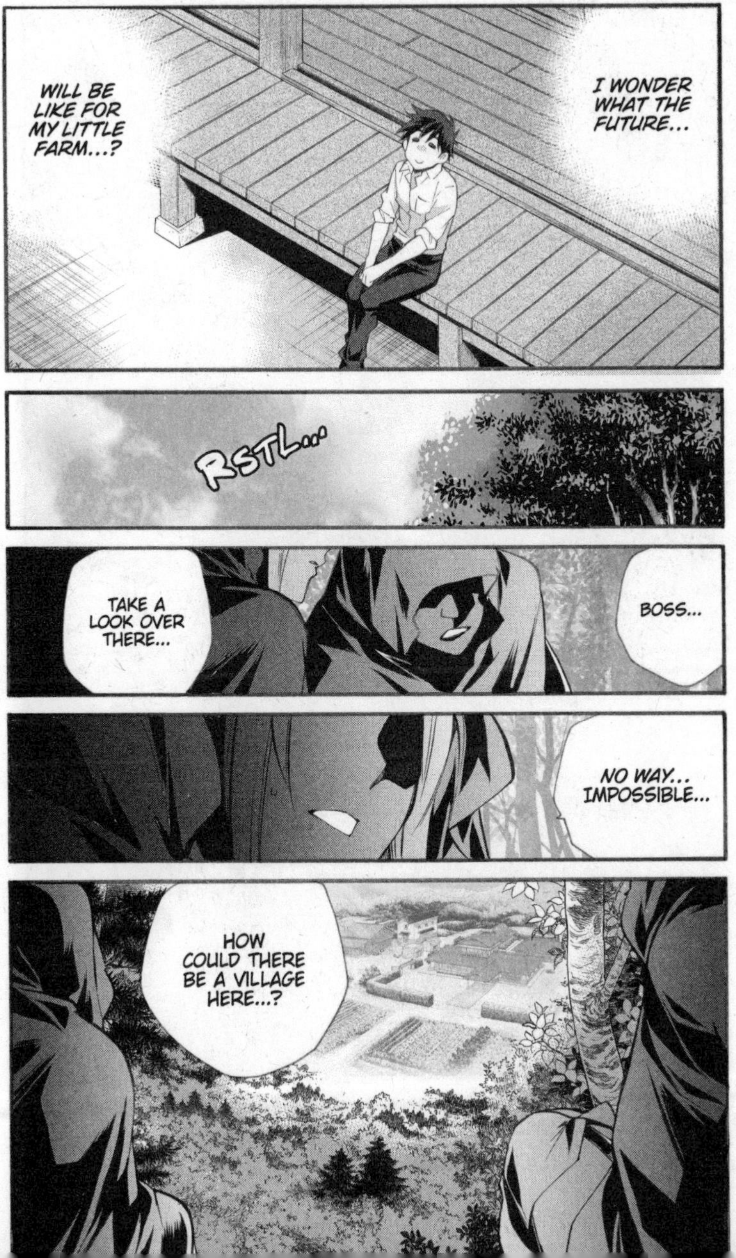
I WONDER WHAT THE FUTURE...
WILL BE LIKE FOR MY LITTLE FARM...?
RSTL...
BOSS...
TAKE A LOOK OVER THERE...
NO WAY... IMPOSSIBLE...
HOW COULD THERE BE A VILLAGE HERE...?

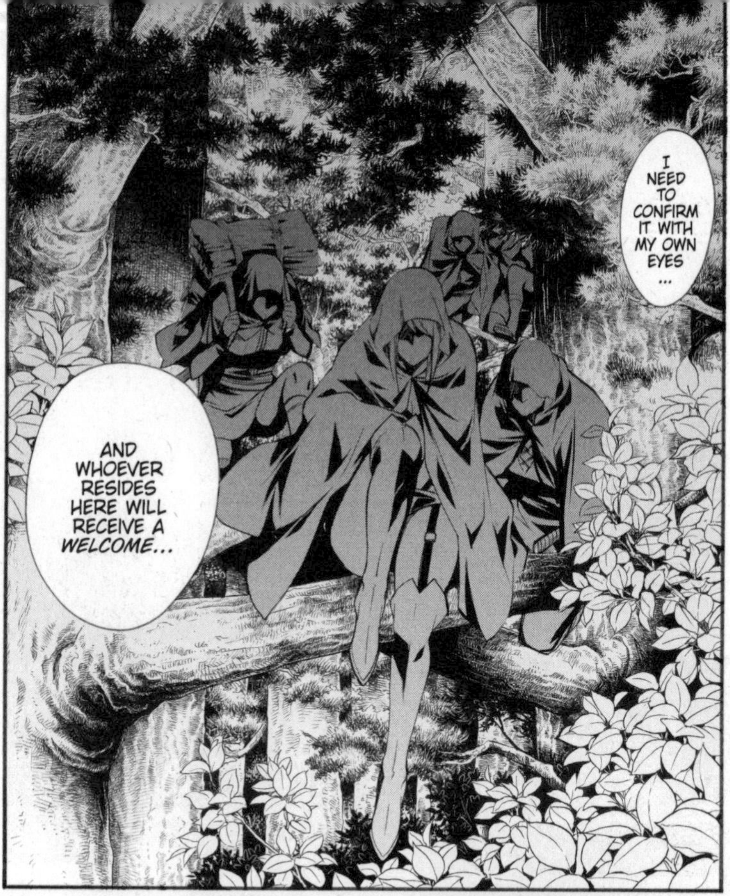
I NEED TO CONFIRM IT WITH MY OWN EYES ...
AND WHOEVER RESIDES HERE WILL RECEIVE A *WELCOME*...

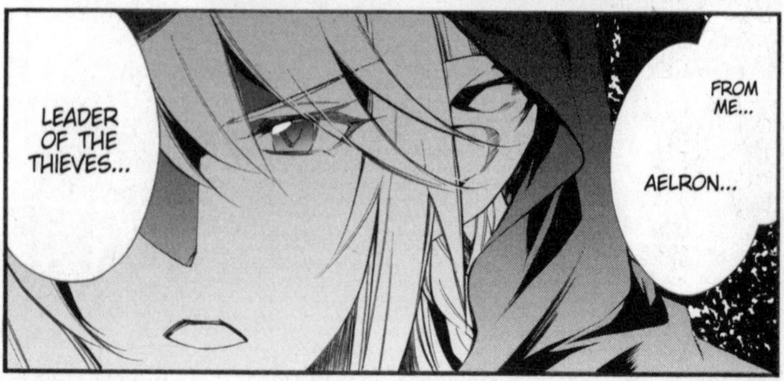
FROM ME... AELRON...
LEADER OF THE THIEVES...

LET'S BUY THE LAND and CULTIVATE IT IN A DIFFERENT WORLD

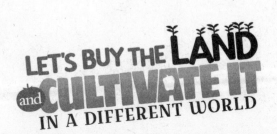

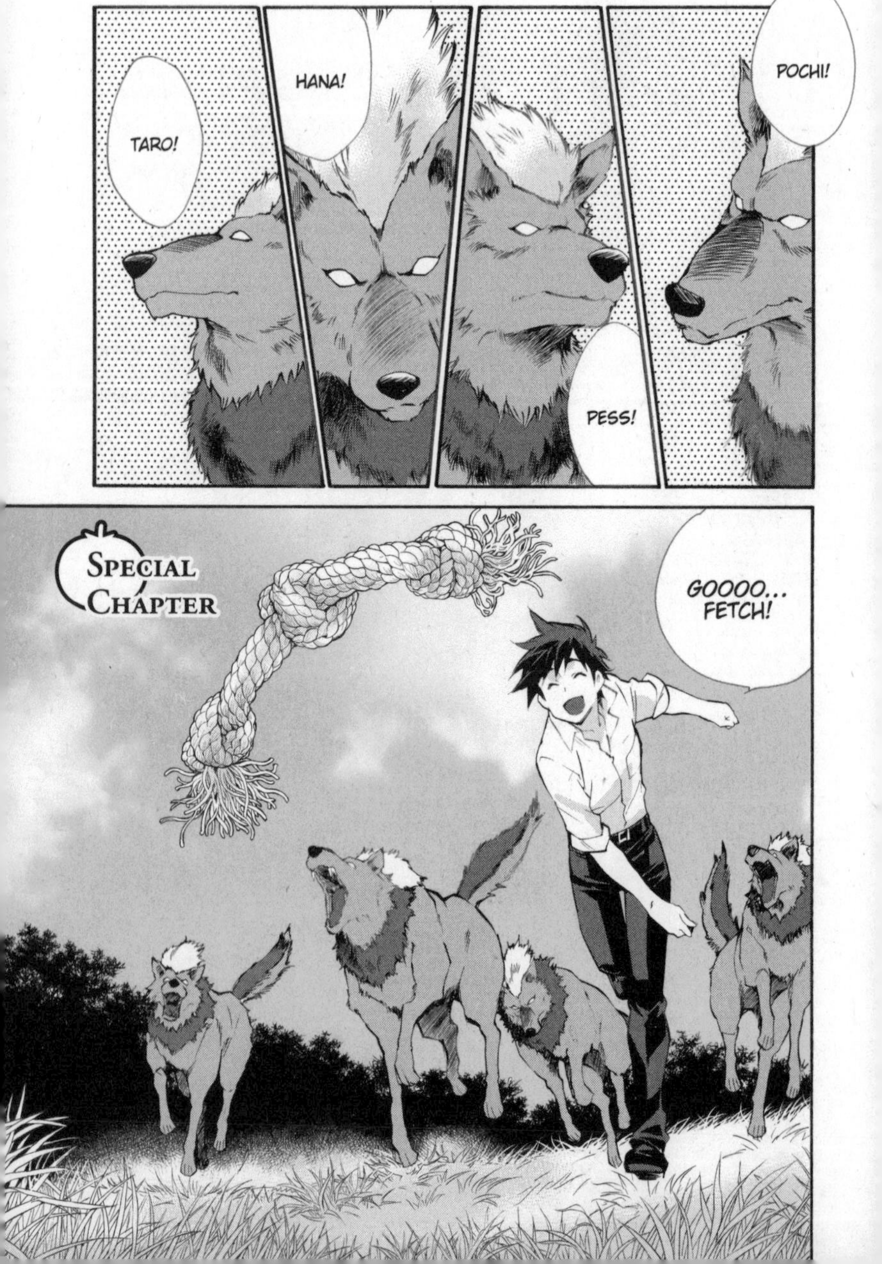
POCHI!
PESS!
HANA!
TARO!
GOOOO... FETCH!
SPECIAL CHAPTER

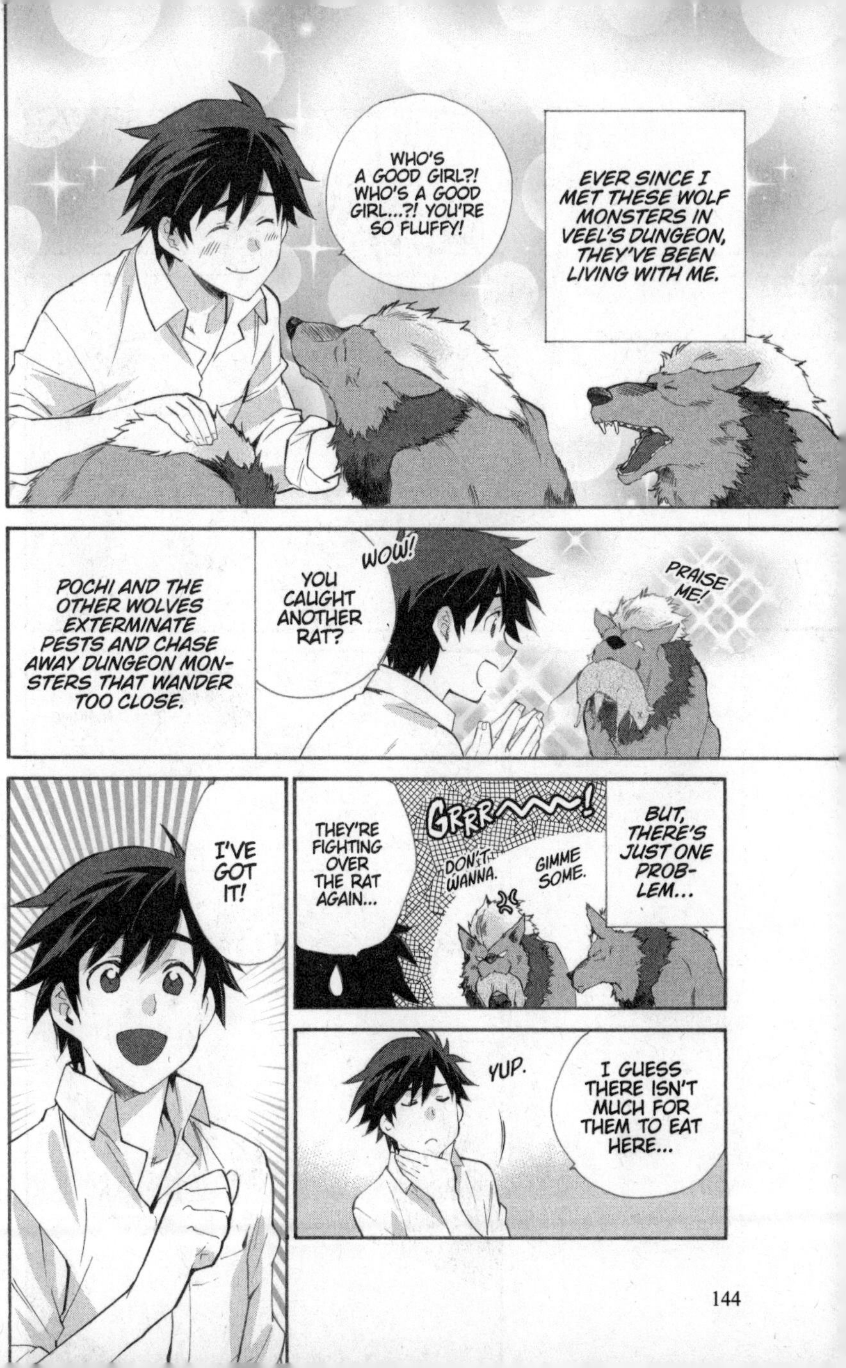
EVER SINCE I MET THESE WOLF MONSTERS IN VEEL'S DUNGEON, THEY'VE BEEN LIVING WITH ME.
WHO'S A GOOD GIRL?! WHO'S A GOOD GIRL...?! YOU'RE SO FLUFFY!
PRAISE ME!
WOW!
YOU CAUGHT ANOTHER RAT?
POCHI AND THE OTHER WOLVES EXTERMINATE PESTS AND CHASE AWAY DUNGEON MONSTERS THAT WANDER TOO CLOSE.
BUT, THERE'S JUST ONE PROBLEM...
GRRR~~~!
GIMME SOME.
DON'T WANNA.
THEY'RE FIGHTING OVER THE RAT AGAIN...
I GUESS THERE ISN'T MUCH FOR THEM TO EAT HERE...
YUP.
I'VE GOT IT!

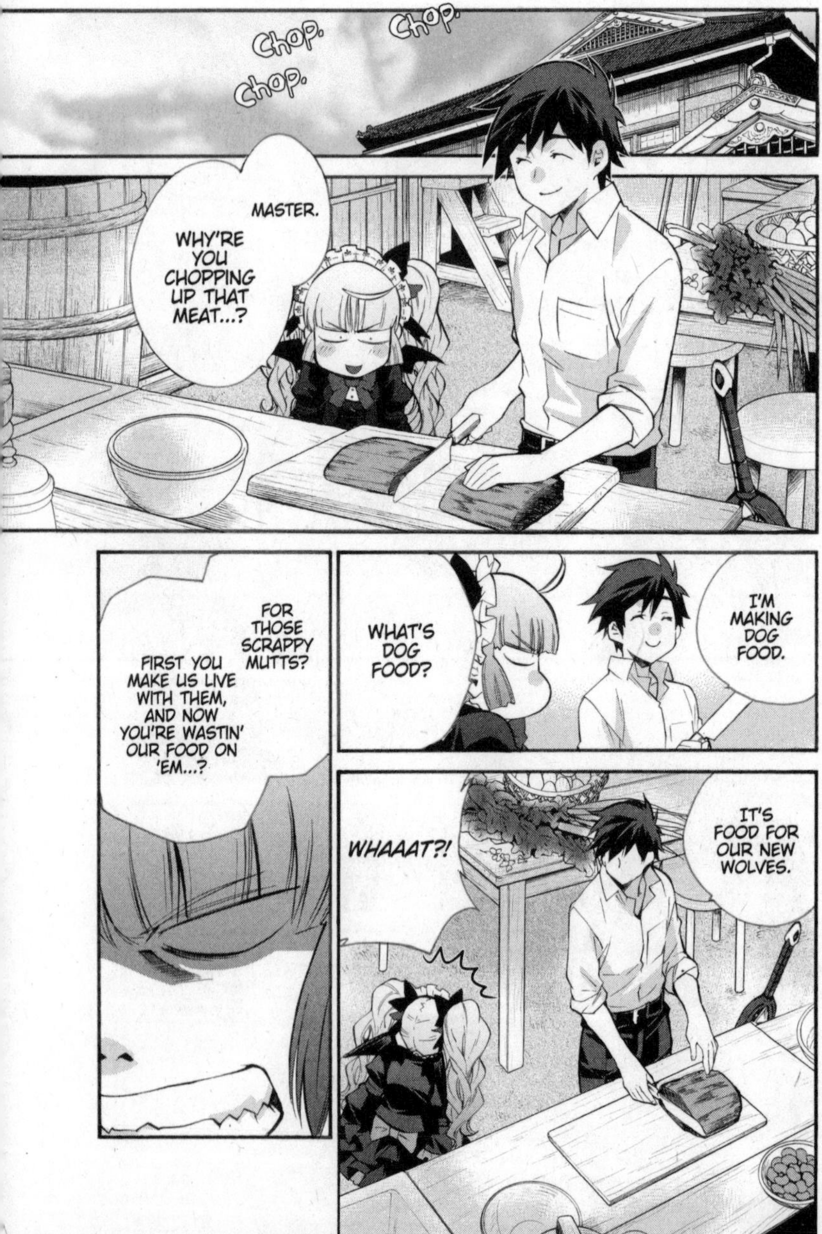
Chop.
Chop.
Chop.
MASTER.
WHY'RE YOU CHOPPING UP THAT MEAT...?
I'M MAKING DOG FOOD.
WHAT'S DOG FOOD?
IT'S FOOD FOR OUR NEW WOLVES.
WHAAAT?!
FOR THOSE SCRAPPY MUTTS?
FIRST YOU MAKE US LIVE WITH THEM, AND NOW YOU'RE WASTIN' OUR FOOD ON 'EM...?

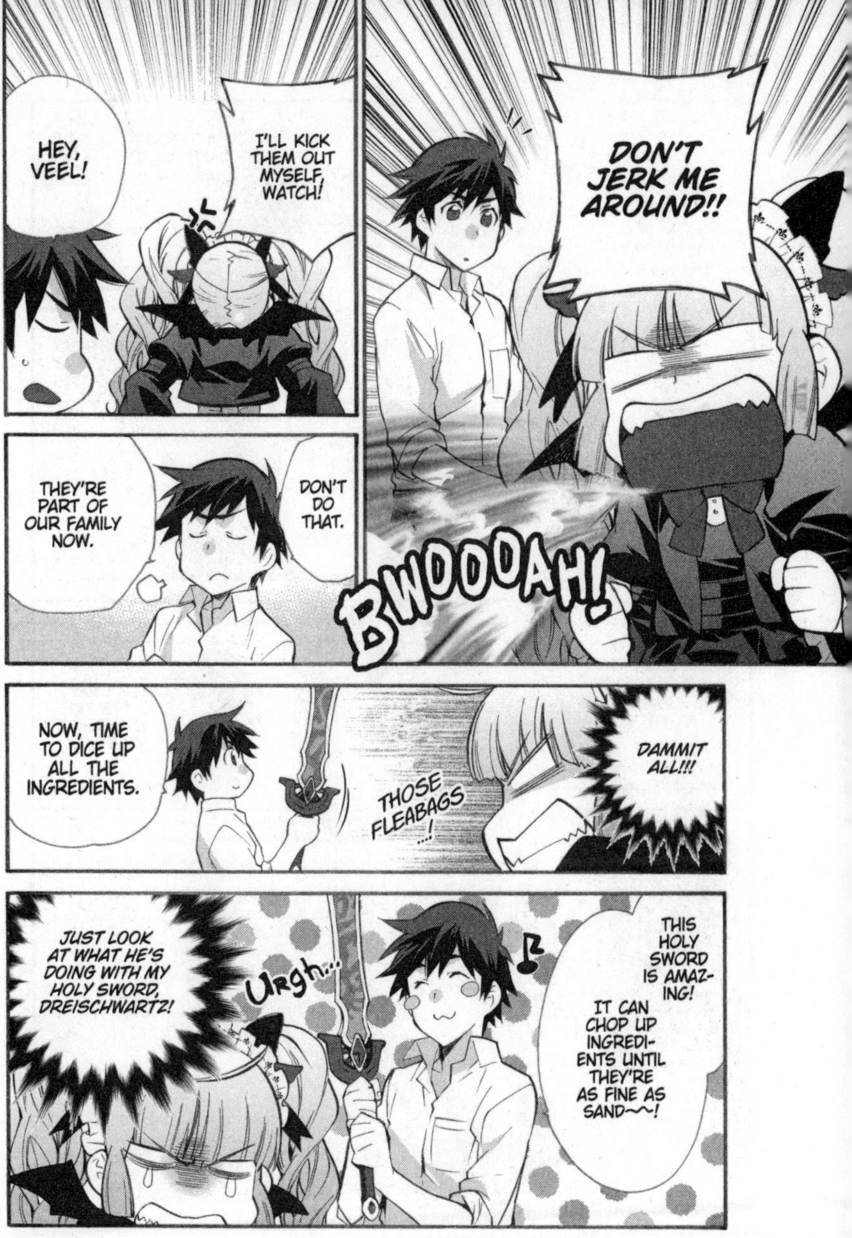
DON'T JERK ME AROUND!!
BWOOOAH!
I'LL KICK THEM OUT MYSELF, WATCH!
HEY, VEEL!
DON'T DO THAT.
THEY'RE PART OF OUR FAMILY NOW.
DAMMIT ALL!!!
THOSE FLEABAGS ...!
NOW, TIME TO DICE UP ALL THE INGREDIENTS.
THIS HOLY SWORD IS AMAZ-ING!
IT CAN CHOP UP INGREDI-ENTS UNTIL THEY'RE AS FINE AS SAND~~!
Urgh...
JUST LOOK AT WHAT HE'S DOING WITH MY HOLY SWORD, DREISCHWARTZ!

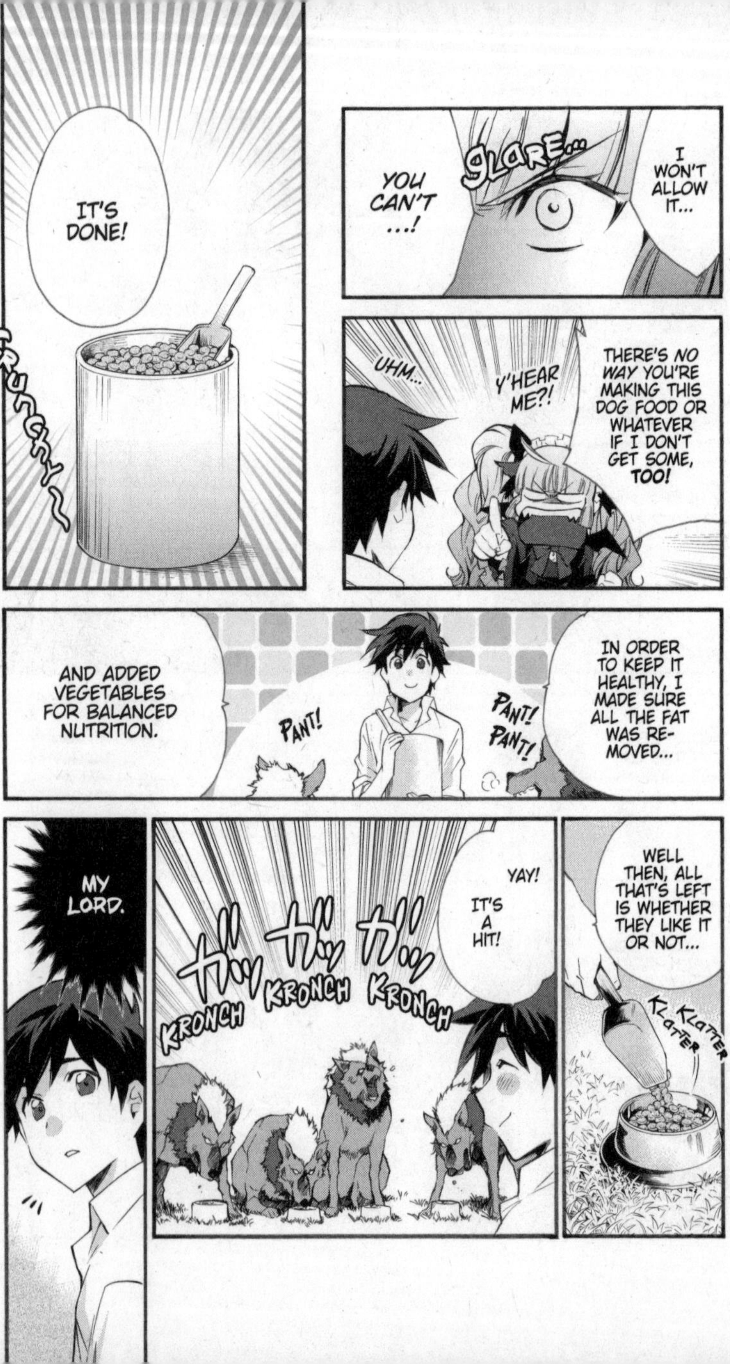
I WON'T ALLOW IT...
GLARE...
YOU CAN'T ...!
THERE'S NO WAY YOU'RE MAKING THIS DOG FOOD OR WHATEVER IF I DON'T GET SOME, TOO!
Y'HEAR ME?!
UHM...
IT'S DONE!
CRUNCHY~
IN ORDER TO KEEP IT HEALTHY, I MADE SURE ALL THE FAT WAS RE-MOVED...
PANT! PANT!
PANT!
AND ADDED VEGETABLES FOR BALANCED NUTRITION.
WELL THEN, ALL THAT'S LEFT IS WHETHER THEY LIKE IT OR NOT...
KLATTER KLATTER
YAY! IT'S A HIT!
ガッ ガッ ガッ
KRONCH KRONCH KRONCH
MY LORD.

……
GIMME MY SHARE.
I'M THE TOP DOG AROUND HERE!
JEEZ...! GUESS I GOTTA ...
TURN BACK INTO A HUMAN AND STICK OUT YOUR HANDS, OKAY...?
VWOOM!
YIPPEE!!
JUST A LITTLE, OKAY?
HERE.
SO THIS IS...
“DOG FOOD”
THANKS FOR THE FOOD!
MUNCH!

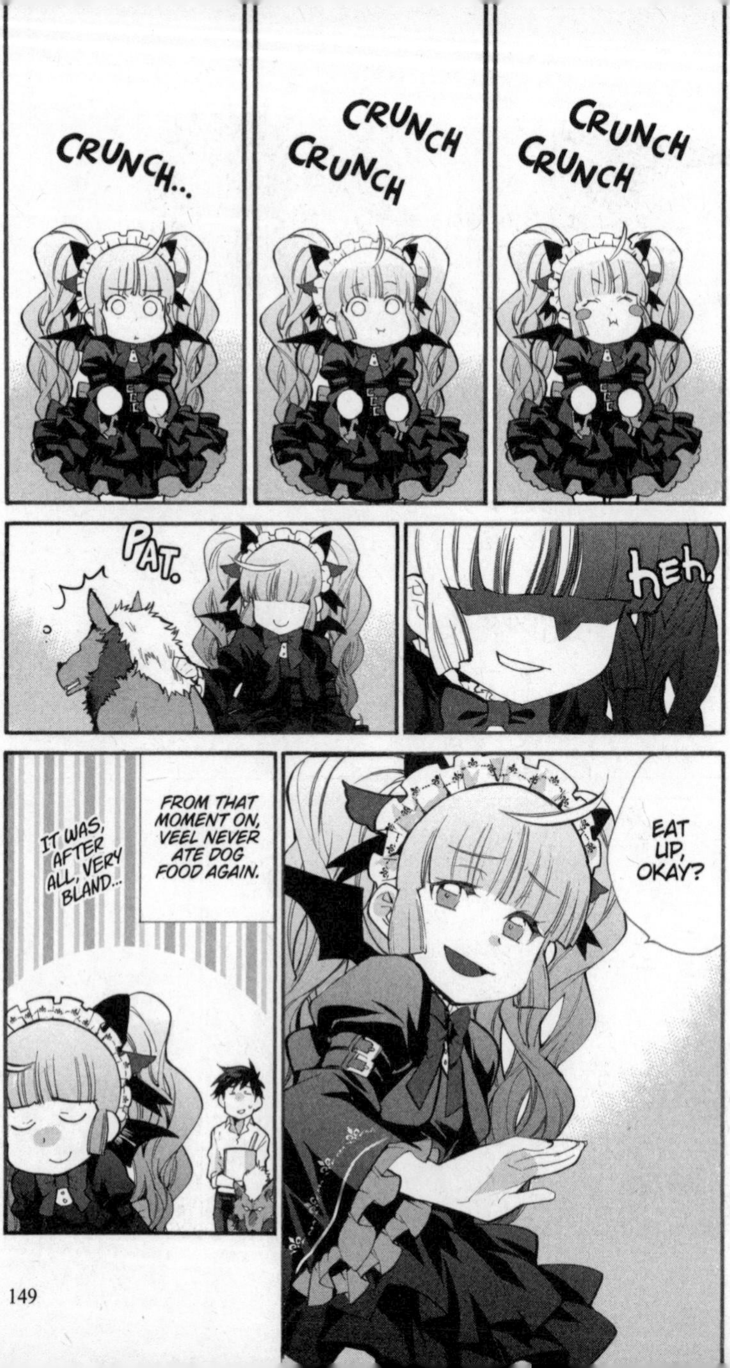
CRUNCH
CRUNCH
CRUNCH
CRUNCH
CRUNCH...
heh.
PAT.
EAT UP, OKAY?
FROM THAT MOMENT ON, VEEL NEVER ATE DOG FOOD AGAIN.
IT WAS, AFTER ALL, VERY BLAND...

LET'S BUY THE LAND and CULTIVATE IT IN A DIFFERENT WORLD

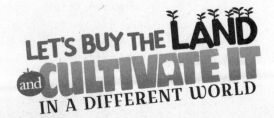

Rokujyuuyon Okazawa
**Veel's Mountain Dungeon:
The Secret Level**

"**S**ecrets are secrets 'cause they're meant to be discover-
ed!" Not long after we finished diving through Veel's
revamped dungeon, she was back to spouting her usual
nonsense.

"Heh, heh, heh. And furthermore, heh! I didn't think that
you'd beat all my dungeon challenges so quickly. But who
said you even encountered *everything* in the dungeon that I,
Veel the Grinzell Dragon, created?"

"What? You don't mean—"

"It's time to announce my dungeon's secret level!"

What did she say?! I thought.

A secret level? Those words made me reminisce about
times I was glued to video games. Secret levels were a big
deal. But the game developers would go nuts and make the
levels impossible to beat, a major heartbreak for serious

gamers. I wonder if she meant wonder if she meant *that* kind of secret level...!

"In order to reach it, you have to enter a special command!"

"Ooooh!"

"Then, let's go! Up, down, up, down, right, left, B, A!"

"Up, down, up, down, right, left, bee, ayy?!"

Reach up! Bend down! Reach up! Bend down! Over to the right! Over to the left! Y-M-B-A! It was beginning to feel like a trick to make us do cardio, but thanks to that special code, the secret level opened before us.

"All right, this is where your hell begins. Abandon all hope now!"

Do you have to say scary things like that?

Trembling, I inched forward, and waiting at the checkpoint was a woman with red hair. "Isn't that Lampeye?"

Why is Lampeye, the Hellfire Witch, here?

Even more perplexing was the fact that she was standing on higher ground, launching some kind of object at us... the strange projectiles traveling in a sweeping arc before hitting the ground exploding on impact!

"Explosions?!"

Is that woman seriously throwing bombs at us?!

Well, she was the Hellfire Witch, so that tracked. As Lampeye lobbed bomb after bomb at us in a consistent rhythm, the explosions almost formed an impenetrable wall of danger.

"You'll have to figure out her timing to dodge if you're gonna advance from here! One mistake and you'll be vaporized into dust!" Veel exclaimed.

"I think I remember a game that was *juuuust* like this...!"

As long as I remained safely in place, there'd be no progress, so I leapt forward and ran at full speed. The bombs falling from the sky detonated as they slammed into the ground. And then, during the short pauses between each new *projectile plummeting from above...run!*

I'm safe! Did I make it to the checkpoint...?!

"Good job. That was a spectacular sprint, and you were fearless in front of the explosions," Lampeye, calm and collected, praised my efforts...

But dodging wave upon wave of exploding bombs was still scary as hell.

"Lampeye, why the heck are you even defending Veel's dungeon?" I asked.

"I was forcibly requested to help," she answered, begrudgingly.

The oxymoron of being "forcibly requested" was not lost on me.

"It seems that the earlier premiere of Veel's dungeon didn't go as planned, leaving our dragon very dissatisfied. So, to relieve her distress, she wanted to hold another event..."

I see, I thought.

I guess if they're willing to bust their humps just to help Veel out, these mermaids must be a good bunch after all.

"And so, until Lady Veel feels better, I'm going all out, okay? Now prepare, as my explosive magic potions will be launched thirty-six times per second," she announced.

"I don't think I can dodge all of them!"

What the hell is with this brutal bomb game?! I thought. But all that being said, I did manage to dodge the rain of bombs by the skin of my teeth, advancing to the next stage where

Puffer, the Glacial Witch, stood waiting.

"It's 'bout time I show you why I'm called the Witch of Frost!"

Since she arrived to my farm, I hadn't been blessed with the opportunity to witness her powers. As I peered ahead to check the layout, a sheet of whiteness spread out on the floor before my eyes.

"The floor's frozen!" If she could freeze the entire floor into a sheet of ice, then she definitely earned that title of hers!

And if the floor's frozen, then that means...!!

"Ooh, slippery! I'm slipping! I'm slipping! *I'm slippinggg!!*"

So, this is how it's gonna be! I'm pretty sure I saw this exact mechanic in video games before, hadn't I? "And, when there's a slippery floor, there has to be... *Aaagh!* Holes! I'm gonna *falllll!*"

Holes on a stage like this meant instant death! It didn't matter that there weren't any enemies, one fall was all it took to kill you. And with me stuck slipping and sliding on this ice, there was no doubt that I was in deep trouble...!

Dammit! At this rate, I'm seriously gonna fall in a hole! At a time like this, I wish I had a double-jumping dinosaur I could use...!

Oh, right.

"Veel, come 'ere! Turn into a dragon so I can ride your back!" I yelled.

"What's this? You need my help? How pathetically desperate of you, my lord!" Veel snarked.

All right! Now that I have Veel as a platform, I can avoid falling to my death!

Everything I learned from back home saved my butt

again! Gotta hand it to modern knowledge.

"Phew, I made it…! I know it's a basic trope, but I still hate ice levels…!" I exhaled a sigh of relief.

"But for real, what a feral way to solve that stage's puzzle," Puffer snidely remarked, judgment plastered across her face.

What are you talking about? The way I did it was absolutely genius!

And just like that, I cleared the second stage. Time to move onto the next one. A pattern was slowly emerging, so I had a pretty good idea of what she was gonna throw at me next.

First, it was Lampeye, the Hellfire Witch…

Then, Puffer, the Glacial Witch…

That meant there was only one option remaining from the little group Lampeye and Puffer formed on my farm.

Will the boss of the third level be Garra Rufa, the Witch of Pestilence…?!

"I'll do my *beeest!*" shouted a keen voice.

See! It is Garra Rufa.

If my hunch was right, I could assume her potions would feature microscopic pathogens. How was that going be implemented at her checkpoint?

"Here are the obstacles I've prepared for you!"

"Zombiiiiieeeessss?!"

If it was gonna be any kind of viral disaster, did it have to be this?! They were zombies! And a whole lot of them, too!

Usually, a zombie was the result of evil curses, but this time they were created by a mysterious virus! And she was acting like they were her children! Though, I guess zombies were pretty on-brand for Garra Rufa. But now because of her dang zombies this had became a survival horror game!

"Aaaah! Whoooaaa! Just where did all these zombies come from…?!" I emptied my lungs screaming. Then I glanced over to see… "Huh? Orkubo?!"

Have all of the orcs and goblins turned into zombies?! How could she do that to them?!

"Milord! Milord, we're fine!" Orkubo reassured me. "We're only acting like we're zombies!"

Huuuhhhh?!

Though, thinking about it, while Garra Rufa certainly loved pathogens, she didn't actually confirm their existence before coming to my farm. Which meant there was no way her ability to use them in her magic potions would be this advanced yet. I wondered how much time we had ahead of us before a zombie virus caught the attention of a certain umbrella-branded pharmaceutical company?

Well, knowing that the orcs and goblins were just pretending, I decided to just roll with it and have some fun.

"If Milord is bitten, then he'll turn into a zombie, too! Everyone, get him!"

"This isn't a zombie game anymore! It's just a game of *taaaaag!*"

Everyone was running at me! Though personally, for the sake of immersion I would've preferred zombies that don't run! Either way, I was still somehow able to dodge Orkubo and the other zombie actors. That surprised even me. I guess I thrived under pressure.

And thus, the third stage was cleared. I hoped this was the end of Veel's Secret Level…

Since my farm only had those three witches, and Veel exhausted all of them, I felt pretty confident I aced the

challenge.

"Hmph, clearly your level of awareness isn't high enough, Hubby," a familiar voice coolly chimed in.

"Plattie?"

"They're not the only witches around here. I wouldn't want you to forget about me, the Crown Witch!" Plattie shouted.

D'oh, I forgot! My own wife, Plattie the Mermaid Princess, was also a witch! Not just that, but out of the six witches, she was the most formidable one: *the Crown Witch*. What did she prepare for her level?!

"Feast your eyes on the most difficult stage of them all! While running on a frictionless ice floor, eight thousand bombs will rain down on you! Then, ten thousand invincible zombies will chase you down! And wait, there's more! At the end of the stage, I've planted traps that can insta-kill you!"

This game was impossible. Of course there was no way for me to win, so I just quit.

"Plattie, once you put your mind to something, you seriously go ham."

"I'm totally gonna crush you! You broke my game's balance!" Veel raised her voice in anger.

Even the dragon had enough. The secret level ended right there, and Plattie's final level ended up amounting to nothing.

Like I've been saying, game balance is important.

***

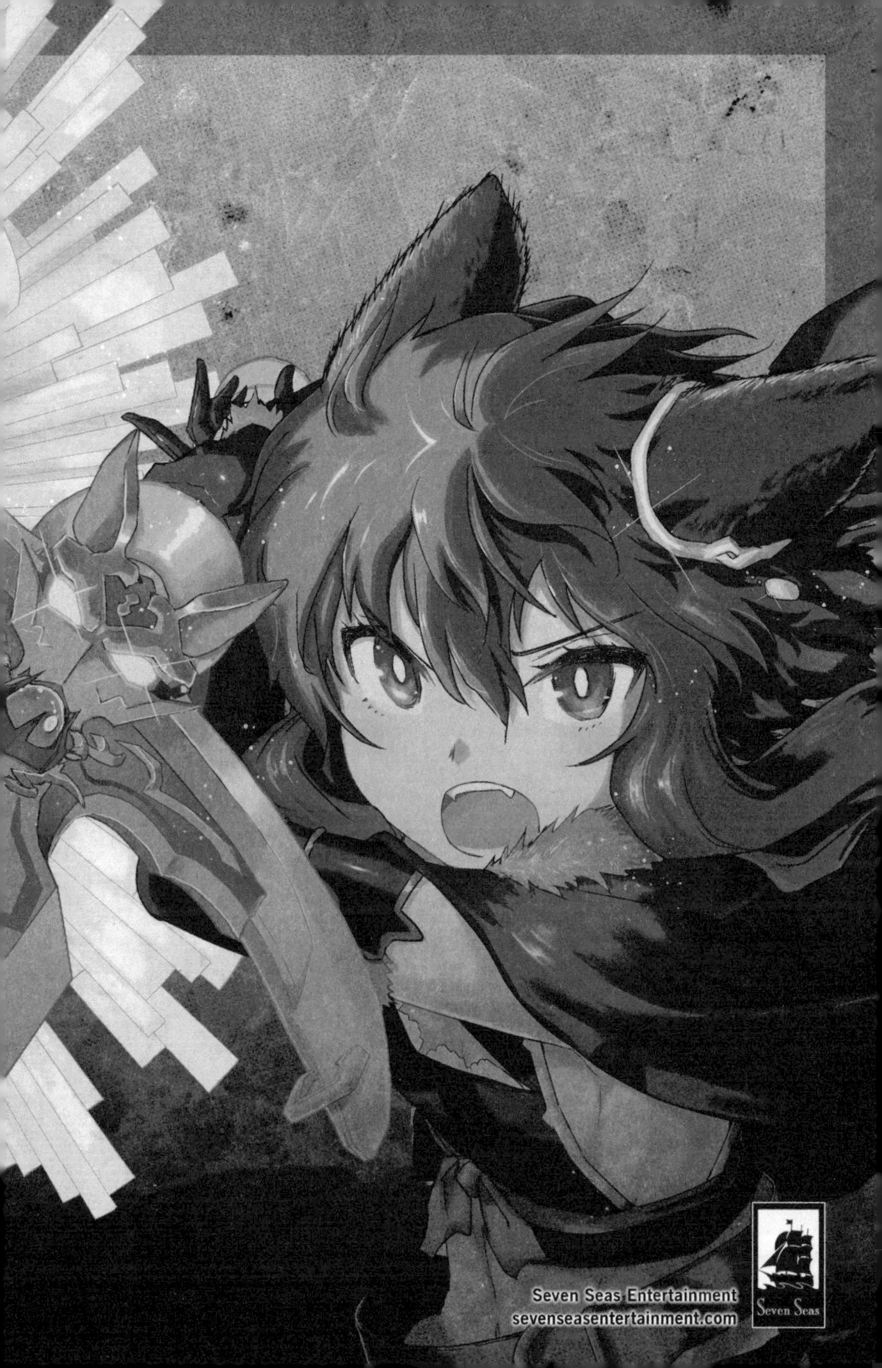
Seven Seas Entertainment
sevenseasentertainment.com
Seven Seas

KIDAN

Originally named "Itonami Norio," Kidan was a run-of-the-mill office worker, until one day he was suddenly summoned to another world. Though initially exiled for not being gifted with a skill, he actually possessed a literally god-given power called the Supreme Wielder, which makes him the master of any tool he holds in his hands.

PLATTIE

Hailing from the Merpeople Kingdom, Plattie is a prideful mermaid who looks down on the land-dwelling races. But ever since being fished up by Kidan, she's committed herself to being his wife. She is a renowned expert on potions and has made great contributions to Kidan's projects.

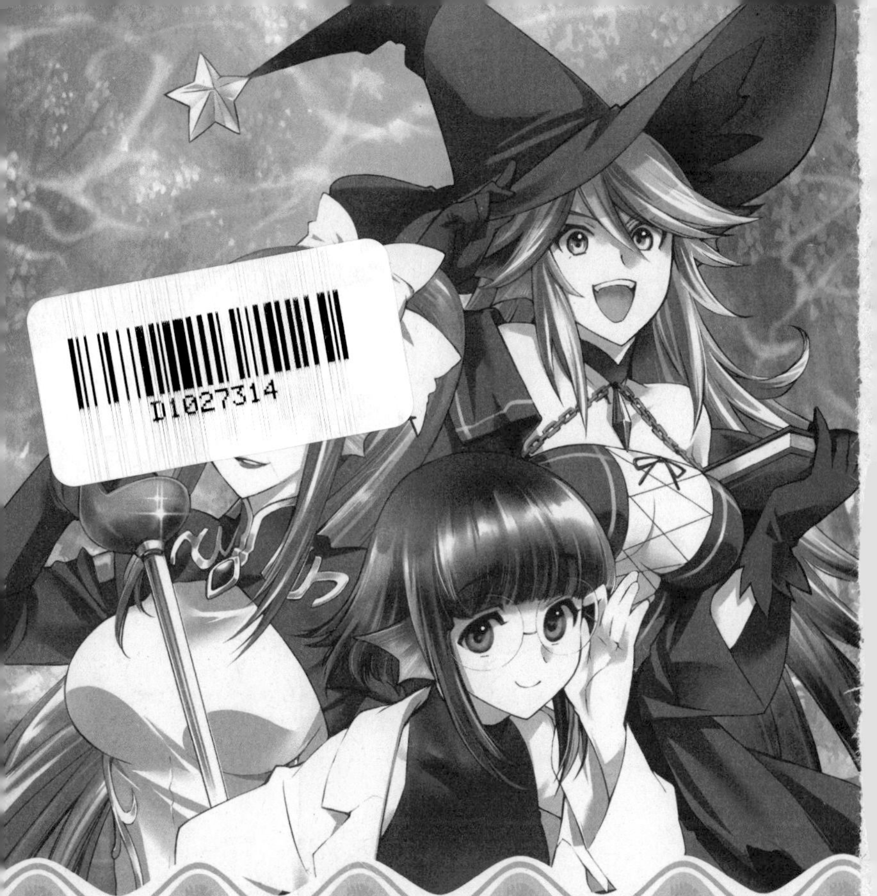

LET'S BUY THE LAND and CULTIVATE IT IN A DIFFERENT WORLD 4

story by
ROKUJYUUYON OKAZAWA

art by
JUN SASAMEYUKI

character design by
YUICHI MURAKAMI